THE LETTERS OF PAUL

Also by Calvin J. Roetzel

The World That Shaped the New Testament

the letters of Paul

CONVERSATIONS IN CONTEXT

Third Edition

Calvin J. Roetzel

Westminster/John Knox Press
Louisville, Kentucky

Published by Westminster/John Knox Press
Louisville, Kentucky

PRINTED IN THE UNITED STATES OF AMERICA
9 8 7 6 5 4 3 2 1

Library of Congress Cataloging-in-Publication Data

Roetzel, Calvin J.
The letters of Paul : conversations in context / Calvin J. Roetzel. —
3rd ed.
        p.   cm.
Includes bibliographical references and index.
ISBN 0-664-25201-X

    1. Bible.   N.T.   Epistles of Paul—Criticism, interpretation, etc.
I. Title.
BS2650.2.R63 1991
227'.06—dc20   91-11977

In Memory of My Parents

οἱ πτωχοὶ τῶν ἁγίων

Contents

Preface to the First Edition

THIS BOOK WAS CONCEIVED in my work with undergraduates. Many of them were trying to read the letters of Paul for the first time and were frankly bewildered. The meaning of these documents was hardly obvious to them, and the identity of Paul's conversation partners was obscure if not hidden altogether. So I wrote this book to assist people like them—those who are systematically reading Paul's letters for the first time as well as those returning to Paul for a fresh look. The book is meant to be read in a few days before turning to the letters themselves, and its purpose is to sensitize the student to the background of Paul and his readers as well as to the dynamic nature of the letters themselves. It is my hope that the modern reader will come to know the letters less as repositories of static truth than as lively and sometimes turbulent exchanges over the nature of the gospel.

The book also aims to sharpen the reader's historical imagination in order that he or she can begin the task of interpreting the letters. Any beginning reader will no doubt change his or her interpretations many times (just as I have changed my own); but intelligent reading of the letters will necessitate some kind of interpretation, and I have tried to clear the ground with this book so that the reader may begin. I have attempted to warn the reader against certain pitfalls, throw light on some issues involved in the letters, clarify the backdrop against which Paul's mission unfolds, and show the structure and function of the letter itself in the ancient world.

Necessarily there is much here that will be commonplace to the seasoned biblical critic, and my debt to the fraternity of biblical scholars is obvious. I acknowledge it with gratitude. My intent has been to make the fruits of the labors of these dedicated and able Pauline scholars available to the nonspecialist and to help those who are discovering (or rediscovering) Paul to appreciate the need for still further interpretation.

Although space prohibits my naming all the persons who had a hand in this effort, special mention must be made of Professor Lloyd Gaston, who read various stages of the manuscript and offered encouragement as well as valuable suggestions; Mrs. Carolyn Carlson, my secretary, whose diligent and patient labors helped in innumerable ways; and the members of my Paul seminars at Macalester College (St. Paul, Minnesota) and White Bear Lake Presbyterian Church, who made many useful comments on the content and style of the work. Without the help of these and others I am certain this book would never have been finished.

Easter 1974
Cookson, Oklahoma

Preface to the Third Edition

THE APPEARANCE OF THE THIRD EDITION allows me to thank the many students, faculty, and reviewers who gave the first and second editions such a generous reception. I was especially pleased when the opportunity came to expand the second edition and thus to take advantage of many valuable suggestions made by those using the book. Since the book was first published in 1975, scholarly research on the social and cultural context of early Christianity has produced a wealth of information that is valuable for any student of Paul. Because of the significance that an understanding of the context has for interpreting Paul's letters, it was useful to augment my earlier treatment of Paul's world. Advances in scholarship always make revision necessary in a book for the nonspecialist. While avoiding some of the complexities of that scholarship, my hope is that this treatment will give the student a feel for the spiritual ferment, the social instability, and the intellectual excitement of Paul's time.

For this edition the chapter "Paul and His World" has been expanded, and supplementary bibliographies have been added for each chapter for those who wish to do further study. Changes in language and references have been made in all chapters. This edition, like the second, includes a discussion of the early interpreters of Paul. After Paul's death, the Gentile mission succeeded so well that the Gentile church was in a position to determine its own direction, to create its own theological idiom, and to chart its own course, heedless of the Jerusalem circle or the sensibilities of a shrinking Jewish Christian membership. The Roman-Jewish war exacerbated divisions between Jews and Gentiles and further threatened the relationship between Jewish and Gentile Christians. The loss of confidence in traditional religious forms combined with a growing disenchantment with social institutions to spark off a vast array of world-denying movements. The Parousia, or return of Jesus, so eagerly expected by Paul, had not come. None of these conditions were foreseen or addressed by Paul. It is a tribute to him, nevertheless, that in his teaching, personality, and example, others in a vastly different age sought instruction and encouragement, consolation and hope. In the treatment of the deutero-Pauline materials, we see certain differences or even contradictions when comparing these letters with the undisputed letters of Paul, but they are important, nevertheless. Their very use of the Pauline tradition shows that those authors associated themselves with Paul even when they departed from him.

My debt to the scholarly community and to friends and colleagues has continued to grow. Even when unacknowledged in footnotes, it will be evident to the seasoned critic on almost every page. My special thanks go to students and faculty members who have offered valuable suggestions for improving the book. My earlier debt to David Rhoads, Robin Scroggs, Lloyd Gaston, Ernst Käsemann, and the late Norman Perrin has grown. I am especially grateful to my colleagues in the Pauline Theology Group of the Society of Biblical Literature for stimulation and correction, and to Walt Sutton and Carl Helmich of Westminster/John Knox Press, who have been most helpful with the revision.

Calvin J. Roetzel

Introduction: Contrary Impressions

FEW WHO KNOW HIM are neutral about Paul. Some love him; others hate him. And so it has always been. Within his own churches he was worshiped by some and maligned by others, called courageous and scoffed at as a coward, viewed as true and dismissed as an impostor. In some quarters he was unwanted; in others warmly welcomed. In the second century, Polycarp revered him as "blessed and glorious"; a Jewish Christian sect rebuffed him as the Devil incarnate. And so to this day Paul continues to provoke and excite, to challenge and antagonize.

A female student, for example, feels insulted by Paul's views of women. She is offended by the popular legend that calls Paul's "thorn in the flesh" a woman, and she is disgusted by the command in 1 Timothy 2:12 that no woman is "to teach or to have authority over men." Rather, as it says there, they are to be silent and submissive, earning their salvation by bearing children (2:11–15). How revolting, she says, that Paul should advise male believers, "It is well for a man not to touch a woman" (1 Cor. 7:1), or that he should think it shameful for women to speak in church gatherings (1 Cor. 14:35). Instead, he advises them to bring their queries to their husbands in private (14:35). Why, she asks, should girls grow up thinking there is something dirty or inferior about being female? Why doesn't Paul command the women not to touch a man? Why must he assume that subordination of women to men is an essential part of the divine order (1 Cor. 11:3)? In order to realize her full humanity, must a woman feel she is defying the Creator? Are Christianity and full humanity for women mutually exclusive?

Another student of Paul, however, argues that Paul was not a male chauvinist but a feminist. Paul, in his view, has suffered the double misfortune of being misunderstood and having a bad press. At the risk of sounding defensive, he asks, "What has 1 Timothy to do with the views of Paul?" On this issue scholars are in near-total agreement— Paul did not write 1 Timothy (or 2 Timothy or Titus). In the popular mind, however, the viewpoint expressed in 1 Timothy continues to color the interpretation of the genuinely Pauline letters. Such a passage as 1 Corinthians 14:33b–36 is not, it has correctly been noted, Paul's

13

work. It was added later by another hand to make Paul's view conform to that expressed in 1 Timothy. Scholars point out that the verses clearly interrupt Paul's discussion of prophecy. Moreover, the imposition of silence on women in church in this passage flatly contradicts 1 Corinthians 11:5ff. There Paul takes for granted the active, verbal participation of women in the service. Even 1 Corinthians 7:1 ("It is well for a man not to touch a woman") has its positive side. Paul prefers celibacy not because women are "dirty" or because sex is evil but because he feels that the special urgency of the times requires emergency measures. With the end in sight, he feels Christians should brace themselves for traumatic suffering. In the face of the impending distress (7:26), normal domestic concerns must be suspended.

However, what is overlooked in this chapter is the evenhanded way Paul addresses men and women. Concerning marriage Paul says, "Each man should have his own wife and each woman her own husband" (7:2). Concerning sexual intercourse Paul says, "The husband should give to his wife her conjugal rights, and likewise the wife to her husband" (7:3). Concerning sexual abstinence Paul addresses the husband and wife together. Concerning divorce Paul says, "The wife should not separate from her husband . . . and . . . the husband should not divorce his wife" (7:11). Concerning mixed marriages Paul says, "If any brother has a wife who is an unbeliever, and she consents to live with him, he should not divorce her. If any woman has a husband who is an unbeliever, and he consents to live with her, she should not divorce him" (7:12–13). So, throughout the passage, Paul argues for mutual responsibility and the equality of man and woman.

The same impartial treatment is given in 1 Corinthians 11. First Corinthians 11:3 is usually translated "the head of a woman is her husband." It should read, however, "the source of a woman is her husband." Paul is obviously recalling Genesis 2 where woman is made from a rib taken from man's side. Later, Paul notes that God makes woman the source of man (through giving birth) and thus underscores the interdependence of man and woman (1 Cor. 11:12).

It is Galatians 3:28, however, that best expresses Paul's view: "There is neither Jew nor Greek, there is neither slave nor free, there is neither male nor female; for you are all one in Christ Jesus." Paul felt that "in Christ" believers already shared in God's new community of the end time. In this new age all barriers that divided the human family are removed, and all obstacles to fulfillment are torn down. Although Paul nowhere attacks prevailing customs that assign women inferior roles in society, he obviously believes they are full partners "in Christ." When one treats women as full and equal citizens in the kingdom of God, it is difficult to hold disparaging views of them.

In response to this, the female student may still harbor doubts. Can she be sure that 1 Corinthians 14:33b–36 was inserted later? Does it really help to say men and women are equal "in Christ" if old patterns of discrimination persist? And in spite of the short exercise in biblical interpretation, she does not like the tone of 1 Corinthians 11:7 where Paul says man is the glory of God but woman is the glory of man. Finally, even if 1 Timothy is not Pauline, it is still in the New Testament and she finds the view of woman expressed in that book unacceptable.

Even in these days of renewed interest in religious studies, many students have a cordial dislike for Paul. In their view, whereas the teachings of Jesus are clear, simple, and basic, Paul's writings are abstract, abstruse, and complex. Where Jesus speaks of a childlike trust in the father God, Paul constructs a complicated system of belief. The death of a sparrow brings a groan from the God of Jesus (Luke 12:6); the God Paul knows cares nothing for animals (1 Cor. 9:9–10). Jesus is warm where Paul is harsh; Jesus is patient where Paul is impatient. Jesus is an unassuming, unpretentious—even unlettered—Galilean peasant with a gift of prophetic insight and empathy for the poor and social misfits. Paul, the learned rabbi, on the other hand, is seen as a kind of bully, forcing his dogma on others and merciless in his attacks on opponents. In the view of Paul's critics, this apostle to the Gentiles deflected Christianity away from the path, style of life, and teachings of its founder.

Where some see Paul as a corrupter of the religion of Jesus, others see him as the greatest theologian of all time. They point to his brilliant and incisive interpretation of the gospel for the Hellenistic world. It was Paul who took a message that was Hebraic in concept and idiom and adapted it to a non-Jewish setting without dilution or compromise. It was Paul who faced the hard questions—about the gospel versus Jewish law, the church versus society, Christians versus this world—that had to be answered if the Christian gospel were to remain intact.

Moreover, Paul was a daring and imaginative apostle. As the great pioneer of the Gentile mission, he crisscrossed Asia Minor and plunged into Europe. Tireless in his mission and undeterred by hardship or persecution, Paul pressed on and on and on. And he died with his boots on, still longing to go to Spain, the western horizon of the known world.

Where some portray him as a dogmatic grouch, others point to the strains of tenderness in his letters. He tried to be as gentle as a nurse with the Thessalonians. He seemed overwhelmed that a brother in Christ, Epaphroditus, would risk his life to serve him. He thought of his converts as his children, and he rejoiced at the restoration of a disciplined member of the congregation. His pastoral concerns surface time and again. Unquestionably, his gentle admonition can give way to harsh polemic. But was this because Paul was dogmatic and inflexible, or because he felt the essential character of the gospel was being compromised?

Some accuse Paul of male chauvinism, and some think he diverted

Christianity from its pure source in the simple religion of Jesus. Many Jews see Paul as the father of anti-Semitism in the West. It was he, they claim, who uprooted the Hebraic heritage from Palestine and turned it into a rival of the synagogue. It was he who lashed out in frustration and anger when the Jews resisted his gospel. It was he who warned that acceptance of circumcision meant damnation. And it was he who, as an apostate from Judaism, misrepresented the Hebrew religion. Jews find it difficult to understand why Paul the rabbi would call observance of the law dark and joyless. Had he never read Psalm 19, which speaks of the law "reviving the soul" and "rejoicing the heart"? Was he ignorant, they ask, of the traditions of the rabbis, which speak of the "joy of the commandments"? In their view the acceptance of Paul means the rejection of Judaism. And all too often it has been but a short step from the repudiation of Judaism to the persecution of Jews.

Some Protestants would wince at the suggestion that their theology is anti-Semitic. Nevertheless, many, perhaps most, would feel that Christianity according to Paul is the exact opposite of Judaism. They would question whether all Jews find delight in the law. At least the story of Richard Rubenstein would seem to suggest otherwise.

Rubenstein grew up as a secular Jew and started keeping the law in his late teens. He tells of wanting a "cosmic Lawgiver" who would provide order through discipline. But later Rubenstein came to despise this Lawgiver. His hatred of this exacting Judge ran so deep he wanted to murder him. Then while mourning the death of his son, he suddenly realized that the law could never give him what he desperately wanted, a triumph over mortality. Finally, while going through psychoanalysis, he discovered a kindred spirit in Paul. The release from the law that Paul found in Christ, Rubenstein found through his psychoanalytical experience. Paul's unshacklement from a troubled conscience in bondage to the law perfectly described, Rubenstein felt, his own release from deep personal anguish. Thus he came to know Paul as a "spiritual brother."[1]

According to the usual Protestant view, Paul, like Rubenstein, found the law oppressive. Through Christ Paul learned that salvation has an "in spite of" quality. That is, God loves the individual not because of anything he or she does but in spite of his or her inability to become worthy of love. God simply accepts each person as he or she is. It was Paul's emphasis on this "grace" that was distinctive.

Others get the impression that though Paul differs with Judaism he does not break with it. They note that frequently the traditional juxtapositions of Paul and Judaism have been weak. They observe that Judaism also speaks of salvation by grace. They note that the neat dichotomy between faith and works is not really a judgment against Judaism, for Jewish religion did not make that distinction. Last, and most significant, they find no evidence that Paul ever felt oppressed by the law. Instead, Paul is viewed as a faithful Jew who came to believe that the Messiah had come. This belief did not separate him from Judaism but confirmed his place in it. Thus they feel that Paul did not reject his Jewish heritage but reinterpreted it in light of his experience of Christ. So which was Paul—a Semite turned anti-Semitic, a Christian who rejected his Judaism, or a Jewish Christian who saw his life in Christ as a fulfillment, not a rejection, of Judaism?

The impressions registered here are only a small sample of the opinions about Paul one could assemble. Most readers will bring some notion about Paul to their reading of the letters. Even seasoned biblical critics hardly come to the epistles with a blank tablet. But the honest critic is always testing preliminary impressions against the evidence and correcting them if necessary. The aim of this study is to help the novice read the letters in light of their social and cultural background. Through such a reading perhaps new data will be brought to light that may require the alteration or even surrender of our first impressions. My hope is that such a change will bring our views of Paul into closer conformity with the reality of the man himself.

1. Paul and His World

MOST OF US can empathize with Polycarp, who complained that neither he nor anyone like him was "able to follow the wisdom of the blessed and glorious Paul" (*Letter to the Philippians* 3.2). Many parts of the letters are "hard to understand" (2 Peter 3:16). Nevertheless, more information about Paul and the world of his addressees should make comprehension less difficult. Ultimately, Paul's letters are understandable only in the light of his genius and the gospel he preached. However, Paul's religious and cultural context does help to illumine the writings. It may not explain them entirely, but it does shed light. In the discussion below we shall look at some of the ways Paul's milieu, both Hellenistic and Jewish, influenced his message, and on the other side, how the *Sitz im Leben,* or real life setting, of his readers affected their response. This convenient division is made to aid discussion, even though, as we soon shall see, there was no unhellenized Judaism in the first century and no part of the Hellenistic world totally isolated from the Jewish experience. So what we separate for purposes of discussion was not in fact separated in the first century.

Paul's Hellenistic Habitat

As the Acts of the Apostles suggest, Paul probably grew up in Tarsus, an important commercial, administrative, and cultural center on the southeast coast of Asia Minor (9:11; 21:39; 22:3).[1] In this capital of the Roman province of Cilicia, which rivaled Alexandria and Athens in importance, Paul learned Greek as his first language. There he became familiar with the Septuagint, the Greek translation of the Hebrew scriptures. There he was most likely taught to read, write, and imitate Greek literary and rhetorical forms. There he received his Greek name, *Paulos,* rather than the Hebrew, *Shaul,* which appears nowhere in his letters (but see Acts 13:9). There he acquired an understanding of Hellenistic culture—its anthropology, its political and religious institutions, its cosmology, sports, and its ecumenical tendencies. There he became acquainted with Greek methods of disputation.

This rich, cosmopolitan tradition filtered to Paul through his ancestral religion, Judaism, and lingered to shape his messianist thinking in highly original ways. The nucleus of that Jewish tradition was found in the scriptures so important to Diaspora Jews, that is Jews at home in the Greco-Roman world outside of Palestine. An awareness of the role of the Septuagint in Paul's religious outlook is crucial for understanding the letters.

1. The Septuagint (LXX) as Paul's Bible

Just as for Helen Keller the discovery and use of language possessed almost magical properties, so also Paul's identity was profoundly influenced by the popular Greek of his day. Language, we know, is no mere passive mirror of the world or a tool to be discarded after the task of world construction is done. Rather, language shapes our understanding of reality itself—our understanding of God, Christ, history, the church, and even our very own self. Much of the language shaping Paul's identity came from his Greek translation of the Hebrew scriptures, which we call the Septuagint. Within a Jewish community steeped in that language, Paul gained his understanding of life and death, fate and freedom, sin and piety, isolation and reconciliation.

As an important feature of Paul's Diaspora Judaism, the Septuagint was the Bible not just of the elite scholars but of the common people. While retaining some of its Hebrew flavor, the Septuagint, composed in the ordinary Greek of the day,[2] was fully intelligible even to the illiterate person who heard it read or cited in synagogue settings. Popular legends sprang up supporting its claim to authenticity. According to one fanciful tale, for instance, seventy-two Hebrew scribes from Jerusalem conversant in Greek translated the entire Torah, or first five books of the Hebrew Bible, in seventy-two days. Translated for the library of Pharaoh Ptolemy II Philadelphus (284–247 B.C.E.), the independent renditions of these scholars, according to later legend, all agreed in every single detail.[3] (Because of this combination of seventies, we call the book the Septuagint, or LXX, the Roman numeral for seventy.) In reality, the translation was not translated in a little over two months but evolved slowly over two centuries at least, and its faithfulness to the Hebrew varies greatly from book to book.

Once available, however, the text soon was surrounded by a vast body of commentary collected to interpret its significance for the Jewish community in the varying circumstances of the Greco-Roman world. In his multivolumed works, Philo of Alexandria, a first-century Jew, concerns himself almost exclusively with the interpretation of Torah for his generation. The commentary in the romantic tale of Joseph's marriage to the beautiful Egyptian woman, Aseneth, had special relevance for Diaspora Jews who fell in love with and married non-Jews.[4] And Aristobolus, writing in the second century B.C.E., attempted to explain anthropomorphic references to God in the Bible to make them more palatable to sophisticated, educated people of his time.[5] By their interpretation of the Septuagint these works, and others besides, all underscored the authority of the Septuagint as God's preeminent vehicle of revelation.

More than a text generating interpretation, however, the Septuagint itself *was* an interpretation. Coming from different periods, from many hands, and written in the Hellenistic vernacular of the day, the LXX concerned itself with the exegesis of the "Old Testament" text as well as with its preservation in Greek. Inevitably, the theological outlook of the translators tinged their translation. So even though the translators may have striven to remain true to the spirit of the Hebrew text, certain Greek ideas inevitably crept into their translation. In at least three important areas those ideas insinuated themselves into the Greek text.

First, the view of God in the Septuagint reflects a Hellenistic bias. Especially noteworthy is the disappearance of the personal name for God so common in the Hebrew text. The Septuagint indiscriminately renders the proper nouns Yahweh and Elohim with the generic noun *theos* (god). *Shaddai,* the common Hebrew proper name for God, is rendered in Greek with the abstract "Almighty" *(pantokrator)* or "All-Powerful," etc.

This trend toward abstraction surfaces in Exodus 3:14, where we find Elohim's ambiguous response to Moses' clever attempt to learn the secret, powerful divine name. Using a play on words, Elohim answers the slightly impertinent Moses, "I AM WHO I AM. . . . Say this to the people of Israel, 'I AM has sent me to you.' " In order for the play on words to work, a knowledge of the Hebrew verb "to be," from which the word "Yahweh" is formed, is required. Such a word-play, however, is missing entirely from the Septuagint. The Septuagint has instead, "I am The Being. . . . Say to the children The Being has sent me." Consequently, Yahweh is depicted as the Self-Existent One, the Absolute, or the cosmic divine being of the Greek philosophers.

A comparable level of abstraction is achieved when the Hebrew God Most High, or El, becomes "the supreme deity" in the Septuagint. Likewise, Adonai, whose name implies a cultic relationship between deity and worshiper, becomes "sovereign Lord" *(Kyrios)* in the Septuagint.

The Hebrew word *Elohim,* which symbolized the one revealed to Abraham, Isaac, and Jacob and the one who gave the Law to Moses, is known in Greek as "God" *(Theos)* or "gods" following the Hebrew plural form. Thus for the Hebrew of Exodus 22:28, "You shall not revile *Elohim,*" the Greek has, "You shall not revile the gods." This small change to the plural form has major implications for faith for the Hebrew religion, which traditionally centered on the one God to the exclusion of all others. In the Septuagint the commandment encourages

tolerance of all forms of religious piety. While the community is urged
to respect all religious traditions, it is not necessarily encouraged to
subscribe to them.

While it is true that Paul's rigorous monotheism contradicts the
Greek spirit of tolerance seen in the Septuagintal translation of Exodus
22:28, he was hardly untouched by the ecumenical tendencies at the
heart of Hellenism. Moreover, Paul's churches in the Hellenistic orbit,
more open to that spirit than he (e.g., 1 Cor. 10:7ff.), in some cases
dictated the issues under consideration in the letters. In the tendency
toward abstraction both Paul and his readers were affected by the
Septuagint, and in one specific case, Paul's understanding of the term
"Lord," *Kyrios,* was informed to a degree by his Greek Bible.

Second, we see in the Septuagint an understanding of law that is
shared by Paul. One of the most prominent features of postexilic Jewish
religion (i.e., after 537 B.C.E.) was the emphasis on Torah. The word
torah in its root form means "to direct" or "to instruct." It may refer
to instruction given students by their teacher, direction given Israel by
Yahweh, guidance spoken by the prophets appealing to the "word of
Yahweh," or the instruction derived from the rich and varied story of
God's dealing with Israel. In the Greek translation, the word *torah*
almost always appears as *nomos* (law), which lacks many of the nuances of the Hebrew word. Usually *nomos* refers to a code that governs
community life or an individual's conduct. In some cases *nomos* refers
to a cosmic principle like the law (or principle) of gravity. In this latter
respect especially, the Septuagint departs from the Hebrew understanding of *torah,* drawing near to the Greek understanding of natural law.
While Paul is aware of the meaning of the Hebrew *torah,* he uses *nomos*
to convey certain Greek shadings of meaning. In Romans 8:2, for
example, when he speaks of being "set free from the law of sin and
death," we should read "set free from the principle of sin and death."
Paul nowhere equates, as this passage would seem to, the Torah with
sin and death. Similarly in Romans 7:23 where Paul speaks of the "law
of my mind" and in 3:27 where he refers to the "law of works" as
opposed to the "law of faith," the most likely meaning of "law" is
"principle."

Third, the perception of "faith" in the Septuagint is also significant
for understanding Paul's thought. The word for faith in Greek translation *(pistis)* comes from the Hebrew noun, *'emet,* whose basic meaning
is firmness, stability, or reliability. When the Hebrews wanted to speak
of faith in someone or something deemed reliable, a verb form was
always used. We see, therefore, that the Hebrews made precise distinctions between reliability (or faithfulness) and faith or belief in that
which is reliable.[6] The Septuagint on the other hand made no such
distinction, and the Greek word for "faith" *(pistis)* is ambiguous
enough to allow for both meanings. While this point may seem trivial,

it does have relevance for understanding Romans 1:17. In this pivotal passage in Romans, which Luther called the most important passage in all of the Bible, Paul is quoting from some version of Habakkuk 2:4. But was that version the Greek or the Hebrew? The Hebrew of Habakkuk 2:4 is clear and can be translated: "the righteous will live by his [or her; i.e., the person's] faithfulness." The Septuagint, perhaps following a slightly different manuscript, reads, "The righteous shall live by my [i.e., God's] faithfulness." Paul renders the passage without the pronoun "my" and takes "faithfulness" to refer to individual belief: "The righteous man [or person] shall live by faith." Does Paul use the word "faith" *(pistis,* or here *pisteōs)* to refer to "belief in" God's work in Christ? Is he referring to the importance of fidelity to God's covenant or faithful obedience to God's will? Or is he referring to God's fidelity? Scholars have long debated this issue without producing a consensus. In using the Greek text Paul may be purposely using a term that is sufficiently ambiguous to include more than a single meaning. In any case, the point is that the passage is notoriously difficult at least in part because of the ambiguity of the language Paul uses and that ambiguity is only possible if Paul is using the Septuagint.

In this sample of passages, we can see how the Hellenistic spirit influenced the translation of the Hebrew scriptures into Greek and how the outlook so evident in the language of the Septuagint is shared at some points by Paul. While it is true that this intrusion of the Hellenistic spirit did not compromise the fundamental character of the Hebrew religion, it would be inaccurate to say that no change in viewpoint occurred. In the comparison below we observe some of those shifts of emphasis.

Comparison of Translations of Hebrew and Greek Texts

(* = Author's translation; italics = Emphasis added)

Translation of Hebrew Texts	*Translation of the Septuagint* *
Who has known the Spirit of the Lord . . . (Isa. 40:13)*	Who has comprehended the mind of the Lord . . . (cf. 1 Cor. 2:16)
He bore the sin of many, and made intercession for the transgressors. (Isa. 53:12)	[He] bore away the sins of many, and on account of their lawlessness was he handed over. (cf. Rom. 4:25)
Now the rabble that was among them had a strong craving. (Num. 11:4)	Again the people who were among them had an eager desire . . . (cf. 1 Cor. 10:6)

Translation of Hebrew Texts	*Translation of the Septuagint* *
[T]he righteous shall live by their faithfulness. (Hab. 2:4)*	"The righteous shall live by my [i.e., God's] faithfulness . . ." (cf. Rom. 1:17)
"By you all the families of the earth will bless themselves." (Gen. 12:3)	"In you shall all the peoples of the earth be blessed." (cf. Gal. 3:8)
Moses went up to God. (Ex. 19:3)	Moses ascended to *the mount of God.*
And they [Moses and the elders] saw the God of Israel. (Ex. 24:10)	And they saw *the place on which* the God of Israel *stood.*
[Isaiah said to Ahaz,] "Behold, a young woman shall conceive and bear a son, and shall call his name Immanuel." (Isa. 7:14)	"Behold, a *virgin* shall conceive and bear a son, and shall call his name Immanuel." (cf. Gal. 4:4)
Elohim said to Moses, "I AM WHO I AM." (Ex. 3:14)*	And the God spoke to Moses saying, "I am the Being."
"You shall not make light of Elohim." (Ex. 22:28)*	"You shall not speak evil of the gods."
I said, "I shall not see Yah(weh) in the land of the living. I shall not look upon mortals again." (Isa. 38:11)*	I said, "I shall never again see the *salvation* of God in the land of the living, never again will I see the *salvation* of Israel on the earth."
Wisdom says, "Yahweh created me at the beginning of his way, the first of his deeds of old." (Prov. 8:22)*	Wisdom says, "The Lord created me, the first principle of his ways, for his works."

While no comprehensive treatment of Septuagintal tendencies and their theological significance is currently available, scholars recognize that those tendencies influenced Paul's theological outlook. Heard in the home, memorized in the school, read and discussed in the synagogue, the Septuagint was in Paul's blood as surely as the Authorized Version of the English Bible was in the blood of Milton. Lodged in his soul, this language came to the fore in his discussion of the great issues of sin and justification, law and liberty, election and exclusion, life and death. The language of the Septuagint molded Paul's understanding of faith, legitimated his mission to the Gentiles, and defined the eschatological congregation as the *ekklēsia* or church. Thus we see that Paul's relationship to the Septuagint was dynamic. Its language defined his world, even his innermost being, and that understanding then curved back on the text itself to illumine its message for Paul the apostle of Christ.[7]

2. Paul's Nonbiblical Hellenistic Language

While the Septuagint was nuclear to Paul's theology, much of his language and important religious expressions came from the wider Hellenistic culture. The word for conscience *(syneidēsis),* for example, commonly appears in the writings of the Stoic philosophers but is missing entirely from the Jewish scriptures. While allowing that the "thing" may exist even where the "word" does not, conscience, as used by Paul, strongly resembles its Hellenistic parent even when resembling its Jewish forebear. Used by Paul to refer to the inner tribunal of the self, "conscience" appears in the apostle's defense of himself against the charge of insincerity (2 Cor. 4:2), and he calls on the conscience of the Corinthians to acknowledge the integrity of his apostleship (2 Cor. 5:11). In the first reference Paul seems to allow that conscience is culturally conditioned, and thus at least partially flawed, for he argues that even though no charge is brought against him by his conscience he is not, therefore, necessarily innocent. For he will ultimately have to answer not to his conscience but to a judging God ("I am not aware of anything against myself, but I am not thereby acquitted. It is the Lord who judges me," 1 Cor. 4:4). Elsewhere, however, he speaks of the important function of the conscience for the Gentile unbeliever (Rom. 2:15) as well as the "weak" Christian (1 Cor. 8:7, 10, 12). So Paul's understanding embraces both concepts—a conscience that serves as an inner tribunal of the self (but which he recognizes is culturally bound) and an awareness of ultimate accountability to the one God of Israel. The two are in tension in Paul's thought even though both play important roles.

Elsewhere Paul draws on the tradition of the Hellenistic church that predated him. But even if Paul borrowed these traditions from others they were no less his own. For in adopting and using the traditions of others Paul shared the views expressed there even if he did not author them. In the closing admonition of his letter to the Philippians, for example, Paul cites a tradition full of words from the Hellenistic milieu. There he says, "Whatever is true [*alēthē*], whatever is honorable [*semna*], whatever is just [*dikaia*], whatever is pure [*hagna*], whatever is lovely [*prosphilē*], whatever is gracious [*euphēma*], if there is any excellence [*aretē*], if there is any recognition [*epainos*], ponder these things" (Phil. 4:8). The terms noted all come from the Hellenistic world, as indeed, does the tradition itself.[8] A short list of definitions will show how this passage mirrors a world quite apart from that of the Old Testament:

alēthēs—true, truthful, honest.

semnos—that which is august, sacred, or worthy of honor. Anything in which a higher order may be detected, including such diverse things as the majesty of the king's throne, gorgeous dress, eloquent speech, beautiful music, or graceful motion.

hagnos—much used in Hellenism to mean the purity of the sanctuary.

prosphilēs—lovely, pleasing, or agreeable.

euphēmos—auspicious, praiseworthy, attractive, or appealing.

aretē—a prominent word in Greek philosophy and literature referring primarily to excellence of achievement, or mastery of a field. May refer to valor, special merit, honor, good fortune, success, or fame.

epainos—recognition, approval, or praise.

The alert reader will also recognize the nonbiblical character of other materials in the Pauline epistles. Scholars have long recognized, for instance, that the lists of virtues and vices like the ones seen in Galatians 5:19–23 were quite popular in the Hellenistic world.[9] In this collection Paul first catalogs the "works of the flesh" as "fornication, impurity, licentiousness, idolatry, sorcery, enmity, strife, jealousy, anger, selfishness, dissension, party spirit, envy, drunkenness, carousing, and the like," and then names the "fruit of the Spirit" as "love, joy, peace, patience, kindness, goodness, faithfulness, gentleness, self-control." While such lists may have come to Paul either through Hellenistic Judaism or through the Hellenistic church, they go back to Greek philosophy. Except for the references to "love," the virtue list contains nothing that would be unusual in a catalog of conventional Greek ethics. The way these "virtues" are subordinated to the Spirit and thus given an eschatological dimension, however, is Paul's own doing.[10] Paul's use of such lists further demonstrates how fully he inhabited the Hellenistic world and how totally free he felt to appropriate its idiom in daring new ways.

Paul also makes copious use of metaphors from the Greek milieu. A statement not literally true, the metaphor aims to provoke the hearers to thought, and in the process to engage the conversation partner in the creative process of communication. If one should say, "Sam Jackson is a horse," or "Stephanie Grant is a gazelle," the hearer knows that these statements are not *literally* true even though at some level they are true. In that recognition the hearer is invited to become a partner with the speaker in the search for the hidden truth and vastly expanded world concealed in the metaphor.

So also in Paul's letters such figures abound invoking images from sport, politics, nature, and religion. In 1 Corinthians 9:24–27, for example, Paul refers to track and boxing. Whereas track stars compete for the honor of wearing a fading laurel wreath, believers run, so Paul suggests, to win an imperishable spiritual wreath. Boxers aim to defeat the opposition in a slugfest to gain a coveted prize, but Paul pommels his own body into submission to make it serve Christ (see also Phil. 3:12–15). Since the message of neither of these statements resides in its literal meaning, the metaphor gives the readers a new set of glasses through which they may view afresh their place and purpose in the world. Similarly, when Paul declares that believers in Philippi have a commonwealth, or colony *(politeuma)* in heaven (3:20), he invites them to ponder their status as foreigners in this world and compare that to their status as citizens of God's commonwealth beyond this world. Elsewhere, fractious Corinthians, whose self-constructed spiritual hierarchy has led to disgusting forms of charismatic snobbery, hear that they are the "body" (1 Cor. 12:27) of Christ. How silly it would be, Paul suggests, for the ear to say, "Because I am not an eye, I do not belong to the body" (12:16). Designed to puncture inflated pretensions, this metaphor aims to move believers from a self-absorbed, individualistic, arrogant spirituality into a concern for others and the welfare of the whole community. Whether Paul succeeded we shall never know. Similarly, the Cynic expression "gentle . . . like a nurse," found in 1 Thessalonians 2:7, reminds Paul's readers of his care for them and their responsibility for each other.[11] All of these metaphors spring from a Greek context and for their maximum impact rely on readers' familiarity with that world.[12] Yet note how skillfully Paul exploits this language to serve his mission, to educate the church, and to teach believers the implications of the gospel.

Observing Paul's use of these metaphors is instructive, for in doing so one may learn how his exploitation of their plurisignificance exposes the gospel's complexity. Paul's play with metaphors often reveals development in his own thinking and his struggle with seemingly intractable problems. In Romans 9:30–33 and 11:11, for example, Paul describes a strange scenario when, while running a race, Israel comically (or tragically) trips on a rock placed on the track by God only to be beaten to the finish by Gentiles who were not even competing. This farcical use of the racing metaphor, after its introduction in 9:30–33, ferments for more than a chapter when Paul returns to it in 11:11: "So I ask, have they [the Israelites] stumbled so as to fall?" "Absolutely not!" Paul emphatically retorts. Now we see a curious implication of Paul's metaphor. Unlike other races in which winners require losers, this one has only winners; Jews who ran the Torah race and Gentiles who did not will both be victorious. When we come to discuss Romans 9–11 and Paul's response to the question: "Now turning to the Gentiles, has God reneged on promises made to Israel?" we shall see how this metaphor works to develop and explain Paul's own thinking. In a flash, the metaphor seems to provide a way out of Paul's own dilemma.

Mixed with this language drawn from his Hellenistic environment are also metaphorical expressions that are unmistakably Jewish in origin. He calls the church "God's temple" (1 Cor. 3:16–17), refers to the Philippian believers as "the circumcision" (Phil. 3:3),[13] and invites the Romans to present their bodies as a "living sacrifice, holy and acceptable to God" (Rom. 12:1).

Inasmuch as Paul's background contains a dynamic blend of Jewish and Hellenistic elements, it should hardly surprise us to find a similar synthesis of these elements in his language. This complex and dynamic mixture may account for Paul's success in preaching his Jewish gospel in the Hellenistic world. Sensitivity to the history and interplay of these metaphors drawn from Jewish and Hellenistic circles and their function in the letters will give interesting clues to the meaning of the conversations between Paul and his churches.

3. Methods of Argumentation

Since Bultmann early in this century noted Paul's use of the diatribe, Paul's debt to the Stoics has been recognized.[14] Originated as a means of raising philosophical questions with the common lot of humanity, from the third century B.C.E. onward the diatribe was refined by the Cynics to a fine art. Later adopted and adapted by the Stoics, the diatribe came into wide popular use even within Jewish circles. A form of argumentation that places questions on the lips of a hypothetical objector, then offers a response, the diatribe was ideally suited for Paul's response to Christian and non-Christian opposition to his gospel and apostleship. For example, the letter to the Romans is sprinkled liberally with questions like these: "Are we to continue in sin that grace may abound?" (6:1); "What then shall we say? That the law is sin?" (7:7); "Is there injustice on God's part?" (9:14). Although the objection or question is hypothetical, it is rooted in a real life experience. Particularly in Romans Paul uses the diatribe to introduce his discussion of some of the most damaging charges against his gospel of justification by grace for the Gentiles, namely, that it encouraged immorality, that it implied that a good gift of God—the law—was bad, and that in choosing the Gentiles God had reneged on his promises to the Jews.[15]

In recent years critics have found evidence that Paul used methods of oral argument from Hellenistic rhetoric to persuade his audience. The expense of learning and developing these rhetorical skills either in schools of rhetoric or from private tutors was prohibitive for all except the most privileged. Designed to equip persons for service in law or politics, rhetoric also took literary form in the apologetic letter. Hans Dieter Betz, for example, argues that Paul's letter to the Galatians follows this pattern, and he offers an outline of the letter drawn from rhetorical speech.[16] Recognizing its popularity in Roman circles, Betz employs the Latin terms:

    I. Epistolary prescript (1:1–5)
    II. Exordium, or statement of the cause of the letter (1:6–11)
    III. *Narratio,* or autobiographical support for the cause (1:12–2:14)
    IV. *Propositio,* or points of agreement and disagreement (2:15–21)
    V. *Probatio,* or arguments from indisputable evidence, from scripture, from human experience, from Torah, Christian tradition, friendship, and allegory (3:1–4:31)
    VI. *Exhortatio,* or warnings and recommendations (5:1–6:10)
    VII. *Conclusio,* or attack on the opposition (6:11–18).[17]

Although Betz's work gives us a fresh look at Galatians, scholars have expressed reservations about the degree of Paul's reliance on classical rhetoric. Paul, for example, did not enjoy the privilege prerequisite to such an education, and classical rhetoric as practiced by Cicero was primarily an oral vehicle. Did Paul and others adapt classical oral strategies of persuasion to letter writing? Doubts have been expressed.[18] Others have objected that while a consideration of strategy may be important, the truth of Paul's gospel, not his political acumen as a persuader, was invariably his primary concern. While questions about rhetorical criticism will continue to be raised, and confusion about the nature and function of rhetorical criticism will continue to exist, the student of Paul cannot dismiss the concerns of rhetorical criticism. Its interest in the arrangement of the argument and techniques of persuasion throws light on the foreground of the text. Such a focus on the politics of persuasion draws attention to the foreground rather than exclusively on the background of the text and rightfully brings the reader into the text's context.[19]

    As we shall see below, Paul's method of scripture interpretation owed much to his Pharisaism. However, in Galatians 4:21–5:1 with its allegory of Sarah and Hagar, we have a perfect example of a popular Hellenistic method of text interpretation. Allegory is the veiled presentation of meaning, usually in the form of a story, where each part of the story stands for a deeper truth. Unlike metaphor, allegory is self-enclosed, carrying its own explanation and leaving less room for the creative role of the listener (see Mark 4:14–20).

    First used by the Greeks responding to the unseemly and even immoral actions of the gods of the classical myths, allegory was employed by the Stoics to rationalize those actions by seeking in them a deeper meaning. An instance of this use of allegory appears in the explanation of the adulterous relationship between Aphrodite and Ares. Aphrodite invites Ares to "Come and lie down, my darling, and be happy! Hephaistos [my husband] is no longer here but gone" (Homer, *Odyssey*

292–293). But their tryst ends abruptly when the suspicious husband, Hephaistos, returns and finds them out, snaring them in his net. Using an allegorical approach, the Greek philosopher Heraclitus found in this text not just a bawdy affair but the harmonious relationship between love and conflict (*Homeric Questions* 69). Allegory thus became the key that unlocked the treasure of texts dealing with gods at war, deceit, and treachery.

While a few instances of allegory appear in the Old Testament and the Qumran texts, and apocalyptic allegory is present in Jewish pseudepigraphical writings, it is the literature of Diaspora Judaism that exploits the allegorical method to the fullest extent. One of the most skillful in the use of allegory was the first-century Jewish philosopher Philo of Alexandria. Like the Greeks, Philo believed that the literal meaning of a text was only its surface and most superficial meaning. The literal text, however, pointed beyond itself to a deeper reality. Philo openly expressed his contempt for unimaginative literalists, calling them "slow-witted" (*On Flight and Finding* 179), "obstinate," and "rigid" (*On Dreams* 2.301), and he noted by example that it is silly to think God actually *planted* a garden of "soulless" plants. The reference to God's planting a garden in Genesis 2:8, Philo argued, was not to literal plants, trees, and herbs, but to divine plants that have virtue, insight, and wisdom to distinguish between the ugly and the beautiful (*On the Creation* 154). Similarly, since no botanist knows of a "tree of life" (Gen. 2:9), Philo suggests that reference is to "reverence toward God . . . by means of which the soul attains to immortality" (*On the Creation* 154). When we come to discuss Paul's use of allegory (e.g., the story of Sarah and Hagar in Galatians 4:21–5:1), Philo's use of allegorical interpretation will be instructive. Although Paul never knew Philo, he grew up in a Diaspora setting that in some ways resembled that of Philo, and for that reason a consideration of Philo's writings will prove useful.

4. Hellenistic Religion and Philosophy

In the Hellenistic world the line between religion and philosophy was blurred. The philosopher's search for wisdom was often informed by religious piety, and even when philosophers were self-consciously atheistic, as were some Sophists in the fifth century B.C.E., they vigorously engaged religious issues. Even the Epicureans from the third century B.C.E. to the first did not, as is sometimes suggested, deny the existence of the gods. They asserted instead that it was useless to solicit their aid in prayer or to propitiate them with sacrifice for they either were indifferent to human concerns or chose not to intervene in them. Conversely, major religious figures of the day like Apollonius of Tyana and Philo of Alexandria worked in the current philosophical idiom. We are being faithful to the spirit of the time, therefore, when we link religion and philosophy in this discussion. Both were vital parts of Paul's world and that of his churches.

Any suggestion that Paul's hearers had no religious faith before baptism is, of course, erroneous. Although Gentiles made up a great, if not the greater, part of Paul's congregations,[20] some were acquainted with Jewish traditions, institutions, and scriptures. As "God-fearers," i.e., people who were sympathetic or even partial to Judaism but not yet converts to it, they might have been more receptive to Paul's Jewish gospel. Others, however, worshiped the popular deities of the Greco-Roman world. Aware of their participation in the religious rites of the Hellenistic world, Paul reminded his converts how they had "turned to God from idols" (1 Thess. 1:9). He frequently warned his addresses about a lingering reverence for the powerful religious symbols associated with their pre-Christian devotion. He urged the Corinthians to "shun the worship of idols" (1 Cor. 10:14). He warned that idolaters, i.e., converts who cling to old religious practices, will not inherit the kingdom of God (Gal. 5:20). But sometimes the line between life in the new age and the previous existence was dim, moving Paul to forbid participation in the local cults even while permitting the consumption of meat offered to idols (1 Cor. 8:1–13; 10:14–22). Paul's mission, therefore, was not to pour his gospel into a religious vacuum but to contend with other religions for the truth of his gospel in a highly pluralistic setting. Sparked off by the conquests of Alexander in the third century B.C.E. that opened up the whole eastern Mediterranean to a dynamic exchange of ideas, the old religions jockeyed with the new for converts. And all were affected by a disenchantment that characterized the age.

The causes of the first-century malaise go back to the third century B.C.E., a period of severe hardship in Greece. Depression, civil war, near-collapse of the judicial system, and the decline of the city-state worsened the suffering brought on initially by famine and hunger. Infanticide was common. The decline of social institutions and the rise of a spirit of skepticism virtually destroyed the old religions. To be sure, certain primitive forms of religion and new religions remained. But even though people still stood in awe of the power and mystery of certain primal forces, belief in the old gods—Zeus, Aphrodite, Apollo, etc.—was on the wane.

After the collapse of traditional religion, Hellenistic piety assumed many forms. In some cases the old corporate theology gave way to a type of individualistic piety fixed on some particular minor god or even foreign deity. In other cases belief in an impersonal, divine force present in the world replaced the venerable old tradition. And in still other instances many felt no kinship with any divine principle that gave the cosmos order. The feeling was pervasive that the world was controlled by an oppressive, blind, impersonal, cosmic fate called *heimarmenē*. Ruled by a dark necessity that was a stranger to love, many felt like reeds at the mercy of a mindless wind. With this shift in mood came a darkness of spirit that cast its menacing shadows over all Greek culture and reason. The great Hellenistic dream of one world free of barbarism and corruption soured. As the first century approached, interest in science and clear, logical thought waned. The hope that Rome or any political power could deliver the good life evaporated. As Helmut Koester notes,

> In Athens, the city in which the most magnificent cultic buildings were erected, the visible presence of splendid temples did little but create the impression that this city was only a museum of classical greatness. The more the old traditions received support and were subsidized by the government, the more the cultic activities of the temples were estranged from the religious consciousness of the majority of the population.[21]

This eclipse of the old had far-reaching implications. For example, in place of the earlier Greek fascination with the body and appreciation for beauty and order in the universe, there appeared a devaluation of the world and a repudiation of the body. The Greek word for "athlete" *(askētēs)* came to mean "ascetic."[22] Gilbert Murray aptly characterizes this period:

> This sense of failure, this progressive loss of hope in the world, in sober calculation, and in organized human effort, threw the later Greek back upon his own soul, upon the pursuit of personal holiness, upon emotions, mysteries and revelations, upon the comparative neglect of this transitory and imperfect world for the sake of some dream-world far off, which shall subsist without sin or corruption, the same yesterday, to-day and forever.[23]

Even granting this wasting away of the old or traditional religions, their decline hardly left a landscape barren of religious expression. Fertility cults remained viable in the rural areas, the mystery religions enjoyed a resurgence in the cities, the healing cult of Asclepius became increasingly popular, and religious movements from the East[24] grew in favor in the cosmopolitan West. Because of the urban character of Paul's mission, the latter three are of special interest to us here.

a. *The Mystery Religions*

We know little about the mystery religions in first-century Greece,[25] perhaps because they were so successful in guarding their secrets. What we do know harmonizes well with the spirit of the time. Although participation in the mysteries was most often corporate, the central concern of the mysteries was for personal salvation through direct identification with the deity. This knowledge was less intellectual than mystical, less rational than relational. Through the prescribed rites the participants received more than a vision, they experienced solidarity with the god. Preparation included elaborate cleansing rites (lustrations or baptisms), and in some of the mysteries sexual union in a cultic setting offered ecstatic union with the god. Through ritual merger with the deity, initiates experienced the state of blessedness: the terror of history was overcome, release from the corruption of this world achieved, and immortality became a present reality.

The Eleusinian Mysteries. The dying and rising god or goddess at the center of the mystery cult normally had his or her first home in agriculture with its vital interest in the turning of the seasons. In that context the deity's life and death had practical issue as the renewal of crops. Now, however, under the influence of mystery religions, the ancient fertility rites changed focus, from the renewal of crops to the renewal of life after death.[26] In the words of Firmicus Maximus we see how the fate of the god became the fate of the initiate:

> Take courage, ye initiates! As the god was saved,
> So too for us comes salvation from suffering.[27]

Most typical of this pattern was the Eleusinian Mystery. The crisis begins when Hades-Pluto kidnaps Kore-Persephone, the beautiful young goddess of fertility, carrying her off to the underworld to rape her. In her absence Demeter, her mother, mourned. The earth languished, the grain wilted. Demeter's desperate search for her daughter met success only after her persistence persuaded Zeus to intervene and rescue the people from starvation and death. As a result, Kore-Persephone spends eight months of every year on earth and four months in the underworld. (The four months were the hot, dry summer months when the grain lay dormant.) Though little is known of the rituals marking these seasonal passages, surely rites of mourning and celebration existed. But evidence from the Roman period proves that the Eleusinian mysteries had a reach far beyond their obvious agricultural home. Cicero, one of the most important Roman jurists and philosophers of the Roman period, was an Eleusinian initiate and spoke of the power of the mystery to enable believers to "live with joy . . . and die with a better hope."[28] A number of emperors accepted initiation into the cult (Augustus, Hadrian, Marcus Aurelius, and others), but the expense of the initiation discouraged participation by the poor and slaves. The attention given in the mystery to ties with the dead heightened its appeal. Yet there was no community of Eleusinian initiates, and the mystery's highly individualistic character separated it radically from the early Christian community.

The Isis-Osiris Mystery. One of the most popular mysteries of the first century was the Isis-Osiris (or Serapis) cult, a transplant from Egypt

Pluto → Persephone — Demeter — Zeus

that flourished in the cities ringing the Mediterranean. Isis was an Egyptian goddess and consort of Osiris, who after being murdered by Seth departed to become lord of the nether world. Though linked to the realm of the dead, Osiris held the secret to the powers of life and fructification. He brought the benevolent Nile floods that caused the Delta to bloom. He caused the wine to ferment, the bread to rise, and the crops to yield their fruit. Osiris's green face still evident in tomb drawings from the second millennium B.C.E. symbolized his intimate association with verdant nature's abundance.

Although the history of the Osiris myth informing the first-century mystery is complex, the basic outline of the sacred story is known. Both born of the sun god Ra, Seth, the older, jealous brother, murdered Osiris, dismembered him, and heaved the mutilated carcass into the Nile. Stricken with grief, Isis, Osiris's consort, scoured the land in search of her lover. Eventually, she located the fragments of his body, reassembled them, breathed life into the reassembled corpse, and consummated her love. From this sexual intercourse issued Horus, Osiris's heir to the throne and the Pharaoh of upper and lower Egypt. Later interred by Anubis, the jackal-headed god of the dead, Osiris returned to the nether world to become lord of the Nile, causing it to flood annually, and joining issue with the soil to assure abundant harvests. Meanwhile, Horus, his son, ruled the land from a throne shaped like the lap of his mother Isis.

Depicted often as a black or Apis bull, a powerful symbol of fecundity, Osiris became the guarantor of life after death and the god with whom Egyptian women and men identified as they faced their own mortality.[29] Through their participation in this myth, they expressed their hope to someday join the great god Osiris and thus be "absorbed in the great rhythm of the universe."[30] Osiris's name when combined with Apis, the name of the beautiful, virile black bull in which he was manifest, produced Serapis (from Osiris and Apis), the Greek version of the Egyptian cult that became highly popular well into the Roman period. In the translation into the Greek experience by Alexander's successors, the Ptolemies, however, it was Isis, not Osiris, who became the dominant figure. So this primal myth, so deeply rooted in Egypt's fertile land, promised victory over mortality to its initiates and became influential with the masses in the great urban centers of the Greco-Roman world. To establish its importance it is unnecessary to see parallels, as does Koester,[31] between Paul's account of dying and rising with Christ (Rom. 6:3–5) and participation in the Isis initiation. Certainly, many in Paul's congregations would have been aware of the cult and may have even been attracted to its wondrous vision of Isis:

> . . . the mother of the universe,
> The mistress of all the elements,

> The first offspring of time,
> The highest of the deities,
> The queen of the dead.[32]

From depictions of Mary influenced by the Isis myth decades after the death of Paul we are aware of the continuing appeal of this mystery religion. But few would have been unaware of the profound differences between Paul's gospel and the message of Isis. Whereas the Isis cult promised a triumph over death in the present, the defeat of death for Paul remained a future prospect. And, of course, although both begin with the story of a tragic murder (Jesus and Osiris), Paul's gospel has a historical dimension that the Isis-Osiris myth lacks and a radical monotheism that would have been totally alien to the Isis-Osiris mystery.

The Dionysiac Mystery. No discussion of the mysteries would be complete without some reference to Dionysus, the most popular Greek mystery of the Hellenistic age. Although a venerable god of distant antiquity, Dionysus's land of origin is disputed.[33] However that dispute turns, all recognize that Dionysus was revered in Greece before the sixth century B.C.E. and still had wide appeal into the first.

Dionysus was conceived in a tryst between the god Zeus and the mortal Semele, the daughter of Cadmus the king of Thebes. His birth, like his conception, stood outside the order of nature. Jealous of Semele's success with Zeus, Hera tricked Semele into begging Zeus to reveal his full splendor to her. After initially resisting, Zeus reluctantly agreed, but in the theophany Semele was struck down, consumed by a bolt of lightning. Dionysus was rescued from the dying Semele (birth one) and carried to full term by Zeus in his thigh, whence he eventually emerged (birth two). Devotees, identifying with Dionysus, spoke of themselves as "born-again" or recipients of a "second birth." Once fully grown, Dionysus descended to Hades to rescue his mother, Semele, and return her to Mount Olympus to live with the gods. In addition to heading a cult of rebirth, he was best known as the bringer of wine, and his victory over death was symbolized by a green ivy headband, a symbol of immortality.

Vase paintings from the sixth and fifth centuries B.C.E. depict maenads or female worshipers in wild, ecstatic nocturnal dances. Under the power of Dionysus they had broken free of onerous work at looms and shuttles. Other sources describe the feast of *sparagmos* in which women in a fit of ecstasy tore flesh from a living animal, devouring it raw in a reckless act of abandon and divine possession. Since Dionysus was present in both the wine and wild animals, to eat the sacred flesh and drink the wine was the mythical basis for their enthusiasm (literally having "god within"). And given the prominence of both the bloody sacrifice and wine from the crushed grape, the symbolic association of blood and wine as living sacrifice was natural. Whether the church's association of blood and wine in the Eucharist was influenced by the Dionysiac mysteries is uncertain. What is certain is that the command to drink the wine as Jesus' blood, so repulsive to Jews, would have sounded entirely natural to Paul's hearers who were familiar with the Dionysiac mystery.

Men also worshiped Dionysus, though usually segregated from women. In their stag parties they drank copious amounts of the wine symbolically containing the spirit of the god. Only in the spring festival apparently did women and men join together in one joyous act of celebration. But whether segregated or integrated, men and women throughout Greece, the islands, and onto the coast of Asia Minor hailed Dionysus in intoxication and dance as the " 'Raw-Eater,' 'Man-smasher,' 'Great Hunter,' 'Steer,' 'Roarer,' 'The-one-with-the-black-goatskin,' 'Erect,' 'Tree-like,' 'Flowerer,' 'Liberator.' "[34] These metaphors with which Dionysus was named reveal some of the complexity and irreconcilable ambiguity of this god. He stood for blood and gore as well as rescue and salvation. His dark side touched on bloodshed and pollution; his light side on release and freedom. His savagery and destructiveness linked him with death; his rescue of his mother from Hades made him the giver of life. His association with life and death, light and darkness, the world above and the world below, the untamed world and refined culture inevitably meant he was filled with contradictions, contradictions that are endemic to daily human experience.

In the Hellenistic period, however, from the third century B.C.E. to the first, the gravity and complexity of the earlier Dionysus gave way to a vision of the god much more in tune with Hellenistic ideals. Now more a symbol of the sophisticated, refined lifestyle of the Hellenistic period, and an advocate of the ecumenical vision of the one civilized world, Dionysus increasingly was used by the rulers to reinforce their political agendas. Nevertheless, Dionysus did not lose touch with the common lot of humanity. His gospel promised strength to endure life's trials and offered rescue from death in the world to come. His association with wine making, dance, and drama remained unshakable, and his powers remained sufficiently broad to be implored by emperor and slave alike. His tolerance for excess made it easy for his followers to identify with him.[35] His affirmation of the physical legitimated the sensual element in the human experience and offered release from the mundane. Caroline Houser aptly summarizes the basis of Dionysus's appeal: Dionysus, she notes, "is a realist who knows the dark and frightening side of nature as well as the light and joyful side. He promises transcendence or metamorphosis, not annihilation."[36]

In sum, one might say that the primary emphasis of the Dionysiac mystery was on the struggle between life and death. The emphasis on the life-giving power of the phallus must be seen against an awareness of death as the one great absolute. As early as the fifth century the mystery was concerned with the terror and bliss of the afterlife. This emphasis on funereal elements continued well into the Roman period. Yet the Roman version of the worship of Bacchus (for Dionysus) differed in the way it exaggerated certain elements in the Greek version. Devotees of Bacchus, for example, were much more direct in their pursuit of erotic pleasure, and the Roman maenads (or female devotees) much more provocative than their Greek counterparts. Although Paul's warnings against drunkenness and lust may not have been specifically aimed at the devotees of Dionysus, surely the context requires such warnings, for Paul would have been acutely aware of the hold of this mystery on some of his followers.

b. *The Healing Cult of Asclepius*

No person ancient or modern is a stranger to illness, and that human extremity often prompts an appeal to a higher power for help. In the Hellenistic world that request often was lifted up to Asclepius, the god of healing. Son of the god Apollo and the mortal Coronis, according to one account, Asclepius was born at Epidaurus, which later became the location of an impressive sanctuary in his honor. According to the myth, Asclepius died as a mortal but returned to earth as a god to live and serve humanity as the compassionate god of healing. Devoted primarily but not exclusively to the poor and disadvantaged, Asclepius was known as the kind, compassionate god. Seeking relief from sickness at any one of more than three hundred sanctuaries dedicated to him at Epidaurus, Athens, Corinth, Pergamum, the island of Cos, and other places, the ill came in great numbers. There were 160 rooms for guests at Epidaurus alone. As precursors of modern holistic medicine, these centers ministered to the mind and spirit as well as the body. The facilities at Epidaurus included libraries, gymnasia, theaters, baths, clinics for physicians, and a holy place *(abaton)* where the ill slept, hoping for a healing encounter with the merciful god Asclepius. For example, we are told that Ambrosia, a young girl who was blind in one eye, was visited by Asclepius as she slept in the *abaton.* "The god appeared before her, telling her that she would be cured and that she had to dedicate in the sanctuary a pig made of silver as a token of her ignorance. Having said this he cut out the bad eye and immersed it in medicine. She awoke at dawn, cured."[37]

While no such centers of healing existed in Jewish or early Christian circles, there was, nevertheless, as the Gospels show, a profound interest in the powers of charismatic healers. One difference, however, was that the emphasis on healing in the Asclepius cult was thoroughly individualistic, whereas the corporate dimension of Jewish and Christian healing stories is unmistakable. Although Paul's addressees, like all people of the time, suffered the usual number of illnesses and physical handicaps, Paul himself pays little attention to these issues. He does note that he was able to perform mighty works (healings? Gal. 3:5) and that he suffered from various afflictions, but he more strongly emphasizes God's strength made manifest in his weakness (2 Cor. 12:9) in contrast to those who display their miracle-working powers as proof of the truth of their gospel. Yet certainly healing cults were very much a part of the environment in which Paul proclaimed his gospel and may have influenced his hearers more than we know.

c. *Stoicism*

The personal agony and social upheaval of the third century B.C.E. provided the ingredients for the formation of Stoicism. With a shaking of the foundations, questions of theodicy were raised in the sharpest possible way. Social upheaval, civil war, famine, and tyranny prompted many to ask: If they care about the plight of humanity, why do the gods fail to redress the wrongs inflicted by this hostile world? Why is life unjust and unfair if providence favors justice and fair play? The Stoics answered by affirming rather than denying the divine presence in the world. "God" for the Stoics was less a divine personality who actively engaged in the affairs of human beings than a divine principle (*logos* or reason) that pervaded and governed the universe. As Edwyn Bevan noted, for the Stoic "the whole universe was only one Substance, one Physis, in various states" and "that one Substance was Reason, was God."[38] The world itself, like humans, had a soul that directed its affairs, and existence was seen as fundamentally rational. Even natural disasters such as floods, earthquakes, or famine advanced the divine purpose; perhaps they controlled population or served purposes hidden from humanity. Chrysippus once remarked that even the lowly bedbug was an instrument of the divine *logos* because it kept people from sleeping too much or too long. The humble pig, likewise, reflected the divine reason. Its "soul of salt" allowed its flesh to be preserved for eating, and its tendency to fatness made its meat delicious and nourishing. Chrysippus had the rather optimistic view that if the world could have been better arranged, the divine reason would have made it so. In the third century B.C.E. the famous Stoic Cleanthes well articulated this vision in his hymn to Zeus:

> For nought is done on earth apart from thee,
> Nor in thy vault of heaven, nor in the sea . . .
> But skill to make the crooked straight is thine,
> To turn disorder to a fair design
> Ungracious things are gracious in thy sight
> For ill and good thy power doth so combine.[39]

Once a person understood the universe to be fundamentally rational, he or she could accept whatever happened with equanimity (or *apatheia*). *Apatheia* was not mere resignation (as its English cognate *apathy* would suggest) but a source of strength based on the conviction that all things were controlled and directed by the divine reason. *Apatheia*, therefore, was the gateway to true freedom, for the truly disinterested person was untrammeled by the concerns and cares of the world. In the Stoic view, a kind of self-sufficiency or spiritual autonomy characterized the life of the truly liberated person.

Although Stoicism was pantheistic (the universe was infused with divine soul), it was no mystery religion. Its emphasis on the inner life, however, did give it a highly individualistic character. Its stress on personal detachment and the orderliness of the cosmos undermined any interest in history. Since the world moved in ways predetermined by cosmic reason, there was a certain sameness about it that minimized the importance of either a past or a future. As Bultmann says, "The Stoic believes that it is possible to escape from his involvement in time. By detaching himself from the world he detaches himself from time. The essential part of man is the Logos, and the Logos is timeless."[40]

Paul's early years were spent in Tarsus, a center of Stoic teaching. Certainly his letters show signs of Stoic influence. His use of the diatribe to argue his case[41] in Romans and his creative appropriation of the allegorical method of scripture interpretation both owe something to the Stoics. His tendency to view believers as citizens of heaven (Phil. 3:20) rather than of the *polis* (or city-state) strongly resembles a Stoic vision. Possibly even the inclusivism of his vision of an *oikoumenē* (or whole inhabited world) that included Jews *and* Gentiles may be informed by a Stoic cosmopolitanism (Rom. 10:18). At other points, however, Paul's worldview differs markedly from that of his Stoic contemporaries. His gospel is fundamentally historical; it is rooted in a historical event, based on a historical person, anticipates a fulfillment in the historical (real) future. Unlike the Stoic view of freedom as spiritual autonomy, freedom for Paul means liberation from hostile powers (death, sin, etc.) for service to Christ. The Stoic is confident that persons can win freedom through their own efforts; Paul sees freedom as a gift of God. And whereas the Stoic's concern centers on freedom, and thus on the individual, Christianity, says Paul, concerns life, and thus the interaction of human beings. We see, therefore, that while Paul uses the Stoic idiom, he always subordinates it to his gospel and in the process transforms it. But what was true of Paul was not always true of his converts, who were often inclined to familiar and easy spiritual options. Such natural compromises often led to sharp exchanges between Paul and his churches.

d. *Cynicism*

Strictly speaking not philosophers but advocates of a life-style and a method of teaching among the common people, the Cynics were called philosophers by their contemporaries nevertheless, and because of their influence they deserve our attention. The word Cynic comes from the Greek for dog *(kyōn),* an epithet hung on these sharp critics of the prevailing culture and norms of their time. The Cynics traced their lineage back to Diogenes of Sinope (fourth century B.C.E.), and their presence in the urban centers of Paul's day was significant. Claiming to live by nature *(physis),* they expressed their contempt for the well-dressed by wearing rags, for the well-groomed by their unkempt appearance, for the wealthy by begging, and for the politically powerful by insisting that only the wise had true power. As keen observers of nature, they modeled their lives by its rules. Like animals they defecated in public places and had sexual intercourse wherever they felt the urge. Like other creatures they sought to reduce life to its barest simplicity. So impressed was Diogenes, for example, by a child's drinking from cupped hands that he discarded his cup saying, "A child has beaten me in the plainness of living."[42] Greatly elevating boldness of speech, they appropriated for themselves a freedom of speech that was usually reserved for citizens in the assembly. For instance, so overawed was he by Diogenes's example that Alexander the Great reputedly told the philosopher, "Ask me any boon you like." To which Diogenes replied, "Stand out of my light."[43] Paul himself speaks, like the Cynics, of having the boldness "in God to speak to you the gospel of God in the face of great opposition" (1 Thess. 2:2). Although they were not atheistic, Cynics might have found such pious language discomfiting, for they usually saw such language as an expression of popular religion, which they sharply criticized as a superstitious endorsement of the status quo.

Understandably, many found Cynic behavior—their ragged, dirty clothing, their dirty hair, their matted, unkempt beards, and surly manner—to be revolting. Writing in the middle of the first century, Seneca scoffed at their behavior and at "their repellent attire, unkempt hair, slovenly beard, open scorn of silver dishes, a couch on the bare earth and . . . other perverted forms of self-display."[44] In spite of popular disdain for them, Cynics, nevertheless, did at points influence New Testament writings. Paul's use of the diatribe came at least indirectly from Cynics and Stoics. Some of his language (e.g., "boldness of speech") shows some debt to the Cynic philosophers. The list of hardships that he notes in his letters (e.g., 2 Cor. 11:23–29) closely follows a Cynic pattern.[45] Paul's own understanding of the radical character of his wandering mission may have owed something in one way or another to the Cynic practice. Yet, at other points, Paul seems at pains to distance himself from wandering popular preachers who were mere hucksters preying on the goodwill of their hearers for support. Paul shows little inclination to engage in a radical critique of society. Why should he? He was convinced that it would all be replaced soon, anyway, by the coming rule of God. And Paul, much more than any Cynic preacher, saw the necessity of religious institutions and corporate support for the life of radical obedience to God. So in being aware of this conceptual context in which Paul preaches, we must also exercise caution—conceptual parallels may not suggest agreement. It is important to see that Paul's critique of the world and his readers is based on the gospel he preached, which was significantly different from Cynic philosophy.

e. Neo-Pythagoreanism

Because of its ability to synthesize diverse traditions, Pythagoreanism[46] enjoyed a widespread revival in the first century B.C.E. With the venerated name of Pythagoras to legitimate their teachings, the Neo-Pythagoreans forged a union of philosophy and religious piety that had genuine popular appeal. Far from being just an exercise in speculation, this philosophy concerned itself with cultivating a sensitivity to the divine element within the self. That "like seeks like" was the primary axiom of both Pythagorean (sixth century B.C.E.) and Neo-Pythagorean thought (first century B.C.E.). This meant that human nature, being divine, constantly seeks to return home to its cosmic source; the aim of life is to strip off the body to allow the spirit to rejoin the divine soul. Naturally this loyalty to one's higher nature required repudiation of the flesh, because it is by flesh that the spirit is tethered to this world. This emphasis on liberation from the body often led to a repression or a sublimation of sex, and to a life of poverty free from earth's trappings. Sometimes a vow of silence was taken to mitigate traffic with this world and afford fuller contemplation of the world of spirit.

Since the soul was divine, and the divine eternal, Neo-Pythagoreans firmly believed the soul was immortal, and this led to belief in transmigration. Soul was not the exclusive property of people: the divine element went beyond the human family to include animals. The Neo-Pythagorean conviction that the divine ether was present in animals led them to ban the eating of meat and to forbid the wearing of clothes made from animal pelts or wool.

A strong mystical current ran through Neo-Pythagoreanism. Like the god-intoxicated worshipers of the mysteries, they called themselves *entheoi* (those in whom God dwells) or even *ekstatikoi* (those possessed or beside themselves with the spirit). This enthusiasm (literally, infusion with God) often manifested itself in miraculous works. In some circles miracles revealed the divinity of the one performing them. In this view, charismatic figures who are by nature divine perform divine (i.e., miraculous) deeds.

For some Neo-Pythagoreans, numbers held a fascinating significance. Far from being mere abstract quantitative ciphers, numbers were divine. Apparently this reverence for numbers sprang from the conviction that harmony was the essence of divine nature. The precise rhythm of the cosmos as well as the delicate and perfect balance between good and evil suggested to them the control of a divine principle. Numbers, in their view, did far more than just count or measure; the harmonies they evinced corresponded exactly to the harmonies of the cosmos, and both were forms of the divine principle. For example, the balance between odd and even numbers, between finity and infinity, and between the one and the many was seen as a fundamental reality that manifested itself also in the division between male and female, light and darkness, good and evil, and so on.

Given this worldview, it is hardly surprising that astrology assumed a prominent place in Neo-Pythagoreanism.[47] Although their interest in astrology and numbers did prompt the Neo-Pythagoreans to an accurate reading of the heavens, their aim was not scientific but religious. The heavenly spheres were more than the expression of divine order, they were also its source. The astral bodies were viewed as divine beings whose will could be known through study of their movements. Knowing that will was important because those bodies were thought to determine the destiny of the world. The goal of knowledge was to penetrate to the very heart of the cosmos and to find truth "as something at once beatific and comforting." This philosophy "presents the human being as cradled in a universal harmony."[48] The saving quality of this knowledge was especially precious in the first century B.C.E. because of the loss of inner security that had come with the increase in knowledge, the decay of social structures, and the loss of faith. Neo-Pythagoreans took comfort in their belief that there was some connection between the "fixed glare of alien power and necessity" in the stars and the destiny of the world.[49]

In the view of some, Neo-Pythagoreanism was a degenerate philosophy.[50] The movement did address itself, however, to a major concern of the time. Increasingly, many felt ruled by powers they could not understand. Life seemed capricious and unfair; the only certainty was uncertainty. The elder Pliny articulated a widespread feeling in the cities when he said,

> We are so much at the mercy of chance
> that Chance herself, by whom God is
> proved uncertain, takes the place of God.[51]

Added to this sense of helplessness before powerful forces was a growing suspicion that the powers were careless. Many felt as though they were mere playthings of Fate *(Moira)*, Chance *(Tychē)*, or Necessity *(Anankē)*. Life, they believed, was determined by forces that were fundamentally irrational and blind to any moral distinctions. Although Neo-Pythagoreanism was not rational and did not encourage reason, it did offer an alternative to surrendering before Fate. It promised the desperate a way out of this world. By touching the divine within, believers could anticipate liberation of the divine spark from its fleshly prison and a reunion of it with the source of all being and truth. Freed from the tyranny of capricious, irrational powers, life assumed meaning and purpose that made it tolerable.

The character of first-century Neo-Pythagorean thought is perhaps best exhibited in Apollonius of Tyana. Although his highly romanticized biography was not commissioned until 216 C.E. (more than a century after his death),[52] the piety reflected in it conforms rather well to Apollonius's actual first-century outlook. Renouncing wine, meat, and marriage, Apollonius wandered about barefoot, clad only in "earthwool" (linen—which did not strip animals of their clothing). Through gifts to the poor he rid himself of the burden of wealth, and through a vow of silence that lasted for five years he screened out this world to concentrate on the divine. His travels carried him as far east as India and as far west as Rome. He conferred with the sages in Nepal, preached and performed miracles through Asia Minor and Greece, visited naked sages on the upper Nile, and advised public officials in Rome.

His preaching emphasized a strong link between salvation and self-knowledge. Inasmuch as knowing the self means knowing the divine within the self, self-knowledge is synonymous with knowing or even becoming god. Consequently, to know oneself is to know all things, since God knows everything. Moreover, the truly good person is divine, that is, one whose actions reflect what he or she essentially is. These divine acts reach beyond high moral concerns to include miraculous deeds. In the biographical account, for example, Apollonius not only denounces Roman tyranny, repudiates gladiatorial combat, exhorts the common people to improve their morals, and admonishes all to be responsible citizens, but he also predicts a plague, raises a dead girl, heals a boy bitten by a mad dog, exorcises demons, and quells riots. There is little cause for wonder that Apollonius is asked at his trial, "Why do people call you god?" And his answer is not surprising: "Every man believed to be good is honored with the title god."[53]

Persecuted under Nero for his "meddlesome business," he was apparently martyred under Domitian near the end of the first century. One tradition, however, speaks of an end befitting an immortal, namely his mysterious disappearance and ascension before the date set for his execution.

Although the biography of Apollonius is late, his activity as a wonder

worker, wise man, lawgiver, and patron of the mysteries is in tune with
the spirit of the age. Whereas the literary portrait of Apollonius painted
by Philostratus reflects some later concerns, the basic outline of his
sketch closely resembles the picture of first-century Neo-Pythagoreanism presented by others.[54] Given the spiritual hunger and the fatalistic
outlook of the period and given the hopeful emphases of Neo-Pythagoreanism, its success among rich and poor, privileged and slave,
intellectuals and illiterates, is hardly surprising. And considering its
broad popular appeal, the likelihood is great it influenced some of
Paul's hearers, perhaps rather significantly.

f. *Gnosticism*

Gnosticism (from the Greek word *gnōsis,* meaning knowledge) was
an important element in the experience of the early church. Although
the background of Gnosticism is extraordinarily complex, it is likely
that the spirit of the Hellenistic age played some role in its genesis and
formation. Although it is unlikely that Gnosticism was merely an acute
Hellenization of Christianity, as Harnack claimed generations ago, it
surely was at home in the Hellenistic context.

Whether Gnosticism antedated Christianity is much debated, but
Gnostic materials with sources that go back to the second century C.E.
were discovered at Nag Hammadi in southern Egypt in 1945. These
materials, now published, should assist us in sketching with some precision the contours of thought in this movement.[55] The description of
Gnosticism given by the church fathers was formerly discounted because of its polemical nature. Already we have learned from the Nag
Hammadi materials that the picture of Gnosticism drawn by the Fathers was not the caricature we had suspected. Since our earliest knowledge is of second-century Gnosticism, it is not always applicable to
Paul, but certain features of the second-century version were undoubtedly present in the first.

The presence of the divine *logos* in the natural world allowed the
Stoic to view his environment positively. The Gnostic, however, saw the
world as incurably evil. It was assumed, therefore, that its creator must
also be evil. Yahweh of the Hebrew Bible, the god of this evil world,
was called an antigod or demonic god, opposed to the true, high god.
This radical dualism between the god above and the god below, between
matter and spirit, between light and darkness, between knowledge and
ignorance, formed the nucleus of Gnostic thought. And the denigration
of matter profoundly influenced Gnostic anthropology or view of the
human. The product of an evil conspiracy, imprisoned in a demonic
world, unconscious of the divine spark within, all humanity wanders
aimlessly in perpetual stupor. Were it not for the great high god who
takes pity on humanity and sends a redeemer to remind them of their

true destiny, all would be hopelessly lost. But once awakened from the ignorance of one's divine origin, Gnostics enjoy total salvation here and now. Liberated from the bodily prison, the "spiritual" person already knows absolute freedom, a freedom that embraces both stringent asceticism and voluptuary license. In their repudiation of the flesh (asceticism), Gnostics demonstrate their freedom *over* the body. In their indulgence of the flesh (promiscuity), Gnostics demonstrate their freedom *from* the body, in that what is done in the body does not affect the real self. Moreover, the laws broken were given by the old fallen god Yahweh, anyway, and breaking the laws demonstrates one's liberation from the god of this world.

In reading 1 Corinthians we see many of these tendencies, and while it is anachronistic to argue for a second-century movement in the first century, it is quite likely that in some of Paul's congregations we have the embryonic expression of a pre-Gnostic phenomenon that would only later come to dominate the church in Egypt and parts of Syria. Moreover, we see in the later church Gnostic misunderstandings of Paul's letters that may reflect much earlier tendencies. Certainly, Paul was no Gnostic, but some of his statements (like "flesh and blood cannot inherit the kingdom of God," 1 Cor. 15:50), if taken out of context, were certainly open to misinterpretation by Christians with Gnostic tendencies.[56]

Summary

Each of the movements described above is in some ways peculiarly its own and in other ways fully representative of the spirit of the age. And apart from these movements, what had previously been central to Hellenism continued—namely, an openness to other cultures and a broad tolerance and even adoption of views from every quarter. Although such cross-fertilization could be and often was fruitful, the risk was great that the new gods and foreign ways would radically alter or even supplant traditional religious views.

One other motif survived—a sense of community or *sympatheia*[57] with the divine. By the first century the heroic period of Hellenism had faded, but if the traditional gods of classical Greece had lost their power to save, they had also lost their enervating characteristics. Most still felt related to a divine principle if not to a divine personality. It was this divine element in everyone that bound all together as kinfolk, erasing artificial distinctions between man and woman, barbarian and Greek, slave and free. Moreover, it was the godly ether shared by the animals that linked humanity with them through *sympatheia*.

The most significant development, however, in the Hellenistic period was the emerging split between the celestial and terrestrial worlds. Matter was viewed more and more as an independent principle and the source of all evil, and a terrifying rupture emerged between flesh and spirit, between the world below and the world above. Whether this dualism was homegrown or imported from the East is unclear. What is clear is that it found conditions favorable for growth in Hellenistic soil. Even if many of Paul's readers had never read or listened to the philosophers, their views were strongly influenced by the spirit of the age. Once we realize that Paul's gospel ran counter to this Zeitgeist, we can begin to locate the points at which Paul's readers would find it difficult to understand or to accept his message. Without question, Paul's gospel was a source of joy and hope to many, but the acceptance of his kerygma did not change cherished ideas overnight. Only reluctantly did Paul's converts surrender their view that matter was evil, that salvation was an individual not a corporate experience, that history was circular, or that God could be apprehended directly without the need of historical media like scripture or apostles. It was over these issues that Paul and his hearers frequently clashed. Once these points of friction are spotted we can begin to see the letters as real conversations over real concerns.

In the discussion above we have seen important elements of the social, cultural, and spiritual environment inhabited by Paul and his churches. Their Greek Bible inevitably contained a Greek idiom that reflected a Hellenistic outlook. Paul's language and that of his hearers also affected their understanding of the human condition and the Christian gospel. Hellenistic religious and philosophical movements, furthermore, were lively conversational cohorts of Paul and his churches. For that reason, Paul's letters are dynamic interactions with that world, providing flashes of insight that generate new symbols, inspire new visions of the present and the future, destabilize patterns of religiosity that were taken for granted, and infuse existing structures with ferment and even protest. Paul's letters are a record of that process.

Paul's Jewish Environment

Some have claimed to see the influence of Hellenistic tradition in Paul's allusion to dying and rising with Christ (Rom. 6:5) and in his references to the eucharistic tradition. Such cultic identification of a person with a divine figure, they say, is compatible with Greek but not Jewish piety that insists on the distinction between the Creator and the creature. Even if one discounts any Hellenistic influence on Paul's understanding of the sacraments, other evidence reveals his awareness of the Hellenistic world and his openness to it. This is hardly surprising: some Hellenistic influence should be presupposed if Paul did indeed spend his formative years in Tarsus, a bustling trade center with a sizable and energetic Stoic school. But was the Hellenistic influence dominant? John Knox is so firmly convinced of the dominance of that

Hellenism on Paul's thought that he wonders if Paul ever did, as Luke claims, study under Gamaliel in Jerusalem (Acts 22:3).[58]

There is no need to know, if we ever could know, whether Hellenism dominated Paul's thought. What is clear is that Paul employs certain literary forms and devices, expressions, methods of argumentation, and concepts that come from a Hellenistic tradition. The special language and outlook of his Greek Bible, the creeds, hymns, and language of the Hellenistic church and/or the Diaspora synagogue, as well as a host of influences from the culture at large, as we have seen, all informed Paul's thought to a significant degree. Yet, in spite of his openness to the Hellenistic world, Paul was proud of his Jewish heritage. These traditions too had a profound influence on the apostle's thinking. It is to a consideration of that part of his history that we now turn.

1. *Paul the Pharisee*

In Philippians 3:5f. Paul refers to himself as "circumcised on the eighth day, of the people Israel, of the tribe of Benjamin, a Hebrew born of Hebrews; as to the law a *Pharisee* . . . , as to righteousness under the law blameless." In Acts, Luke likewise speaks positively of Paul's Pharisaism. Going beyond what Paul himself reports in his letters, Luke suggests that Paul remained a loyal Pharisee until his death. Given the unflattering picture of the Pharisees in the Gospels, Luke's positive assessment of Paul's Pharisaism may surprise many.[59] But the harsh polemic against the Pharisees in Matthew reflects the struggle between church and synagogue in a later period and should not be read as an objective description. Much work has been done in recent years on the nature of first-century Pharisaism and a brief consideration of some of that work will help us to understand Paul.

Although the picture of the Pharisees painted by the Gospel writers is a distortion of historical reality, much that is historically reliable can be learned about the Pharisees from the Gospels. From them we learn about the Pharisaic emphasis on ritualistic purity. Careful to eat the right kind of foods, to purify (not merely wash) vessels used in food preparation, and to exclude the unclean (such as tax collectors and prostitutes) from table fellowship, the Pharisees are obviously treating all of life as a ritual. Unlike the priests who took the laws in Leviticus relating to sacrifice, eating temple food, and cultic preparation to apply only to the temple itself and its worship, for the Pharisees the "setting for law observance was the field and the kitchen, the bed and the street."[60] Taking quite literally the command in Exodus 19:6 to be a "kingdom of priests," the Pharisees attempted to act as if all of the common life was a temple service.

This preoccupation with ritual purity noted in the Gospels is an important though single dimension of Pharisaism. Other aspects of this movement are mentioned in the writings of Josephus, a first-century Jewish author. In his history of the Jewish War (66–70 C.E.), Josephus says:

> The Pharisees, who are considered the most accurate interpreters of the laws, and hold the position of the leading sect, attribute everything to fate and to God; they hold that to act rightly or otherwise rests, indeed, for the most part with men, but that in each action Fate cooperates. Every soul, they maintain, is imperishable, but the soul of the good alone passes into another body, while the souls of the wicked suffer eternal punishment.[61]

This "leading sect," we are here told, affirms a classic paradox—belief in divine predestination (Fate) and the demand for responsible human behavior. Moreover, the value of every soul is linked with the belief in the resurrection of the righteous, which is to occur at the grand, final assize when God will vindicate the pious people and punish the sinners. Here Josephus notes the Pharisees' accurate interpretation of the law; elsewhere he admires their simple life-style, their repudiation of luxury and the "respect and deference" that they show to their elders and their teachings. They, unlike the Essenes, live among the townfolk and are intensely involved in the workaday world.[62] In the respect they pay to the traditions of the elders and in their acceptance of the concept of the resurrection, whose origin was probably as late as 165 B.C.E., Pharisaism displays an openness to innovation that is remarkable.

While Neusner argues that the Pharisaism of Paul's day was concerned primarily with ritualistic purity and, therefore, was apolitical, Rivkin objects that Pharisaism in the first century was revolutionary and concerned with issues ranging far beyond ritual cleanness.[63] As scholars devoted to the study of both the oral and the written law, the Pharisees gradually replaced the priestly class as authoritative interpreters of the law and gained sufficient power to impose their rulings on the society at large. As the dominant political and religious force in Israel, the Pharisees were in a position not only to interpret law but also to promulgate new law.

According to Rivkin, the Pauline letters and the Gospels corroborate this version of Pharisaism. Paul speaks of his Pharisaic past when he was "so extremely zealous . . . for the traditions of my fathers" (Gal. 1:14). The Gospels disparage the Pharisees as those who "sit on Moses' seat" in positions of authority (Matt. 23:2), and recognize the deference shown them in the marketplace, the honor they enjoy in the synagogue, and the special authority they have to persecute Christians (Acts 9:1–2). While Rivkin's critique of Neusner is telling at points, his own thesis suffers from its strict dependence on Josephus and from its reading of Gospel texts written after the destruction of Jerusalem as if their portrait of the Pharisees applies equally to the prewar period (i.e., before 66 B.C.E.). Although flawed in this regard, it is entirely possible that Rivkin's work will require some expansion of Neusner's rather narrow definition of Pharisaism to include concerns that go considerably beyond ritualistic purity. In such a case, Paul's harassment of Messianists (or Christians) may have been motivated if not authorized by his Pharisaism.

But can we go further? Did Paul continue in the way of the Pharisees after his apostolic call? Luke tells us that he did. In Acts 25:8 Luke has Paul say in his own defense, "Neither *against the law of the Jews*, nor against the temple, nor against Caesar have I offended at all" (italics added). In his speech before Agrippa Paul says, according to Luke, that "according to the strictest party of our religion I have lived as a Pharisee" (Acts 26:5). Certainly Paul does, as his letters testify, still share many Pharisaic beliefs. His view that the resurrection of the just comes at the end of the age, his concept of predestination linked with an emphasis on human responsibility, his liberal estimate of what was scriptural, his involvement in the workaday world, his spiritualization of sacrificial language, and his method of scriptural exegesis all seem to reflect his Pharisaism. But there is evidence on the other side as well. His free association with Gentiles, his casual attitude toward the laws of purity, the role the Messiah plays in his thought, and his interpretation of the Law all divide him from his Pharisaic brothers. Certainly by the strictest interpretation Paul appears to compromise his Pharisaic tradition, but to say that he rejected it outright is going too far. It would be more accurate to say that Paul's letters reflect a fresh appraisal of those traditions in light of his conviction that in the cross and resurrection of Jesus God's final eschatological breakthrough was occurring.

2. Paul's Jewish Methods of Scripture Interpretation

The apostle's ties to his Jewish heritage are also evident in his method of scripture interpretation. First, it must be noted that his scriptures were exclusively and emphatically Jewish. As we noted above, Greek ideas did intrude through the Greek translation of the Septuagint, but the story of the Jewish people told in the scriptures is fundamentally a Jewish story about God's election and the responsibilities that went with that call. In the full light of that story Paul crafted his gospel. His various methods of interpretation were designed to show how Jesus as the Messiah, crucified and risen, fulfilled the hopes and expectations of those scriptures. Many of those methods Paul learned from his Jewish teachers. His use of midrash, his appeal to Jewish legend, his use of scripture to interpret scripture, his collection of random texts that cluster around a common theme, his reading of the prophets as seers, his reasoning from the lesser to the greater, and his attempt to draw analogies through link words are all methods of exegesis that Paul shares with the learned Jewish interpreters of his day. (One must be careful to note, however, that even these methods of interpretation were influenced to a degree by Hellenistic methods of textual interpretation.)

One important method of scripture interpretation used by the rabbis was midrash, which we see Paul using in 1 Corinthians 10. (Midrash is a method of exegesis from the rabbis that seeks to find in a text its inner significance, to discover principles or laws for living, or to reveal what is authentic in religion.) In this passage Paul draws on Israel's wilderness experience to instruct a church in which some viewed the sacraments as a magical guarantee of salvation. Paul cautions against such overconfidence, reminding his readers that their life as a sacramental community was prefigured in Israel's wilderness wandering. Israel too ate sacred food (manna) and Israel also drank the supernatural drink (water from the rock). Yet, Paul warns, Israel's status as a sacramental community in no way exempted it from divine accountability. Murmuring brought death to many, and idolatry brought the fall of more than 20,000 in a single day. Thus Paul draws a lesson from the biblical account of Israel's wilderness experience for a wayward church that takes salvation (and God) for granted.

Certain images Paul uses come from legendary materials related to biblical traditions but not specifically mentioned in the Old Testament. In Galatians 3:19 he speaks of the role the angels played in the giving of the law. In 1 Corinthians 10:4 he refers to the moving rock in the wilderness, and in 1 Corinthians 11:10 he notes a command given to women to cover their heads in the service of worship "because of the angels." At the very least Paul's willingness to cite these legendary materials that go beyond the literal meaning of the biblical story shows how broad his understanding of the sacred tradition was.

In 2 Corinthians 3:6ff. Paul uses one text to interpret another. First he contrasts the covenant made with Moses with that forecast by Jeremiah: "The written code kills, but the Spirit gives life" (3:6). Then he tells the old, familiar story of the giving of the Law to Moses "carved in letters on stone" (2 Cor. 3:7). Because the brilliant splendor of this event was reflected by the face of Moses, he veiled his face to shield the people from the blinding light. Paul suggests in allegorical fashion that like Moses' face, the true meaning of the Torah, which was veiled up to now, has been revealed. The glory associated with the giving of the Law, as great as it was, is now surpassed by that of the Christ event. Paul then concludes with a quotation from Isaiah that he believes forges a link between this glory of Christ and the outpouring of the Spirit to come at the end time: "Now the Lord is the Spirit, and where the Spirit of the Lord is, there is freedom" (2 Cor. 3:17).

Another instance of the interpretation of one passage by another is seen in Galatians 3. While discussing the promise given to Abraham, Paul quotes Genesis 12:3: "In you shall all the peoples of the earth be blessed" (Septuagint). In another version of the same account the expression "in you" is changed to "in your seed [or offspring]" (Gen. 22:18). After concluding that the phrase "in your seed" refers to the statement "in you," Paul makes a rather dramatic interpretive leap. Reading "seed" as singular, he takes this key word to refer not to Abraham's many descendants but to one descendant (or "seed") and one only, namely, Christ. Thus Paul interprets Genesis 12:3 by way of Genesis 22:18 to mean, "in you [i.e., Christ] shall all the nations [i.e., the Gentiles] be blessed" (Gal. 3:8).

While such a method of exegesis may strike us as highly arbitrary or even historically incorrect, Jeremias was correct when he wrote that Paul is here using a method of scripture interpretation commonly utilized by the rabbis.[64] Such methods, however arbitrary they may appear to us, seem to link the messianic movement that Paul knows with Israel's history in a dynamic way.

In his collections of random texts clustered around a common theme, we also see a method of exegesis commonly used in Jewish circles. In Romans 3:10b–18, for example, we see six quotations threaded together like beads on a string. Held together by a theme that Paul wants to emphasize, these citations from diverse Old Testament contexts address a common topic—the universality of human sin or culpability. The cumulative effect of such clustering is to underscore a major point of the first three chapters of Romans, namely to establish beyond excuse or special pleading the need of all people, Jew and Gentile alike, for the gospel.

In another instance, Paul reads scripture, the prophets in particular, as if they were forecasting the apostle's imminent future. Paul either alludes to or quotes the Old Testament prophets more than forty times.[65] An examination of those references will show that Paul understands almost all of these references to refer to his present and near future. The prophets, he believed, predicted the coming of the eschatological age now dawning (Rom. 1:2; 3:21; 16:26, etc.). They foresaw the rejection of Jesus by most of the Jews and the inclusion of the Gentiles now taking place (Rom. 3:29; 9:25–26; 10:20; 15:12). They anticipated the laying of the new cornerstone in Israel in the person of Jesus (Rom. 9:33) and they promised a covenant in the process of being established (2 Cor. 3:14–18). They spoke of the present manifestation of God's righteousness (Rom. 3:21), and their rejection foreshadowed the death of Jesus (1 Thess. 2:15). One clearly sees in his use of the prophets Paul's preoccupation with the "end time." This preoccupation strongly influences Paul's way of reading these ancient texts. In this respect also his method of exegesis was widely shared in Jewish circles. In the writings from the Dead Sea community, for example, we see the same tendency to read the prophets primarily as seers whose predictions are directed to the last generation of humankind before the "day of the

Lord." The Qumran sectarians believed that the secrets (Hebrew, *razin*) of scripture heretofore unknown were revealed to their leader, the Teacher of Righteousness, and after his death to the members of the community. Selected members of the community studied those texts literally day and night to learn their secrets for this community of the end time. While Paul's focus is quite different from this form of inspired exegesis, his basic conviction that scripture contains eschatological secrets was the same.

With the benefit of historical criticism we know that the prophets spoke to their own time and their predictions had a fairly limited horizon. Yet to say that Paul and the sectarians of the Dead Sea community were simply mistaken is to impose unfairly our canons of interpretation on Paul and his contemporaries. At least Paul professed to see in the activity of Jesus the inauguration of the age the prophets envisioned. But more important than the question of whether Paul misreads scripture is how the sacred texts function for him. We have seen that the scriptures do more than rehearse Israel's sacred story. They also, Paul and the Qumraners believe, anticipate a future. Since the scriptures of old embrace the writer's future, a dynamic relationship is established between the storied past and the time of Paul and his contemporaries. In this way of viewing texts, the past provides the key that unlocks the future, and the future provides the lens for viewing the writings of the past. Thus, the ancient texts were never dead letters. Always pregnant with meaning, the scriptures served as a powerful force to legitimate the proclamation of the early church and to secure the gospel in the history of Israel. By attending to the ways the Old Testament comes to life for Paul and how it functions in the letters of Paul, we gain a better idea not only of how the apostle's argument unfolds but also of how the past remains alive for Paul and his community.

Jeremias (and Michel before him) found evidence in the letters that the apostle followed the rabbis in other ways.[66] The first rule of Hillel involved the reasoning from the lesser to the greater. In Romans 5:15, 17, for example, Paul shows how the destiny of many is affected by the decision of one person. First he offers Adam as a negative example. Just as many were partners with Adam in disobedience, so also, Paul argues, many may participate in the act of obedience of one man, Jesus. But the comparison, he continues, is inapt in that the grace experienced "in Christ" is more efficacious than the power of sin experienced "in Adam." The development of Paul's argument, we see, moves from the lesser (Adam) to the greater (Christ) and in so doing follows a pattern of argument from scripture already practiced by the famous rabbi Hillel.

The second rule of Hillel followed by Paul, Jeremias shows, involves drawing analogies through link words. In Romans 4:1–12, where this method is employed, Paul opens with a quotation from Genesis that says that "Abraham believed God, and it was *reckoned* [counted] to him as righteousness" (emphasis added). That Abraham receives the promise through grace rather than works is corroborated, in Paul's view, by Psalm 32:2 where forgiveness of sin is taken by the psalmist to mean that "the Lord will not reckon [count] his sin" (author's translation). Finally, we are told that just as righteousness was reckoned (counted) to Abraham because of faith rather than works, so also Gentiles who believe in God because of God's work in Christ will be reckoned (counted) as righteous (4:22–23).[67] We see here how Paul uses the word "reckon" to link the faith of Abraham ultimately with the inclusion of the Gentiles in the eschatological community. Although the content Paul gives this argument reflects his "life in Christ," the method he uses in making his point belongs to the rabbis.

3. *Paul and Jewish Apocalypticism*

While recognizing that Paul's views on eschatology completely suffuse his interpretation of scripture, let us pause for a moment to note the relationship of Paul's eschatological outlook to Jewish apocalyptic traditions.[68] Such terms as "wrath" *(orgē)*, the "day" *(hēmera)*, "death" *(thanatos)*, "righteousness" *(dikaiosynē)*, "judgment" *(krisis)*, and the distinction between the two ages *(aiōn)* are hardly intelligible apart from their Jewish milieu. And the similarity between Paul and Jewish apocalypticism goes far beyond the colorful terminology they share. Both are dominated by an eager longing for and an earnest expectation of the messianic kingdom. In both burns the intensity that comes from living on the boundary between two worlds—one dying and the other being born. Both share the link with Israel's past, and both hope for the *imminent* fruition of God's promises. Although Paul's understanding of Jesus as beginning God's future age differs from the ideas in Jewish apocalypticism, the two share a conviction that their generation is to be the last. This heightened awareness of God's impending doom influences everything Paul says to the churches. Everything he enjoins—instructions concerning marriage (1 Cor. 7:26), or for settling disputes in the church (Rom. 14:10–12), or for celebrating the Eucharist (1 Cor. 11:32), or for paying taxes (Rom. 13:6–7), or for honoring public officials (Rom. 13:1–5)—as well as his own sense of mission assumes a special urgency because of this belief that time is short.[69]

No discovery has more revolutionized biblical studies than the discovery in 1947 of the Qumran Scrolls by Muhammad ed-Dib, a Bedouin boy searching for a lost sheep. Stored in jars and hidden in caves on the northwest corner of the Dead Sea in anticipation of the arrival of a Roman legion on the march, now after more than 1,800 years the scrolls have emerged to reveal much about the life and religion of an intense apocalyptic sect that had withdrawn from priestly service at the temple in Jerusalem. Convinced that the Hasmonean ruling family had polluted the temple by taking over the high-priestly office, these rebellious priests abandoned this holy place to follow the injunction of Isaiah 40:3: "In the wilderness prepare the way of the Lord."

Archeological excavations have shown the Qumran site to be an impressive establishment. Built around a system of reservoirs and canals catching and delivering water for daily needs and ritual bathing, these facilities included a large assembly hall, a scriptorium for transcribing sacred texts, a kitchen, bakery, pantry, watchtower, and even a laundry and stable. Scholars judge that at its peak the site may have supported more than two hundred members. These impressive facilities supported a community that was chiefly (though not exclusively) celibate for almost two hundred years, and during that time the feverish expectancy of God's final visitation never waned.

The apocalyptic tone of their writings is unmistakable, and though there is no evidence for a direct link between the Qumran community and New Testament writings, indirect influence is evident. Like the Qumran community, Paul himself divides humanity into two camps— the children of light and the children of darkness (1 Thess. 5:4). Like the Qumran community, his conviction that he lived in the last generation of humankind was unshakable. Like the Qumran community, he associated God's righteousness with the redemption of the elect. Like the Qumran community, he discouraged though he did not forbid marriage in anticipation of the final eschatological crisis (1 Cor. 7:26, 32–35). Like the Qumran community, he insisted on purity in the community in preparation for the world's denouement (1 Thess. 3:13; 4:7–8). And like the Qumran community, Paul believed the raging cosmic conflict between God and "the ruler of this world" is replicated in microcosm in the life of every believer, and by God's grace the believer is victorious.

Though abundant precedent exists in Jewish circles for early Christian apocalyptic thought, profound differences exist as well. Paul and the early church held that in Jesus' death and resurrection the end time had already begun. Whereas the Qumran community retreated to the wilderness to prepare for the end, Paul encouraged no such separation. The priestly community at Qumran expected God to inaugurate a purified cult in Jerusalem, but Paul harbored no such expectation. The members of the Qumran community fantasized about fighting in God's final battle for control of the world, but no such expectation is voiced in the Pauline letters. A general resurrection may be implied but is nowhere explicitly mentioned in the Qumran scrolls, but it is a common feature of the Pauline letters. We see, therefore, that Paul's apocalypticism hardly originated with him or even the church before him but was deeply rooted in the Jewish experience. Yet, in important ways his life "in Christ" revalued traditions coming out of that experience.

In all the ways noted above—his views of the resurrection and predestination, his liberal assessment of what was scriptural, his uses of traditional methods of scriptural interpretation, and his extensive use of imagery from Jewish apocalyptic thought—we see how thoroughly Hebrew tradition permeated Paul's thought. Schoeps quite properly states that Paul's argument is obscure if not altogether incomprehensible apart from its relationship to Old Testament traditions.[70] To this we might add the use of that tradition made by the Jewish interpreters of Paul's day.

In the discussion above we have seen that Paul was deeply influenced by both the Hellenistic and Jewish traditions of his day. Yet this combination of Hellenistic and Jewish elements hardly originated with Paul. It came at least partly prepackaged in the Jewish tradition he knew. In the Asia Minor of Paul's youth the Jews had already accommodated themselves to their Greek environment. They attended the theater, took part in sports, gave their children Greek or Latin names, and decorated their tombs with Greek art.[71] This accommodation, however, was made without assimilation. The Jews of the Asia Minor of Paul's youth were well integrated into the community. They were good citizens up to a point. But at that point—where the claims of Gentile society clashed with the claims of Torah—the Law took precedence.

Judging by the archeological evidence, even in Palestine Judaism had been Hellenized almost as much as in Asia Minor. Goodenough has drawn our attention to numerous Greek inscriptions found in Jerusalem itself.[72] A Greek word, "Sanhedrin" *(synedrion),* designated the most significant judging body in Palestine, and Greek manuscripts were found among the scrolls from the Qumran sect on the Dead Sea. We see, therefore, to quote Davies, that "the traditional convenient dichotomy between Judaism and Hellenism was largely false. In the fusions of the first century the boundaries between these are now seen to have been very fluid."[73] Using different information, Martin Hengel has come to substantially the same conclusion in his well-documented study, *Judaism and Hellenism.*[74] Therefore, to attempt to understand Paul exclusively in light of his Hellenistic or his Jewish background is to misunderstand him.[75]

In Philippians 2:6–11, a pre-Pauline Christian hymn that Paul edits to suit his epistolary interests, we see a blending of these worlds. Whether the background of the hymn is basically Jewish or Hellenistic has been hotly debated. The issue is made more complex by the presence of both Jewish and Hellenistic elements in the hymn. The opening line of the hymn transports the reader into the heavenly realm, the primary abode of Jesus who, humbling himself, takes the part of a "slave" in human form and descends to earth. Obedient unto death, he is exalted to assume the place he once occupied with God and now will receive the praises of all humankind. The hymn ends with a paean of praise: "At the name of Jesus every knee should bow, . . . and every tongue confess that Jesus Christ is Lord." Scholars have taught us that this closing doxology is an echo of Isaiah 45:23, which reads, "To me every knee shall bow, every tongue shall swear." In this echo of Isaiah and probably also in the allusion to the role of the "slave" assumed by Jesus, we have vestiges of Old Testament tradition. But in the references to the world above as Jesus' first habitation and the world below as the locus of his ministry, as well as in the descent-ascent motif (i.e., Jesus' coming down to death and ascending to his former home), and in the cosmic Lordship bestowed on the glorified Christ to whom all powers "in heaven and on earth and under the earth" (2:10) will do obeisance, we see evidence of Hellenistic influence. We see, therefore, that the riddle of the hymn's background finds its solution in neither the Jewish tradition nor the Hellenistic milieu alone. What we see in this pre-Pauline hymn is a synthesis of Jewish and Hellenistic elements. Traces of a Jewish heritage remain, but these have coalesced with a Hellenistic cosmology (or view of the world) and soteriology (or understanding of salvation).[76]

Some have claimed to see Hellenistic influence as the dominant influence in Paul's messianism. Others are just as firmly convinced of the overriding importance of Judaism in Paul's thinking. But there is no need to know, if ever we could know, whether Hellenism dominated Paul's thought. What is clear is that he employs certain literary forms and devices, expressions, methods of argumentation, and concepts that come from a Hellenistic tradition. The special language and outlook of his Greek Bible, the creeds, hymns, and language of the Hellenistic church, and/or the synagogue of Diaspora Judaism, as well as a host of influences from the culture at large, all informed Paul's thought to a significant degree. In spite of his openness to the Hellenistic world, Paul's Jewish heritage was a dominant feature of his religious world. Though Paul revalued his Pharisaism he did not abandon it altogether. His scriptures were Jewish, and his methods of interpretation were shaped by his Jewish experience. His apocalypticism is only understandable in light of the Jewish apocalyptic thinking of the day. His understandings of history, election, death and resurrection, and divine vindication of the holy martyrs are deeply rooted in the story of Israel. So to understand Paul as *either* Jew or Hellenist is to misunderstand him. He was both at once, and his ability to move freely in both worlds ideally equipped him to take a gospel that was fundamentally Jewish and translate it into understandable language for the Gentiles.

But the burden of this translation did not rest on Paul's shoulders alone. Given the presence of Jews in all the major cities of the Mediterranean world (Acts 15:21), we must assume Gentiles learned about

Judaism from direct contact with individual Jews and synagogue congregations. Baron's estimate that every tenth Roman was a Jew and
that 20 percent of the population of the Empire east of Italy was Jewish
sounds incredibly high;[77] nevertheless, it is widely granted that the
Jewish minority exercised an influence on the Hellenistic world out of
all proportion to its size.

Paul, for example, can assume that his predominantly Gentile congregation knew Jewish scripture. It is unlikely that this familiarity with
scripture was grounded in Paul's preaching alone. The archaeological
evidence suggests that every major city in the Mediterranean world had
at least one synagogue. We know of nine synagogues in Rome, and that
the largest building in first-century Sardis was the synagogue. The
synagogue in Corinth was strategically located near the heart of the
city. The number, size, and location of these buildings show that
the Jewish presence could not be ignored. Moreover, although many
"God-fearers" (sebomenoi) did not convert to Judaism, they attended
the synagogue and were strongly attracted. It was not unheard of for
such a "God-fearer" to abstain from eating pork, to keep the Sabbath,
to study Torah, and to have a son circumcised, while still holding back
from full conversion.[78]

Through active but not necessarily organized proselytizing, Jews
influenced, if they did not convert, their Gentile neighbors. Baron could
be right that Jews wandered from city to city, contending for the loyalty
of their hearers.[79] Matthew seems to be alluding to this practice in his
condemnation of Pharisees who "traverse sea and land to make a single
proselyte" (23:15). And considering the vast commerce of the Mediterranean, recognition of the Torah was undoubtedly spread by Jewish
merchants.

Alexandria, especially, contained a sizable Jewish population.
Mommsen commented that Alexandria was "almost as much a city of
the Jews as of the Greeks,"[80] and Philo, a contemporary of Paul, suggests that the knowledge of the law by "one half of the human race"
annoyed the other half.[81] Although Philo's statement applies only to
Alexandria, it is notable nonetheless, for it shows that the flow of
influence from the Hellenistic to the Jewish worlds was not all one way.

As important as the Hellenistic world and Jewish tradition was in
shaping Paul's thinking, the most formative item in Paul's experience
was his meeting with the risen Lord (1 Cor. 9:1; 15:8). Evangelists have
frequently called this Paul's conversion, but a generation ago Johannes
Munck argued that by Paul's own description that meeting resembled
less a conversion from the revivalist period than an Old Testament
prophetic call. Like Jeremiah of old, Paul said that God "set me apart
before I was born," and described himself as "called . . . , set apart for
the gospel of God which he promised beforehand through his prophets"
(Gal. 1:15; Rom. 1:1–2).[82] That Paul viewed himself as a latter-day

Jeremiah is unlikely,[83] but it is almost certain that Paul regarded his conversion as a call, like Jeremiah's, and not just a psychological change. In the view of some scholars the Acts account of Paul's Damascus road encounter (Acts 9:1–30; 22:3–21; 26:4–20) does denote a sudden conversion experience. Increasingly, however, others caution us against making the views expressed in Acts normative for understanding Paul.[84] Whereas the term "conversion" suggests a radical break with the past, Paul's Damascus experience produced no such repudiation. Although he did turn from persecuting the church to nurturing it, he consistently linked the church (or its gospel) with God's promises to Israel (e.g., Rom. 9:4–5). His conviction that the Messiah had come *distinguished* Paul from the Jewish majority, but it did not *divorce* him from Jewish tradition.

Paul's relationship to Christ was central but it was not exhaustive. Any emphasis on his relationship to Christ that excludes consideration of his Hellenistic and Jewish habitat, or any stress on the habitat to the exclusion of his gospel, distorts our view of Paul and the gospel he preached. It is important, therefore, while reading the letters to remember that Paul was many things at once—a Hebrew of the Hebrews, a Pharisee, a Hellenistic Jew, possibly a Roman citizen, an apostle of Christ, and a missionary to the Gentiles. And though these aspects of his life do not all hold equal place in Paul's theology, each of them contributes something. Alertness to the way these forces work on Paul should give us a fuller appreciation of the range, complexity, richness, and subtleties of his epistles.

2. The Anatomy of the Letters

ALL CONVERSATIONS have a structure. A "Hi" and a "See you later" bracket an exchange between friends. A "Hello" and a "Goodbye" frame a telephone conversation. A "Dear Jane" and a "Yours sincerely" mark the boundaries of a personal letter. These conventions which we all take for granted provide a framework for conversation and serve as doorways through which a graceful entry to or exit from the conversational circle is possible. And however habitual this litany of meeting and parting may be, it is a vital part of sharing another's presence.

All conversations do have a structure, but not all structured conversations are letters. A telegram, an announcement, and a letter all come in envelopes and all are instruments of communication between separated persons, yet the difference between them is instantly apparent to even the most casual reader. It is the structure as well as the content that identifies the letter as a letter. It begins, continues, and ends in a predictable way. We were all taught early that the sender's return address, date, greeting, body, and conclusion form the skeleton of a personal letter and that all letters have this same structure, more or less. But the skeleton of the letter receives the flesh and blood that make it unique through the information shared and concerns expressed by the writer. Thus letters, like people, share a common frame, and yet each is distinct.

Paul's letters, like our own, have a structure. Fortunately, the discovery of thousands of Greek papyrus letters from ancient times has helped us define more precisely the shape of the letter in Paul's day. Study of those papyri has identified the parts of the ancient letter, as well as the function of each part.[1] We now know that the use of the letter-writing conventions of his time was just as natural (or even unconscious) for Paul as for us. But his use of those conventions was hardly mechanical, for Paul, like writers today, altered the traditional epistolary forms to suit his own purposes. And it is the alterations he made that tell us most about Paul's self-understanding, his intentions, and his theology.

However complex such an analysis may sound, each reader will recall how carefully he or she pondered the structure of an important letter. The letter from a boyfriend, for example, may begin "Dear Sue," which in and of itself may seem insignificant. But suppose the previous letter began "Dearest." Then the form of the greeting may raise a host of questions: "Is he losing interest?" "Is there another?" "Is he taking me for granted?" Or, "Is he worried and distracted?" And on and on Sue goes, combing the letter, looking for clues in the structure to the writer's deep and true intent. So although the anatomy of the Pauline letter may be unfamiliar to us, we are sensitive to the nuances that the structure of letters can carry. Once the letter-writing conventions that Paul used are understood, the alert reader will also find clues to Paul's intent in his creative use of those conventions as well.

The discussion below will treat both the form and the function of main elements in the Pauline letter. Our purpose is to show the working of the separate parts, not to offer an exhaustive discussion of each member. Before turning to our survey of the separate elements of the letter, let us display a typical Greek papyrus letter. From such a model the basic skeleton of the letter will become clear, and we shall better understand how Paul duplicates letter-writing patterns of his own time as well as how he alters them.

Irenaeus to Apollinarius his dearest brother many greetings. I pray continually for your health, and I myself am well.	SALUTATION PRAYER
I wish you to know that I reached land on the sixth of the month Epeiph and we unloaded our cargo on the eighteenth of the same month. I went up to Rome on the twenty-fifth of the same month and the place welcomed us as the god willed, and we are daily expecting our discharge, it so being that up till today nobody in the	BODY
corn fleet has been released. Many salutations to your wife and to Serenus and to all who love you, each by name. Goodbye. Mesare 9.[2]	CONCLUSION (Greetings, final wish, date)

A comparison of the key elements in this letter with those in Paul's letter to Philemon may be illuminating:

	Papyrus Letter	Pauline Letter
I. *Salutation*		
A. Sender	Irenaeus	Paul, a prisoner for Christ Jesus, and Timothy our brother
B. Recipient	to Apollinarius his dearest brother	To Philemon our beloved fellow worker and Apphia our sister and Archippus our fellow soldier, and the church in your house

	Papyrus Letter	**Pauline Letter**
C. Greeting	many greetings	Grace to you and peace from God our Father and the Lord Jesus Christ
II. *Thanksgiving* (Prayer)	I pray continually for your health, and I myself am well.	I thank my God always when I remember you in my prayers
III. *Body*	[Information about his arrival on the grain boat from Egypt]	[Discussion of return of Onesimus the slave]
IV. *Closing commands*	[Absent here but present elsewhere]	receive him . . . charge that to my account . . . Refresh my heart in Christ . . . prepare a guest room for me . . .
V. *Conclusion* A. Peace Wish	[Absent]	[Present elsewhere but absent in Philemon]
B. Greetings	Many salutations to your wife and to Serenus and to all who love you, each by name.	Epaphras, my fellow prisoner in Christ Jesus, sends greetings to you, and so do Mark, Aristarchus, Demas, and Luke, my fellow workers.
C. Kiss	[Absent]	[Absent in Philemon but present elsewhere]
D. Close (Grace Benediction)	Goodbye.	The grace of the Lord Jesus Christ be with your spirit.

Although we can draw no firm conclusions from a comparison of only two letters, the parallels are obvious. Other comparisons would yield similar results. It is evident, however, that Paul's relationship to Christ dictated some change of emphasis. The sender is described as a "prisoner for Christ Jesus," and the close goes beyond "Goodbye" to place both Paul's addressees and himself in the presence of "Jesus Christ." Other similarities and differences will become obvious in our discussion below of the anatomy of the Pauline letter. We shall now take each of the parts in order of appearance.

1. The Salutation

The salutation is one of the most stable elements in the ancient letter. The form is rather precise. Unlike our modern letter, the salutation includes the names of both sender and recipient, as well as a greeting. In spite of the highly stereotyped nature of the letter opening, it remained pliable in the hands of Paul. In Philemon, Romans, and Galatians we will see how Paul molds the salutation to his purposes in the letter as a whole.

In Philemon Paul addresses the master of Onesimus, a runaway slave who had sought refuge with Paul. Through Paul, who was in prison at the time, Onesimus was converted (v. 10), thus setting the stage for the letter. In his letter Paul reminds Philemon that his apostolic mission gave him (Paul) a prior claim on Onesimus. Moreover, while he was in jail he needed the slave's assistance. Nevertheless, Paul reports that he is returning Onesimus with the request that he be treated "like a brother." It is interesting that as early as the salutation Paul identifies himself as "a prisoner for Christ Jesus." Thus the condition central to Paul's plea for leniency to Onesimus (the condition of bondage) surfaces in the opening line of the letter.

It is in Romans that we see Paul's most original adaptation of the conventional letter opening. Writing to a church that he has neither founded nor visited, Paul was eager to establish the "orthodoxy"[3] of his gospel and the legitimacy of his apostleship. In some quarters Paul was looked upon as a theological maverick, and an interloper (if not a troublemaker) in the apostolic circle. It is quite likely that Paul's awareness of his notoriety inspired the baroque formulation in Romans 1:1–7. The salutation found there includes both a summary of Paul's gospel and a definition of his apostolic mission. The message that he proclaims, Paul says, is no dangerous innovation but is derived from the promises that God made "through his prophets in the holy scriptures" (1:2). Drawing on traditional formulations, Paul summarizes his gospel for all to judge. He tells of Jesus' descent from David, God's designation of Jesus as "Son of God" through the resurrection, and his own appointment as apostle to the Gentiles by the risen Christ (1:3–6). We see, therefore, how as early as the salutation Paul is defending his apostleship by relating it back to God and thus establishing his right to be heard. By showing the integral place of his mission in God's plan of history, Paul puts forward a strong claim upon the support of the Roman church for his mission to Spain.

The salutation in Galatians likewise offers a clue to Paul's purpose in the letter. In 1:1 Paul refers to himself as "an apostle—not from men nor through man, but through Jesus Christ and God the Father, who raised him from the dead." Then, with the formalities of the letter opening out of the way, Paul plunges into his main business. What has been hinted at in the salutation now receives careful and prolonged treatment. In 1:10 Paul begins a vigorous defense of his apostleship that stretches through chapter 2. He lashes out at those who seek to discredit his apostleship and who are trying to devalue his gospel. By asserting that his gospel is "not man's gospel," and that he did not "receive it from man" (1:11, 12), Paul seeks to establish his independence of the Jerusalem circle and to defend the authenticity of his message. It is possible, if not likely, that the young Galatian church saw in Peter, James, John, and others a direct link with the Lord, and as Jewish Christians they practiced circumcision. Paul, on the other hand, had received his gospel secondhand from human agents, with the result that the Jerusalem gospel and practice was often appealed to in opposition to him. So even in the salutation, Paul tries to establish the integrity of his credentials ("not from man") and of his gospel. Once again we see him altering a highly stereotyped form to address the specific needs of his readers.

2. The Thanksgiving

More than any other work, Paul Schubert's epochal *Form and Function of the Pauline Thanksgivings*[4] stimulated an interest in the form and function of the various parts in the letters of Paul. Although Schubert's thesis has been refined, his basic hypothesis has not been refuted: that the thanksgiving is a formal element of most Pauline letters and that it terminates the letter opening, signals the basic intent of the letter, and may serve as an outline of the major topics to be considered.[5]

Coming immediately after the salutation, the thanksgiving appears in all of Paul's letters except Galatians. In each case Paul brings into view the situation of the recipients. In 1 Corinthians 1:4–9, for example, references to the charismatic speech and knowledge of the Corinthian Christians are linked with an allusion to the future "day of our Lord Jesus Christ." A study of 1 Corinthians will show that Paul here "telegraphs" the basic concern of the letter. Scholars have long noted that the Corinthian preoccupation with "wisdom" (1:18–4:21) and charismatic speech (chs. 12–14) sprang from a religious enthusiasm that claimed total salvation in this world. Paul's reference in the thanksgiving to the future "day of our Lord Jesus," therefore, indicates his resolve to adjust the eschatological perspective of his Corinthian converts. For Paul's emphasis on a future "day of the Lord" would qualify the enthusiasm of those who claimed to be already experiencing the "day of the Lord" here and now.

The thanksgiving in 2 Corinthians 1:3–7 functions like that in 1 Corinthians 1:4–9 in that it offers a preview of one major emphasis that is to come in the body of the letter.[6] Paul alludes to the abundance of his sufferings through which he participates in the sufferings of Christ. He then invites his addressees to share also in "our sufferings" so that they may also share in "our comfort." Others have noted the connection of these statements to the situation addressed by the letter as a whole.[7] Against those who seek to validate their claims with visions, mighty works, and other prodigies of the Spirit, Paul exalts his imprisonments, beatings, shipwrecks, and other afflictions. What his adversaries take to be the "stench of death" raised by these vicissitudes, however, Paul calls the "aroma of Christ" (2 Cor. 2:14–17). In 2 Corinthians 6:3–10 Paul again defines his ministry (versus that of others) in light of the suffering, persecution, and poverty he has suffered—throughout which the power of God has been manifested. Obviously, he sees his own deprivation as a participation in the sufferings of Christ, and through this he finds comfort and strength for his ministry (see 7:5–12). In 2 Corinthians, therefore, as elsewhere, we see how Paul relates the thanksgiving to the situation of his readers, and how the thanksgiving serves as a peephole through which we see the main point of the letter.

An additional word is necessary. James M. Robinson has shown that in his thanksgivings Paul is not mechanically following a fixed epistolary form.[8] Rather, the apostle has grafted onto this traditional epistolary form materials from liturgical tradition. Thus he has created a hybrid form. The thanksgiving in 2 Corinthians 1:3, especially, sounds a liturgical note: "Blessed be the God and Father of our Lord Jesus Christ." We should be aware that Paul does not slavishly follow precut patterns but creates his own. Moreover, we should not assume that this was a conscious exercise on Paul's part, any more than our own use and modification of the letter-writing conventions of today are conscious.

3. The Body of the Letter

After passing through the thanksgiving, the reader enters a vast and varied conversational world. The landscape is as broad as Paul's theological understanding and as diverse as the needs of the churches. But in spite of the range and variety in the body of the letters, there is a pattern that repeatedly occurs. A request or disclosure formula ("I beseech you . . ." or "I would not have you ignorant . . .") serves as the threshold of the body, while the end is marked by an announcement of Paul's travel plans.[9] Usually these plans include a contemplated visit by the apostle himself.

Galatians alone lacks any reference to Paul's travel plans. Robert Funk's explanation of this omission is attractive. In Galatians 4:12–20 Funk sees a substitute for the usual reference to an upcoming apostolic visit. There Paul reflects on his previous visit and wishes that he could return again (but of course he cannot). In the view of Funk:

> This is a "travelogue" in a situation where travel . . . is out of the question, i.e., in a situation where Paul cannot add the promise of an oral word to the written word, he recalls the previous oral word and wishes he might renew it.[10]

The function of this travelogue is to reinforce the written word with the promise of an apostolic visit.

Others have noted an autobiographical section, or a report by Paul on his activity, near the beginning of the body in most letters. In Galatians he speaks of his relationship to the Jerusalem church (1:10–2:21). In 2 Corinthians he reports on the hardships he has suffered (1:8–2:13). In Philippians he speaks of his imprisonment (1:12–26), and in 1 Corinthians he recalls his ministry among his addressees (1:10–17). In each case this autobiographical note is fully integrated into his theological argument. The report on his situation is made to impinge directly on the situation of his readers. By reciting the demands made on him as an apostle of Christ, Paul is warning his hearers that like demands may be made of them.

We see, therefore, that although the topography of the body of the letter is necessarily less predictable than that of the thanksgiving, there are landmarks to guide our journey through it. Since the body embraces the full range and richness of Paul's theological outlook, we should expect it to offer difficulties, but we should be prepared also for pleasant surprises.

Finally, it should be noted that functionally the thanksgiving and the body of the letter complement each other. In the thanksgiving, using the language of prayer, Paul places himself and his hearers in the presence of God. In the body of the letter Paul interprets the claims made on him and his hearers by God in Christ. As Funk well said:

> The thanksgiving looks back . . . on the effects of grace already experienced . . . the body of the letter calls the readers again into the presence of Christ, that the word of the cross may take effect anew.[11]

4. Paraenesis (Ethical Instruction and Exhortation)

At least three different types of ethical instruction are found in Paul's letters. First, there is the cluster of unrelated moral maxims, strung together like beads on a string. Often there is little to hold them together except their similarity of form, or perhaps a catchword carried over from one to another.

A good example of this type of material appears in Romans 12:9–13 where Paul says:

> Let love be genuine; hate what is evil, hold fast to what is good; love one another with brotherly affection; outdo one another in showing honor.

Never flag in zeal, be aglow with the Spirit, serve the Lord. Rejoice in
your hope, be patient in tribulation, be constant in prayer. Contribute to
the needs of the saints, practice hospitality.

In this short paragraph thirteen different injunctions are given and
at least twelve different topics are mentioned, no one of which has much
to do with any other. We shall continue this discussion in the next
chapter, but it is necessary here to say that Paul is probably dependent
on tradition for this type of material.[12]

Second, scattered throughout Paul's letters we find lists of virtues and
vices in which both Jewish and Hellenistic traditions have merged.[13]
These lists, like the unrelated injunctions above, have only the most
casual relationship to each other. In Galatians 5:19–23 we find such a
catalog:

> Now the works of the flesh are plain: immorality, impurity, licentious-
> ness, idolatry, sorcery, enmity, strife, jealousy, anger, selfishness, dissen-
> sion, party spirit, envy, drunkenness, carousing, and the like. . . . But the
> fruit of the Spirit is love, joy, peace, patience, kindness, goodness, faithful-
> ness, gentleness, self-control.

The third type of paraenetic material is a prolonged exhortation or
homily on a particular topic.[14] Strongly reminiscent of an oral situation,
these materials are highly personal and supportive (e.g., "I became your
father" 1 Cor. 4:15). Pastoral in tone, such exhortations appear frequently throughout Paul's letters. The bulk of 1 Corinthians (chs. 5–15)
probably belongs to this type of material. Paul there deals one by one
with problems brought to him in an oral report by Chloe's people and
by a letter from the church. First Thessalonians 4:13–18 and 5:1–11 will
illustrate this paraenetic style. Both sections treat topics of concern to
Paul's readers—the resurrection of the dead and the unpredictable
suddenness of the end. And both close with an exhortation ("Therefore
comfort one another with these words," 4:18; and "Therefore encourage one another and build one another up," 5:11).

For our purposes it is important to distinguish individual paraenetic
units from sections of paraenetic material. Individual units (including
types 1 and 2) appear haphazardly throughout all of the letters. But the
paraenetic section knits together the body of the letter and stretches to
the conclusion (Galatians, Romans, 1 Thessalonians, and possibly 1
Corinthians and Philippians). Although some of this instruction or
exhortation has little specific relevance for any particular church, Paul
often tailors general ethical traditions to fit particular needs. General
admonitions to refrain from vengeful acts, to do good to outsiders, to
obey the leaders, and to build up the church occur with some regularity
in the epistles. But these act not as a rulebook for solving every problem;
rather, they are examples or illustrations of how the gospel is to take

effect. These ethical sections provide practical guidance, but they also convey information, make requests, and issue reminders (see 1 Thessalonians 4–5). Many sources of wisdom feed into this material, and by no means does Paul proclaim it as original; but his weaving of it shows a masterly hand at turning general moral saws to specific and concrete account.

5. Conclusion of the Letter

Unlike the opening of the letter, the conclusion has received scant attention. Increasingly, however, scholars have discovered in it important clues to the viewpoint of the letter as a whole.[15] Analysis of the conclusion has isolated its various parts with some precision, and in the light of such analysis we can see the particular use of Paul's endings.

Like the letter opening, the conclusion is a stable element in the epistolary structure. We usually find there a peace wish, greetings, and a benediction (or grace). Occasionally, we see an apostolic pronouncement. And generally, all of this is preceded by a battery of last-minute instructions. Bridging the gap between the instruction cluster and the conclusion is the peace wish. Once Paul crosses this threshold with his readers, he has committed himself to parting, and he soon brings the conversation to a close.

The peace wish, of course, did not originate with Paul. The shalom (peace) greeting of the Semitic letter was familiar to him. Used both in meeting and parting, the word expressed a desire for the total well-being (bodily health as well as inner peace) of the person greeted. Reminiscent of the coveted "blessing" of the Old Testament, the shalom greeting often went beyond the simple exchange of amenities to a joint affirmation of faith. This peace wish occupied the ultimate position in the conclusion of the Semitic letter. In this regard it corresponded to the "goodbye" *(errōso)* of the Greek letter or to the final wish for the well-being of the recipient (e.g., "you will do me a favor by taking care of your bodily health"). The peace wish for Paul, however, occupies a penultimate position in the conclusion.

In the letter opening Paul usually greets his auditors with a grace—putting both parties in the presence of God (e.g., "Grace to you and peace from God our Father and the Lord Jesus Christ"). In the conclusion, greetings are sandwiched between the peace wish and the grace, and thus, the closing peace wish echoes the opening greeting and brings us full circle: (opening) grace and peace; (closing) peace and grace. Before parting, however, Paul once again places himself and his hearers in the presence of God, and the note of promise sounded in the peace wish extends God's presence beyond this meeting point of the letter and into the future ("live in peace, and the God of love and peace *will be with you,*" 2 Cor. 13:11, emphasis added). So although the peace wish is a part of the closing bracket of the letter, Paul's mind rushes on beyond this ending to the new possibilities that lie ahead.

For Paul, however, the peace wish is more than a priestly benediction. It also gathers unto itself some of the major concerns of the letters. In 1 Thessalonians, for example, Paul addresses a church demoralized and distressed: some members had died before the expected second coming; others had fallen into sloth—evidently they quit work to wait for the end. Perhaps some excuse themselves from "worldly" concerns because of their special charismatic gifts (1 Thess. 4:9–11). So in the peace wish of 1 Thessalonians, Paul reiterates his major concerns. By declaring that God will preserve the "spirit and soul and body" blameless at the end, he reaffirms a future that some had come to doubt and others mistakenly believed was already realized. So once again we see how Paul bends a conventional form to his own theological end.

Occasionally a prayer request ("Brethren, pray for us," 1 Thess. 5:25) stands adjacent to the peace wish. Although it has no exact parallel in the papyrus letters, it may have its counterpart in the assurance of remembrance in the letter opening and in the closing request to keep the writer in mind. The Hellenistic letter often opened with the assurance "I pray for your health" and concluded by asking, in turn, for the recipient's prayerful thoughts. One writer, for example, complaining that he is having difficulty navigating the river past the Antaeopolite nome, requested prayers on his behalf: "Remember the night-festival of Isis at the Serapeum."[16] Likewise at the beginning of 1 Thessalonians Paul includes the hearers in his prayers (1:2), and before closing he asks his addressees to include him in theirs (5:25; see also Rom. 1:9 and 15:30). By such usage, Paul shows himself to be a practitioner of that vital reciprocity in life that exists in the community of God. In the opening announcement of his prayer for them and in the closing request for their prayer, he demonstrates the corporate rhythm of giving and receiving. Paul and his readers share a world.

Following the peace wish and prayer request, the impending separation between Paul and his readers becomes more and more prominent.[17] The closing greeting from Paul and his co-workers and the command to greet one another signal the imminent end of the epistolary meeting. Even where it is not explicitly stated, it is to be assumed that this greeting will be conveyed by the kiss.

This kiss has often been viewed as a prelude to the celebration of the Eucharist. To be sure, Paul's letters were read to the gathered church, and it is possible that that reading was followed by celebration of the holy meal, but, judging from the text, there is little evidence for this idea. Rather than as a signal for formal liturgy,[18] the kiss stands as simply the usual form of greeting, which Paul harnessed to serve his epistolary interests. The letters were not written to individuals[19] but to congregations. Through the command "greet one another with a holy kiss" Paul is reaffirming the kind of relationship created by Christ between himself and his spiritual family, and also between the members of the congregation themselves (1 Thess. 5:26).[20]

The benediction—"the grace of our Lord Jesus Christ be with you"—is the most stable of the concluding elements. Appearing in every complete letter, this closing formula varies little. Here again Paul has accommodated an epistolary convention to his Christian perspective (e.g., "The grace *of the Lord Jesus* be with you," 1 Cor. 16:23, emphasis added). Occasionally, however, a solemn warning or sober adjuration precedes the benediction. The tone of 1 Corinthians 16:22 is especially threatening: "If anyone has no love for the Lord, let that person be accursed [anathema]." In the other letters similar adjurations appear in the same position (1 Thess. 5:27 and Gal. 6:17). It is improbable that the Corinthian admonition is a eucharistic formula that aims to exclude unworthy or unbaptized persons from the Lord's table.[21] More likely the Corinthian command is a decisive reminder of the central exhortation of the letter. The warning includes those who curse Jesus (1 Cor. 12:3), those who hurt a brother through arrogant use of their charisma, and those who profane the body of Christ. In this pronouncement Paul addresses the total epistolary situation in which the loveless behavior of some believers threatens to destroy the church.

In Galatians 6:17 we see another apostolic warning: "Let no man trouble me; for I bear on my body the marks of Jesus." It is possible that Paul intends to draw an unfavorable comparison between the "good showing in the flesh" (i.e., circumcision) of his addressees and the "marks" of Jesus (scars) that have been inflicted on his body by beatings, shipwreck, etc. Paul apparently understands his own suffering as a replication of Jesus'; consequently, to trouble the apostle, the Lord's representative, is to injure the Lord himself.

These adjurations are especially harsh to our modern ears. They sound mean and vindictive. Yet they are understandable in terms of Paul's sense of his mission. Paul felt himself to be like the prophets of old, who were commissioned to speak the word of Yahweh. Sometimes, of course, the line gets blurred between the prophet's own words and those of God. Paul, believing himself appointed as an apostle of the risen Christ, felt he re-presented Christ to his hearers for judgment and healing; and thus, in his view, the words he spoke had the power and authority of the One who sent him.

Evidently Paul views the letter as an instrument of his apostleship. Thus it assumes an official quality that goes beyond the usual correspondence between friends. The letter, serving as an extension of his apostolic presence, places the community in the Lord's company—with everything such status promises and demands. So although Paul's letters are highly personal and at times deeply moving, we fail to appreciate their scope and power if we ignore their apostolic character.

To summarize, we have noted the importance of reading Paul's letters as letters, and we have seen how Paul constrains to his own use the epistolary conventions of his time. We have noticed that Paul's message informs and even transforms his medium. Although the letter was for Paul the only mode of conversation between separated persons, it was more. It was an extension of his apostleship. A reader of the letters who is aware of the subtle interplay between form (medium), content (message), and agent (apostle) will appreciate more fully the subtlety of Paul's gospel and the influence these letters have had on their readers over the centuries.[22]

OUTLINE OF LETTER STRUCTURE

	1 Thessalonians	1 Corinthians	2 Corinthians	Galatians	Philippians	Romans
I. Salutation						
A. Sender	1:1a	1:1	1:1a	1:1–2a	1:1	1:1–6
B. Recipient	1:1b	1:2	1:1b	1:2b	1:1	1:7a
C. Greeting	1:1c	1:3	1:2	1:3–5	1:2	1:7b
II. Thanksgiving	1:2–10 2:13 3:9–10	1:4–9	1:3–7	—	1:3–11	1:8–17
III. Body	2:1–3:8 (possibly 3:11–13)	1:10–4:21	1:8–9:14 (letter incomplete) 10:1–13:10 (letter fragment)	1:6–4:31	1:12–2:11 3:1–4:1 4:10–20	1:18–11:36
IV. Ethical exhortation and instructions	4:1–5:22	5:1–16:12 16:13–18 (closing paraenesis)	13:11a (summary)	5:1–6:10 6:11–15 (letter summary)	2:12–29 4:2–6	12:1–15:13 15:14–32 (travel plans and closing paraenesis)
V. Closing						
A. Peace Wish	5:23–24	—	13:11b	6:16	4:7–9	15:33
B. Greetings	—	16:19–20a	13:13	—	4:21–22	16:1–15(?)
C. Kiss	5:26	16:20b	13:12	—	—	16:16(?) (see note 22)
Apostolic Command	5:27	16:22	—	6:17	—	—
D. Benediction	5:28	16:23–24	13:14	6:18	4:23	16:20(?)

3. Traditions Behind the Letters

WHY DO WE APPEAL to tradition? Why do we quote famous people, poets, novelists, orators, and scholars? Why do we appeal to scripture, legends, and fairy tales? It is not just to enliven our speech, though it does do that. It is not just to overcome the impoverished nature of our vocabulary, though it also does that. It is not just to amuse, though it even does that. Rather it is because the tradition opens up in us a level of insight or being that we had not known before. Through the shared experience of the ages we are delivered from our trivialized view of the human and nonhuman world to appreciate more fully the heights and depths of the human spirit. This is the authority tradition carries. For Paul these heights and depths were known through the historic interaction between God and Israel. Paul appealed often to the traditional deposit stored up through the centuries. Through our study of his use and interpretation of those materials we stand to gain a better appreciation of Paul the man, and of the word he speaks to the churches.

From the outset a difficulty faces our investigation of the traditions behind the letters. In Galatians 1:11–12 Paul declares, "The gospel which was preached by me is not a human gospel. For I did not receive it from human beings, nor was I taught it, but it came through a revelation of Jesus Christ." Elsewhere, however, Paul draws on church tradition, cites the primitive Christian kerygma, repeats liturgical formulas, quotes Christian hymns, prayers, and confessions, and uses traditional ethical admonitions. These were all composed by people—so how can the apostle maintain that his gospel did not come from a mortal being?

The statement in the Galatian letter does not reveal an inconsistency in Paul's thought so much as the severity of a problem in the Galatian church. Paul's Galatian enemies charged that his reliance on the Jerusalem apostles ("human authority") invalidated his claim to be an apostle of Christ. And this attempt to impugn his apostleship was nothing less than an attempt to discredit his kerygma (the gospel that he preached) and reject it altogether. How, his opponents asked, can an impostor preach an authentic gospel? The Galatians viewed his kerygma as woefully deficient, so they supplemented it with the observance of "days, and months, and seasons, and years" (4:10), with circumcision, and with worship of "elemental spirits" (slavery, in Paul's view; 4:9).

Paul scorned this Galatian amalgam, calling it "no gospel at all," and he condemned their doubt of his gospel as a fundamental distrust of the God who gave it. In Galatians 1:11–12 he is not denying that he uses human formulas in his preaching. He is saying that his motive—his authority—for that preaching came directly from Christ. A gospel with that authority must be complete and sufficient. Once the polemical cast of 1:11–12 is recognized, Paul's claim to be dependent on no person for his kerygma does not contradict his admission elsewhere of dependence on tradition (e.g., 1 Cor. 15:3–4). Moreover, Paul can ascribe to Jesus in person what actually came through the church (1 Cor. 11:23–25). Obviously, he viewed the church as the Lord's agent; and thus, to his mind, what came from the church was also from the Lord. The identification of traditional elements is valuable for understanding Paul. His choice of materials tells us something about his theological emphases, his view of scripture (though not all of his traditional materials are scriptural), and possibly also his own background. His use of that material, however, is fully as important as the selection he makes. For in every letter he adapts traditional material to a specific problem or issue. Tradition for Paul was no "thing in itself" whose meaning was transparent. The past required interpretation and application. It is important to realize that these materials were not inert deposits embedded in an archaic past. The tradition was for Paul a dynamic reality coming out of a living past, impinging directly on the present, and anticipating the future. In the discussion below we shall list representative traditional materials that Paul incorporated in his letters.

1. The Kerygma

C. H. Dodd taught us that the apostle shared with the rest of primitive Christianity a basic outline of doctrine. Although the emphasis of Paul's preaching and his interpretation of the kerygma differed from that of his predecessors, the Jerusalem apostles nevertheless approved his gospel (Gal. 2:2), presumably because on essential matters it coincided with their own. The primitive gospel as defined by Dodd contained six elements:

    a. The arrival of the messianic age as foretold by the prophets.
    b. The inauguration of this age in the ministry, death, and resurrection of Jesus.
    c. The exaltation of Jesus.
    d. The presence of the Holy Spirit in the church as a sign of Christ's "power and glory."

   e. The imminent return of Jesus as the consummation of the messianic age.

   f. The call to repentance coupled with an offer of forgiveness.[1]

Although all of these elements appear nowhere together in the same place, most of them surface somewhere or other in the Pauline letters. The following list shows where some of those elements are found:

a.	Prophecy fulfilled	Rom. 1:2
b.	Messianic age inaugurated in Jesus who was	
	born of the seed of David	Rom. 1:3
	died according to the scriptures	Gal. 1:4
		1 Cor. 15:3
	was buried	1 Cor. 15:4
	was raised	1 Thess. 1:10
		1 Cor. 15:4
		Rom. 1:4; 8:34
c.	Who was exalted	Rom. 8:34
		Phil. 2:9
d.	Presence of Holy Spirit	Rom. 8:26ff.
		1 Cor. 12:1ff.
e.	Who will come again	1 Thess. 1:10
		Rom. 2:16
f.	Call to repent	Rom. 10:9

First Corinthians 15:3–7 is a classic example of primitive tradition that Paul has incorporated to advance his argument:

For I delivered to you . . . what I also received,
that *Christ died for our sins* in accordance with the scriptures,
that *he was buried,*
that *he was raised* on the third day in accordance with the scriptures,
   and
that *he appeared* to Cephas, then to the twelve (emphasis added).

2. Eucharistic and Baptismal Formulas

In his hortatory or instructional materials Paul often alludes to traditions that his addressees knew. The reference to being washed in 1 Corinthians 6:11 is a clear allusion to baptism. A baptismal tradition also appears in Romans 6:4–5, where Paul says, "We were buried therefore with him by baptism into death, . . . [and] if we have been united with him in a death like his, we shall certainly be united with him in a resurrection like his." And in 1 Corinthians 11:23–25 Paul directly quotes the eucharistic liturgy:

I received from the Lord what I also delivered to you, that the Lord Jesus on the night he was betrayed took bread, and when he had given thanks, he broke it, and said, "This is my body which is for you. Do this in remembrance of me." In the same way also the cup, after supper, saying, "This cup is the new covenant in my blood. Do this, as often as you drink it, in remembrance of me."

3. The Language of Prayer

Paul frequently alludes to prayer and in some places bursts into a spontaneous doxology (e.g., Rom. 7:25, "Thanks be to God through Jesus Christ our Lord"). Some of his prayers are simply the outpouring of a full heart, but others have a traditional ring (Gal. 1:5; Phil. 4:20). It is often difficult to distinguish between prayers that Paul creates and those that he takes from tradition. It is possible, however, to recognize fragments of traditional prayers in the epistles. Words like *amen* (Gal. 6:18; 1 Cor. 14:16; and 2 Cor. 1:20), *Maranatha* ("Our Lord, come," in 1 Cor. 16:22), and *abba* ("father," in Gal. 4:6; Rom. 8:15) belong to a tradition that antedates Paul.

4. Hymns

For generations before the time of Jesus hymns of praise had been rising to God from synagogue and temple. It was natural, therefore, that the early Christian church, deriving from Judaism, should be a singing church. While the early hymns of the church were from the Psalms, the church soon created new songs appropriate to its Christian status. Traces of this early hymnody appear in Paul's letters as well as the rest of the New Testament (e.g., Col. 1:15–20; 1 Tim. 3:16; Eph. 5:14). The rhythm, parallelism, clearly defined strophes, poetic expression, and the absence of Pauline vocabulary or ideas establish Philippians 2:6–11 as a pre-Pauline Christian hymn. Even in English translation (RSV alt.) its hymnic character is obvious:[2]

Pauline Introduction:

Have this mind among yourselves,
Which you have in Christ Jesus,

Hymn:

I

Who, though he was in the form of God,
Did not count equality with God
A thing to be grasped,

II

But emptied himself,
Taking the form of a servant,
Being born in the likeness of men.

III

And being found in human form
He humbled himself
And became obedient unto death.[3]

IV

Therefore God has highly exalted him
And bestowed on him the name
Which is above every name,

V

That at the name of Jesus
Every knee should bow,
In heaven, on earth, and under the earth,

VI

And every tongue confess,
"Jesus Christ is Lord"
To the glory of God the Father.

5. Words of the Lord

In 2 Corinthians 5:16 Paul says, "though we once regarded Christ from a human point of view, we regard him thus no longer."[4] Some scholars see this statement as evidence that Paul was personally acquainted with Jesus. If Paul did know Jesus during his ministry, however, it is astonishing that he would barely mention the words and deeds of Jesus. If we had to depend on Paul for information about Jesus' life, we would know only that he was "born of woman" (Gal. 4:4), that he was in David's line (Rom. 1:3), and that he died on a cross (Phil. 2:8; 1 Cor. 1:23). We would not know his mother's name, that he had sisters, that he taught in parables, or that his ministry was centered in Galilee. If Paul is silent about the words and deeds because he assumes they are known to his readers, then it is strange that he quotes the Old Testament even when he presupposes that it is familiar to his readers. Moreover, even though Paul often summarizes his own preaching, Jesus' ministry receives little emphasis (1 Cor. 2:1–2).[5] But though Paul expresses little interest in Jesus' ministry or the content of his preaching, he does lay heavy stress on three historical facts: the cross, the resurrection, and Jesus' imminent return. These salvific events are anchored in history, but they possess a significance that transcends history.

As in the Gospels, the words of Jesus that Paul quotes or to which he alludes assume a transcendent character as sayings of "the Lord." The sayings of Jesus occupy little space in Paul's letters, but they add important weight to his ethical teaching.[6]

a. *Quotations from Jesus (emphasis added)*

(1)	1 Cor. 7:10–11	To the married I give charge, not I but the Lord, that *the wife should not separate from her husband . . . and that the husband should not divorce his wife.* (See Matt. 5:32; 19:9; Mark 10:11–12; Luke 16:18.)
(2)	1 Cor. 9:14	The Lord commanded that *those who proclaim the gospel should get their living by the gospel.* (See Luke 10:7, the laborer deserves his wages.)
(3)	1 Cor. 11:23–24	The Lord Jesus . . . said, *"This is my body which is for you. Do this in remembrance of me."* In the same way also [he took] the cup, after supper, saying, *"This cup is the new covenant in my blood. Do this, as often as you drink it, in remembrance of me."* (See Matt. 26:26–28; Mark 14:22–24; Luke 22:19–20.)
(4)	1 Thess. 4:16–17	The Lord himself will descend from heaven with a cry of command,[7] with the archangel's call, and with the sound of the trumpet of God. And the dead in Christ will rise first.
(5)	Also 1 Cor. 14:37, which alludes to but does not quote a saying.	

b. *Echoes of Sayings*

(1)	1 Cor. 4:12	When reviled, we bless, when persecuted, we endure.

b. *Echoes of Sayings (cont.)*

	Rom. 12:14	Bless those who persecute you; bless and do not curse them.
	Luke 6:28	Bless those who curse you; pray for those who abuse you.
(2)	1 Thess. 5:15	See that none of you repays evil for evil.
	Rom. 12:17	Repay no one evil for evil.
	Matt. 5:39	Do not resist one who is evil.
(3)	Rom. 13:7	Pay all of them their dues, taxes to whom taxes are due.
	Matt. 22:15–22	Then the Pharisees . . . [asked,] ". . . Is it lawful to pay taxes to Caesar, or not?" . . . Jesus, aware of their malice, said, ". . . Show me the money for the tax." . . . "Render . . . to Caesar the things that are Caesar's, and to God the things that are God's."
(4)	Rom. 14:13	Then let us no more pass judgment on one another, but rather decide never to put a stumbling-block [*skandalon*] or hindrance in the way of a brother or sister.
	Matt. 7:1	Judge not, that you be not judged.
(5)	Rom. 14:14	Nothing is unclean in itself.
	Mark 7:18–19	"Do you not see that whatever goes into a person from outside cannot defile, since it enters not the heart but the stomach, and so passes on?" Thus he declared all foods clean.
(6)	1 Thess. 5:2	The day of the Lord will come like a thief [*kleptēs*] in the night.
	Luke 12:39–40	If the householder had known at what hour the thief [*kleptēs*] was coming, he would have been awake. . . . You also must be ready; for the Son of man is coming at an hour you do not expect. (See Matt. 24:42–43.)

(7)	1 Thess. 5:13	Be at peace among yourselves
	Mark 9:50	Be at peace with one another.
(8)	1 Cor. 13:2	If I have all faith, so as to remove mountains.
	Matt. 17:20	If you have faith as a grain of mustard seed, you will say to this mountain, "Move . . . ," and it will move.

6. The Paraenetic Tradition

A generation ago Martin Dibelius noticed the traditional nature of Paul's ethical instructions (paraenesis).[8] We know now that the apostle drew on pre-Pauline or even pre-Christian traditions for his moral exhortation. Characterized by a terse, gnomic style, these materials usually fall near the end of Paul's letters (e.g., Gal. 5:13–6:10; 1 Thess. 4:1–5:22; 2 Cor. 13:11) and possess a certain uniformity in content and vocabulary. Admonitions to do good and to avoid evil, warnings against immorality, exhortations to nonviolence, and encouragement of subjection to leaders, edification of the church, and kindness to outsiders all appear in more than one of Paul's letters. Since these concerns are shared in many early Christian writings (1 Peter, Ignatius, Hebrews, 1 Clement, Barnabas, Hermas, the *Didache,* and the pastoral epistles), it appears that the main contours of Paul's paraenetic materials did not originate with him but were the common property of early Christianity.

It is generally agreed that Paul borrowed his ethical injunctions, but whether he deployed them in a way appropriate to each addressee is still debated. Until recently most scholars followed Dibelius, who held that the paraenesis was constructed with no particular situation in mind, but as a general guide to everyday affairs. To attribute all of the sins enumerated in the vice lists to particular churches would be a mistake.[9] Recently, however, support for Dibelius's view has softened.[10] If Paul gives other traditional materials like the thanksgiving and conclusion immediate relevance, would he not also mold the paraenetic tradition to each epistolary situation?[11] Furnish has shown how Paul gives specificity even to the more general lists of virtues and vices. The vice list, for example, in 2 Corinthians 12:20–21 deals with divisive behavior (bickering, pettiness, arrogance, etc.), antisocial acts (anger, selfishness, slander, gossip, etc.), and sexual immorality—all of which characterize Corinthian behavior mentioned elsewhere.[12] Therefore, even the general lists have specific applicability when used by Paul.

In 1 Thessalonians 5:16–18 also, Paul adapts a general paraenetic tradition to a specific situation. In 5:15 he links the adverb *pantote* ("always") to the general admonition to do good: "Always *(pantote)* seek to do good." The catchword *pantote* likewise enjoins the next command, "Rejoice always *(pantote)*"; a synonym of *pantote* follows

the third, "Pray constantly *(adialeiptos)*"; and a related term enforces
the final one, "give thanks in all circumstances *(en panti).*" In the
Greek each adverb comes first, and the injunctions form a neat parallel
structure:

pantote do good . . .
pantote rejoice,
adialeiptos pray,
en panti give thanks.

The parallel construction, the adverb and prepositional phrase ("in all
circumstances," *en panti*) in the emphatic position, and the repetition
of the key emphasis—"always . . . , always . . . , unceasingly . . . , in
all circumstances"—hammers home Paul's main point: the need for
perseverance in these acts of piety.

This emphasis on the need for persistence in the life of faith is stressed
throughout the letter. In 4:13ff. we learn that death has invaded this
inspired community; blinded by disappointment, some want to give up.
Misguided enthusiasts quit work to await the Lord, only to become a
burden on the rest of the church. Both the freeloaders and the disillu-
sioned, the brazen and the timid, receive the same admonition to persevere in the ways that Paul had taught them. For their comfort or
discomfort, Paul reminds them that Christ will return to rescue his
own, whether living or dead. In the meantime, they must persevere in
the life of faith and retain hope, for "this is the will of God" (5:18). Over
and over again Paul urges the faltering to do "more and more" the ways
they know (4:1, 10; 5:11).

We see, therefore, how Paul structures traditional paraenetic materials, adding key words at strategic points, to underscore the fundamental
point of the letter—the need for steadfast endurance until the end. So,
even these materials, as general as they seem, have specific and immediate relevance for the Thessalonian church.

Although Dibelius correctly maintained that the paraenetic sections
are not the property of Paul to the same degree as are the sections of
sustained theological argument, it is hardly accurate to call the paraenetic materials a "bag of answers to meet recurring problems and questions
common to the members of different early Christian communities."[13]

TYPES OF PARAENETIC TRADITION

a. *Wisdom Sayings*

    (1) You reap whatever you sow. (Gal. 6:7, NRSV)
    (2) The one who sows sparingly will also reap sparingly, and the one
        who sows bountifully will also reap bountifully. (2 Cor. 9:6, NRSV)
    (3) Bad company ruins good morals. (1 Cor. 15:33)
    (4) A little leaven leavens the whole lump. (Gal. 5:9)

b. *Vice and Virtue Lists*

   (1) They were filled with all manner of wickedness, evil, covetousness, malice. Full of envy, murder, strife, deceit, malignity, they are gossips, slanderers, haters of God, insolent, haughty, boastful, inventors of evil, disobedient to parents, foolish, faithless, heartless, ruthless. (Rom. 1:29–31; see also Gal. 5:19–21; 1 Cor. 5:10–11; 6:9–10; 2 Cor. 12:20)

   (2) The fruit of the Spirit is love, joy, peace, patience, kindness, goodness, faithfulness, gentleness, self-control. (Gal. 5:22–23; see also Phil. 4:8, which includes prominent Greek philosophical terms like *prosphilēs,* "lovely"; *euphēmos,* "gracious"; *aretē,* "excellence"; and *epainos,* "praiseworthy.")

c. *Imperative Cluster*

Let love be genuine; hate what is evil, hold fast to what is good; love one another with brotherly and sisterly affection; outdo one another in showing honor. Never flag in zeal, be aglow with the Spirit, serve the Lord. Rejoice in your hope, be patient in tribulation, be constant in prayer. Contribute to the needs of the saints, practice hospitality. (Rom. 12:9–13)

d. *Developed Exhortation* (or Topical Moral Essay)

(See the sustained admonition concerning the mutual responsibility of the strong and weak in Rom. 14:1–15:13; also note 1 Thess. 5:1–11.)[14]

In the discussion above we saw how Paul drew on early Christian tradition as well as Jewish and even "pagan" sources. Paul freely used the epistolary conventions of his time and frequently tapped a vast reservoir of Christian and non-Christian paraenesis. The alert reader will spot these and other traditional materials in reading the letters. Sometimes Paul will identify the nuggets of tradition with phrases like "I delivered what I also received, that . . . ," or "it is written that . . . ," or "this we declare by the word of the Lord, that . . ." Elsewhere, however, only a break in the context, an interruption in the stream of thought (e.g., Phil. 2:6–11), or an unusual construction of words or sentences will signal his use of sources. In other cases unusual vocabulary or theological statements that sound uncharacteristic of Paul may arouse our suspicion that traditional elements are present. But we must not merely notice that certain materials are appropriated; we must also see to what specific end. Fully as important as what is used is how it is used in the letter. How, the reader should ask, does Paul use traditional elements to address the specific problems of his readers? How does he relate the traditional elements to the theological arguments of the letter as a whole? Where does his theological outlook require alterations in the understanding of tradition, and what do these changes tell us about the intent of the letter itself? Although these questions are sometimes unanswerable, they are worth asking nevertheless. For through them we gain a heightened awareness of the horizons of Paul's thought. Even our failures may be instructive in teaching us the limits against which we are operating. But more important, by asking questions about Paul's use of tradition, we discover new dimensions of his theology that would otherwise remain hidden to us.

4. The Letters as Conversations

DEALING AS THEY DO with such mundane matters as sex, taxes, diet, lawsuits, circumcision, ecstatic speech, and intramural squabbles, Paul's letters bear the unmistakable imprint of this world. Among other things, the concreteness of the letters shows how seriously Paul took his readers, and how painstakingly he tried to interpret his gospel for them. Once we realize how the ferment in the churches prescribed the scope if not the content of Paul's writings, then it is obvious why in considering Paul we must treat not simply his thought but also the situation in the churches. Study of the epistles isolated from their context is like reading the answers at the end of an algebra book without the corresponding problems. Any one of the excellent summaries of Paul's theology would give the reader a grasp of the range and diversity of his thought.[1] In this study, however, we shall focus on the chief issues under debate between the Apostle and his congregations, hoping the reader will thereby gain an appreciation of Paul's vigor and ingenuity in applying his gospel to particular circumstances.

The precise stages of the relationship between Paul and his churches are not easy to reconfigure. In some ways our task is like that of a detective who, with painfully few clues, must reconstruct what happened at the scene of the crime. The following construction of the discussions between Paul and his addressees could be debated at great length. It is hoped, however, that even if our interpretation does not point to true north, it nevertheless may point to that magnetic north which, with proper allowances, may still guide us through a rugged and confusing terrain.

The Thessalonian Correspondence (c. 51 C.E.)[2]

1. Paul's Preaching

After his release from prison in Philippi (1 Thess. 2:2), Paul came to Thessalonica with his co-workers, Timothy and Silvanus. While working at his trade to earn his bread, Paul began preaching "in power and in the Holy Spirit and with full conviction" (1:5). His preaching was well received and enough converts were made to form a church. Proclamation of the gospel was the first stage in Paul's relationship to the Thessalonians.

But what was the nature of that proclamation and what was its content? Although Paul nowhere records a sermon for us, his letters do contain vestiges of his preaching: e.g., "Now I would remind you, brothers and sisters, in what terms I preached to you the gospel" (1 Cor. 15:1); "For you know what instructions we gave you through the Lord Jesus" (1 Thess. 4:2), and so on. Drawing on allusions to his preaching, we can reconstruct a model of the Pauline sermon on a reduced scale. Although later different problems compelled Paul to give different messages to each church, his initial preaching was approximately the same everywhere. The summary below, therefore, can be assumed to be the first stage in each conversation between Paul and the various churches.

Yahweh is God of the Jews, and through the Jews came his promises, the commandments, the prophets, and finally the Messiah. But Yahweh is not God of the Jews only. In past generations he has never left himself without witness among any people. Through his creation of the world and his gifts of rain and good harvest, God has shown his care for all people. But instead of the Creator, the Gentiles worshiped nature gods and local deities. God has decided to overlook the error and ignorance of the past and is once more making his appeal to all people, not just the Jews. His promise through Abraham was to all nations. Now in the last days that promise is being realized in Jesus the Christ who was crucified and whom God raised from the dead. Jesus will soon return to judge the world and collect all of his people. He will come from heaven with his angels in flaming fire; he will vindicate God's righteousness and punish those who reject God and the gospel. He will grant mercy and peace to all who believe in him. Those who accept his gospel will now taste the joys of the kingdom of God and enjoy deliverance from the present evil age. Repent, for the final days are at hand. Turn to God from the worship of idols. Be baptized into Jesus' death and rise up to walk in newness of life through the gift of the Holy Spirit. Be alert, watch, and wait for the return of the Son of God.[3]

2. The Report of Timothy

To avoid the charge that they were religious hucksters peddling gospel for gain, Paul and his companions worked "night and day" to support themselves while preaching at Thessalonica. Occasionally their earnings were supplemented by money sent from the Philippian church

(Phil. 4:16). At first, Paul's own example gave his gospel an authentic ring and it enjoyed good success. But among the Gentiles Paul met resistance and ultimately left Thessalonica, perhaps involuntarily (1:9–10; 2:13ff.; possibly also 2:16 and 2:17).

All during his journey south, however, Paul was haunted by thoughts of the troubled church. Concerned about its internal quarrels, uncertain whether it would even survive, he felt an almost irresistible urge to return, but, as he says, he was "hindered" from doing so (2:17–18). Unable to bear the suspense any longer, he dispatched Timothy to remind the church of his teaching (3:1ff.) and to encourage it. In due time, Timothy rejoined Paul in Corinth, reporting on the problems of the church as well as what was being said about the apostle. He possibly also carried a letter from the congregation to Paul.

In spite of his best efforts, Paul had not escaped the charge that his preaching was for personal gain. His sudden departure confirmed the suspicions of some that he, like the wandering preachers of "pagan" cults, had breezed into town, covered his greed with false pretenses, lined his pockets with money from the church, and then abandoned his converts when he came under fire from the Gentile officials (2:14). Because of Paul's success among the God-fearers, certain jealous Jews were also accusing Paul of error and uncleanness (2:3): "error" because his gospel did not come from God, and "uncleanness" because he taught disregard for the laws of Torah and thus encouraged libertinism.

Timothy also brought word about tensions within the church itself over the idle, the fainthearted, and the weak (5:14). Preoccupation with the coming world led some to neglect the proper concerns of this world. Some were so engrossed with the things of the spirit that they refused to work. They demanded support from others in the congregation (4:11–12; 5:14, 19–22) and rejected the need for instruction (5:12). Thus, the leisure of some was bought at the cost of added toil for others. Resentments flared up, tensions mounted, and disorder threatened the very existence of the church.[4]

The enthusiasm of some was matched by the disappointment of others. Belief in Christ's immediate return left some unprepared for the death of baptized friends. Inevitably, questions arose: Does the death of brothers and sisters in Christ mean that they were unworthy of seeing the Lord on the day of Christ's return *(parousia)*? Does not the death of some of the faithful raise questions about the salvation of the rest? Is the gospel a fraud? Where is the sign of Christ's coming (4:13–5:11)? With hope flickering, the temptation was strong to revert to the old familiar ways (4:5–8). Immorality, it appears, was taken up again by some. That others might succumb was an ever-present danger.

Nevertheless, except for the parts about the despondent or the idle, Timothy's report was positive. Despite the charges against Paul, a great reservoir of affection for him remained (3:6). Despite the crisis of hope in the community, the faith and love of the Thessalonians endured. But the threat of disillusionment was real, and Paul responded with his letter.[5]

3. Paul's Letter to the Thessalonians

The outline below sketches Paul's response to the Thessalonians. Instead of the harsh polemic seen elsewhere, this letter blossoms with assurance and comfort, gentle admonition and conciliation, encouragement and pastoral care. In one way or another, Paul addresses everyone in the congregation: The idle are admonished to work; those disheartened by the death of baptized friends are given new cause for hope (the dead will precede the living into the eschatological kingdom); those who know the claims of the gospel but who are at the point of giving up are admonished to persevere "more and more" in their life of hope; teachers are urged to use care in teaching, and all are reminded of their need to learn. Some of the teachers have an apprehension of the gospel that contains misunderstanding and disillusionment, but Paul tries to correct the misunderstandings gently and encourage the Thessalonians to persevere in the life of faith and love with hope.

OUTLINE OF PAUL'S LETTER TO THE THESSALONIANS
(1 Thessalonians)

1.	Address and Salutation	1:1
2.	Thanksgiving	1:2–10; 2:13, 3:9–10
3.	Personal Defense	
	a. Recollection of the Mission	2:1–16
	(1) Paul's pastoral work	2:1–12
	(2) Response of the believers	2:13–16
	b. The Mission of Timothy	2:17–3:13
	(1) Paul's desired visit	2:17–20
	(2) Sending of Timothy	3:1–5
	(3) Timothy's return and report	3:6–10
	(4) Prayer	3:11–13
4.	Ethical Exhortation and Instruction	chs. 4–5
	a. The ethical demands of the gospel	4:1–12
	(1) Previous instructions	4:1–2
	(2) Sanctification excludes sexual impurity	4:3–8
	(3) Concerning love for one another	4:9–10
	(4) Idleness	4:10–12
	b. Concerning the dead in Christ	4:13–18

c. Concerning the season of Christ's
coming   5:1–11

d. Miscellaneous paraenesis (Random
instructions)   5:12–22

5. Closing (Peace Wish, Kiss, Apostolic
Command and Benediction)   5:23–28

The Corinthian Correspondence (c. 52–55 C.E.)[6]

Paul came to Corinth in "fear and trembling" (1 Cor. 2:3). Perhaps he was afraid that he would receive the same harsh treatment that had cut short his ministry in Thessalonica and Philippi. What he feared might be a ministry of just a few weeks, however, stretched into a year and a half, and the gospel that first took root in the city enjoyed success in the surrounding countryside as well (2 Cor. 1:1). During his relatively long stay in Corinth, Paul received assistance from Aquila and Prisca, Jewish Christian refugees from Rome who "risked their necks" for him and earned the gratitude of all of the Gentile churches (Rom. 16:3–4; see also Acts 18:1–4).

Most of the membership of the Corinthian church was drawn from the ranks of the uneducated poor. Paul puts it graphically (1 Cor. 1:26–28) when he says,

> Not many of you were wise according to worldly standards, not many were powerful, not many were of noble birth; but God chose what is foolish in the world to shame the wise, God chose what is weak in the world to shame the strong, God chose what is low and despised in the world, even things that are not, to bring to nothing things that are.

Of these "weak" and "despised" ones, no doubt many were slaves (7:21ff.; 12:13) or the free who had won their release. Nevertheless, a sprinkling of leaders from the community did join the church. The Crispus whom Paul baptized (1 Cor. 1:14) was called a leader of the local synagogue in Acts 18:8; and Erastus, apparently a member of the Corinthian church, was the city treasurer (Rom. 16:23). In any case, the majority of both the poor and the privileged were Gentiles. They may have attended the synagogue, and some may even have observed Jewish practices, but they held back from becoming Jewish proselytes.

From the Corinthian letters we learn that the exchanges between Paul and that church continued over several years. Although the history of that relationship is complex, we can, nevertheless, reconstruct the principal stages of it with some certainty. A skeleton outline of that relationship should contain the following elements:

1. Paul preaches at Corinth (eighteen months).
2. Paul departs, settling eventually in Ephesus; he writes his first letter to the Corinthians (lost; see 1 Cor. 5:9).

3. Corinthians write to Paul (1 Cor. 7:1) and also send oral communication (1 Cor. 1:11 and 16:17).
4. Paul writes his second letter (our 1 Cor.), answering both oral and written communications from Corinth.
5. He dispatches Timothy by land with oral instructions. Timothy returns to Ephesus, reporting that his efforts to reclaim the church for Paul were unsuccessful.
6. Paul makes a brief "painful" visit to Corinth (2 Cor. 2:1–2), returning to Ephesus in humiliation (12:21).
7. Paul writes a harsh letter (letter number 3) "out of much affliction and anguish of heart" (2 Cor. 2:3–4, 9; 7:8–12). This letter (possibly 2 Cor. 10–13) was hand-delivered by Titus.
8. Paul travels to Macedonia to meet Titus, who brings encouraging news about the church.
9. Paul dispatches Titus with his fourth letter (2 Cor. 1:1–6:13; 7:2–9:15), a letter of reconciliation.
10. Paul visits Corinth to receive the offering for "the poor" in Jerusalem.

1. Paul's Preaching in Corinth

Much as in Thessalonica, Paul's gospel was enthusiastically received in Corinth. The essence of that gospel was that the deliverance promised by the prophets had now become available through the death and resurrection of Jesus. Through faith in Jesus as the Christ and baptism in his name, Paul asserted, men and women could share in the saving power of his death, and through the Eucharist believers could enjoy the fare of the world to come.

"Now is the day of salvation," Paul could say (2 Cor. 6:2). The time had arrived when God would pour out his Spirit on all flesh (Joel 2:28), when believers would see visions (see 2 Cor. 12:1ff.) and speak the language of angels (ecstatic speech, 1 Cor. 13:1; see Isa. 28:11). His preaching, like his letters, doubtless reflected Paul's conviction that his was the last generation, and his preaching included a call to the community to keep itself in readiness for the end.

While at Corinth Paul evidently spoke in tongues (1 Cor. 14:18) and demonstrated other charismatic gifts ("signs and wonders and mighty works"). In the face of the "impending distress," Paul chose to remain celibate (1 Cor. 7:7, 26). Evidently these examples had profound effect on the congregation, for Paul later devoted extensive discussion to both marriage and ecstatic speech.

2. Paul's Departure and His First Letter

After leaving Corinth, Paul eventually settled in Ephesus for about three years (c. 52–55 C.E.). Among others, Timothy, Titus, Aquila, and

Prisca worked with him there. Apollos also, an Alexandrian Jew, followed Paul in Corinth, enjoyed good success for a time, and ultimately joined him in Ephesus. If the account in Acts is to be believed (18:24–28), the eloquence of Apollos, his agile, imaginative approach to scripture, his enthusiasm, his skill in debate, and his resourceful personality endeared him to the Corinthians. It is unnecessary to assume that Apollos's presence in Corinth caused the problems there, but it may have aggravated certain enthusiastic tendencies already in the church.

While at Ephesus, Paul sent a letter, now lost, addressing certain problems in the Corinthian church (1 Cor. 5:9).[7] We are uncertain what those problems were. Perhaps a rumor of excesses had come to Paul. Or the presence of Apollos may have encouraged forms of enthusiasm that were disruptive to congregational life. Under the power of the Holy Spirit Paul probably uttered ecstatic speech (*glossolalia*—literally, speaking in tongues) while at Corinth. Since life in the kingdom of God was understood as life with the Holy Spirit, it is hardly surprising that what was once an expression of life in the kingdom became a condition for acceptance within the church. Effect was regarded as cause: ecstatic speech was thought to induce salvation, rather than salvation inducing speech. Angel speech, as it was called (see 1 Cor. 13:1), indicated who was in tune with the divine, or, as they put it, who had "knowledge." Those "in the know" felt so secure in Christ and so sure of their power to prevail over this world that they behaved in ways that Paul would have found foolhardy. Since they knew that idols had no real existence, they freely attended pagan celebrations, participated in pagan cultic meals, and ate meat offered to idols. It is possible, if not likely, that this "knowledge" led some to attempt to live above mere accidental distinctions, like sex, since in the kingdom of God by Paul's own admission there is neither male nor female. "Spiritual marriages" would have allowed men and women to live together without sexual intercourse. It is hardly surprising that such well-intentioned practices sometimes encouraged the very thing they wished to avoid (see 1 Corinthians 5). If such a life-style emerged from this "knowledge," then we can understand why the gist of the missing first letter was the admonition not to associate with sexually immoral persons (1 Cor. 5:9).

3. Oral and Written Responses from Corinth

Chloe's people (slaves?) and perhaps others (1 Cor. 16:17) soon arrived in Ephesus from Corinth to report the deteriorating situation in their home church (1 Cor. 1:11). Boasts about exclusive truth and pretentious claims to religious "knowledge" had brought on fiery antagonisms. The church in fact was perilously close to shattering, with each faction devoted to a different leader—Paul, Peter, Apollos, or even Christ. Each faction claimed that only through its leader could "knowledge" be gained, and, intoxicated on its own divine secrets, each group thought only of the glorified life and forgot about the cross. Each faction was eager to give full expression to its eschatological gifts, especially speaking in tongues. These powerful signs, they boasted, demonstrated the truth of their wisdom in Christ. Such spiritual elitism fostered contempt of those with other gifts, led some to disdain the unimposing Paul, and jeopardized the very existence of the church (see 1 Cor. 1:10–4:21).

The cliques also disrupted worship (see esp. 11:17–34). Full of eschatological preoccupation, some celebrated the Lord's Supper as if it were the great messianic banquet reserved for the end of time. In their enthusiasm they stuffed themselves, saving nothing for Christian slaves whose arrival was delayed by assigned tasks. Some were gorged and drunken; not a crumb remained for others. Such self-indulgence and indifference to the needs of others were direct results of the religious enthusiasm referred to in 1 Corinthians 1:10–4:21.

Chloe's people also reported that one member of the congregation was living openly with his stepmother without any objection from the church leaders (5:1–8, 13). Moreover, some believers had gone before the pagan magistrate to settle disputes with other Christians (6:1–11).

In 1 Corinthians 7:1 Paul shifts his attention to the concerns expressed in the letter from the Corinthians ("now concerning the matters about which you wrote"). Using here as elsewhere the phrase "now concerning . . ." *(peri de),* Paul introduces into discussion each topic that the Corinthians had specified in their letter. Indeed, by noting the appearances of that phrase ("now concerning . . ."), we can reconstruct a rough outline of the Corinthians' letter to Paul (see 7:1, 25; 8:1; 12:1; and 16:1). Our hypothesis of that letter is as follows:

Corinthian Letter to Paul

(1) *Concerning Marriage*

Given the urgency of the times, we believe married believers should refrain from sexual intercourse and virgins and widows should not consider marriage—all this, so that believers might devote themselves wholly to preparing for the end. Remember how you said "it is well for a man not to touch a woman"? In this we are only following your example. Moreover, you yourself said that in the kingdom of God there is neither male nor female, and the Lord said that in the kingdom men and women are not married or given in marriage. Since we are members of the kingdom, should not those of us who are married act as if they were not, and should not believers divorce any unbelieving partners?

(2) *Concerning Contact with the World*

You wrote us not to associate with the immoral, but that is impossible; the world is full of immoral people. And how does this square with your preaching? You said that for believers there is no law; all things are lawful. So what is there to fear? Don't we give evidence of our faith by exercising our freedom in Christ? Doesn't God love everyone, moral and immoral alike?

Also, what harm can come from eating idol meat? Since there is only one God, we know that an idol has no real existence. Moreover, we know that physical things cannot defile the spirit—"Food is meant for the belly and the belly for food." Must we decline all invitations to eat with our unbelieving friends and relatives? Must we insult them by asking if the meat they offer us is pure? How can we witness to unbelievers if we offend them?

(3) *Concerning Worship*

Since all are one in Christ, the distinctions between men and women are artificial; such physical accidents mean nothing in the kingdom of God. It is entirely appropriate, therefore, for women to pray with heads uncovered and to share actively in the service. And why should you have reservations now about speaking in tongues? We are merely following your example. It is clear to us that those who are unable to speak the language of angels have not fully surrendered to God's Spirit.

(4) *Concerning the Resurrection*

Through baptism we have already passed from death to the resurrected life. If we have already died, and if today is the day of salvation, how can you say we must prepare for the resurrection of the dead? How can those who have died die again? Also, what do you mean by the "resurrection of the body"? The whole idea of the resuscitation of a dead corpse is repugnant. Salvation brings release from our bodies; what good is salvation if we are still imprisoned in our bodies?

(5) *Concerning the Collection*

Although we are poor ourselves, we shall give something for the poor in Jerusalem. It would probably be best if we sent someone from our church to deliver the offering. You would not want anyone to think you were skimming off part of the gift for yourself.

(6) *Concerning Apollos*

Could you encourage Apollos to return to Corinth? He had a very effective ministry here. Some of our people miss his powerful witness and his persuasive teaching of scripture. They are always asking when he will return to continue his work among us.

4. Paul's Written Reply to the Oral Report and the Letter from Corinth[8]

In what we know as 1 Corinthians we see Paul's reply to two communications from Corinth—one oral and one written. It is interesting that Paul responds in kind, sending 1 Corinthians (which was really his second letter) from Ephesus by sea (1 Cor. 5:9, c. Easter, 55 C.E.) and dispatching Timothy by land (1 Cor. 4:17) with oral instructions. Paul's letter is intact, but for the sake of clarity we summarize his argument below.

Paul's Response to the Oral Report

(1) *Concerning Division* (1:10–4:21)

Why do you boast of your baptism in the name of people like me, Apollos, Peter, and even Christ? Is Christ divided? Were you baptized in the name of Paul? Does some special wisdom come in baptism through your union with Christ? Is that why you call yourselves wise, mature, and spiritual? Your boasting is silly and contrary to the ways of God. Divine wisdom looks like foolishness to society. Through a cross, or through a motley collection of people like yourselves, or through a frail and unimposing figure like me, God reveals wisdom—not in strength and glory but in weakness and shame! Christ crucified, not Christ glorified, was the heart of my gospel, and this Christ forms the foundation of the church. All work laid on that foundation by Apollos or anybody else will be tested on the last day. To those inflated with their own self-esteem and heedless of the welfare of the church, let me say: if they destroy the church, God will destroy them. Is it because you think you are so spiritual that you presume to judge Christ's apostles and think you are above scripture (see 1 Cor. 4:6, *hyper ha gegraptai*)? When I come, I will find out how really spiritual these people are.

(2) *Concerning Immorality* (5:1–6:11)

a. *Incest* (5:1–13)

I hear that a man is living with his "father's wife," all in the name of the Lord Jesus, and worse, you condone it! You say Christians are above such trivial differences as those of sex, and that life in the kingdom transcends sexuality. You tolerate behavior that even pagans scorn. Expel this offender lest he poison the whole congregation. When I wrote that you should not associate with immoral persons, I meant just such as this, not the outsiders.

b. *Lawsuits* (6:1–11)

I hear that some of you are defrauding others, and that someone has taken a case to the civil courts. How ironic that you who someday will judge the heathen, or even angels, now turn to the heathen for justice. Must the injured party turn to the civil courts? You claim to be wise *(sophos)*; are you not wise enough to render a decision on such matters? Great harm can be done to the church and the mission by such action.

(3) *Concerning the Lord's Supper* (11:17–34)

Each one eats, so I hear, regardless of the needs of others and only for self-satisfaction. You claim to be celebrating your life in the kingdom, but instead you profane the Lord's body. Do you not know that Christ is in his community? Your selfish and greedy behavior not only insults your brother and sister, it offends the Lord himself, who is present for judgment. That is why some are sick and some have died.

Paul's Response to the Corinthians' Letter

(1) *Concerning Marriage* (7:1–40)

I fear you misunderstood my remark that it is better for a man not to touch a woman. Because you think you are equal to angels, you claim to be above such worldly things.[9] The pure want to rid themselves of unbelieving partners. Continence within marriage is expected. Widows and virgins are made to feel inferior if they marry. I encouraged all to remain as I am because of the special urgency of the times (the end is near), not because we have overcome the world. Not everyone has the gift of celibacy. It is better to marry than to be aflame with passion.

(2) *Concerning Idol Meat* (8:1–11:1)

It is true that there is no God but one, and that therefore idols have
no real existence. Since idols do not exist, you ask, what harm comes
from eating meat offered to them? But what if my freedom causes a
weaker believer to stumble? Freedom must always be subordinated
to love. I am free, am I not? Yet I freely surrender my "rights" for
the sake of others. Because you are washed and now eat supernatural
food, do not think that you are infallible. Israel too was a sacramental
community, and yet 23,000 died in a single day in the wilderness.
You cannot worship the living God one day and share in pagan
worship the next. One is bound to whatever is worshiped. You cannot
share the cup of Christ and the cup or food of idols. Remember also
that even if you are free in Christ, and even if all things are lawful,
not all things are helpful. Eat in a way that strengthens yourselves
and others.

(3) *Concerning Distinctions Between Men and Women* (11:2–16)

Some of you say that in Christ there is neither male nor female. It
is true that I encouraged women to participate in the service. But you
seek to obliterate all distinctions between male and female. Such are
accidents of birth, you say, and after sharing in the new creation all
such accidental distinctions should be ignored. You claim too much.
We are not yet angels. Let men and women continue sharing in the
service of worship, but let us maintain the distinction between male
and female. Men, cut your hair, and women, cover your heads (or
wear veils).

(4) *Concerning Spiritual Gifts* (12:1–14:40)

You claim to follow my example in practicing ecstatic speech. You
do well to exalt the spiritual gifts, but if those who speak in tongues
despise those who do not, how does that build up the church? Strive
for the higher gifts like teaching and interpreting, which edify others.
Allow all to contribute in their own way with whatever gift they
have, and subordinate all of the gifts to love.

(5) *Concerning the Resurrection* (15:1–58)

Remember the gospel that I preached that Christ died, was buried,
and was raised. Christ's raising was the first of the general resurrection soon to be completed. You say you have already been raised up,
that death is behind you, that only the life of glory remains, and that
therefore there is no future resurrection for you. I hear also that the

whole idea of the resurrection of the body is repulsive to you. Do you not know that God can give us a different body appropriate to that life? But death has not yet been completely conquered; that will come in the future when God puts all enemies underfoot, and the last enemy to be destroyed will be death. Then and only then will we be able to say, "Death is swallowed up in victory."

(6) *Concerning the Collection* (16:1–4)

Have the collection ready when I come. I agree that someone from the congregation should accompany us to deliver the offering.

(7) *Concerning Apollos* (16:12)

I urged him to come, but it was not God's will that he come at this time. He will come later.

5. Paul Dispatches Timothy with Oral Instructions, and Timothy's Return

The second letter, going directly by sea, arrived in Corinth ahead of Timothy, who had taken the roundabout land route. When Timothy arrived in Corinth, he found the church still shaken by internal disputes and gravely suspicious of Paul. Soon he returned to Ephesus to report the bad news. Neither his presence nor the letter had healed the wounds opened by internal conflict.

To add insult to injury, certain Hellenistic Jewish-Christian missionaries had arrived, bidding for the affection, loyalty, and support of the Corinthian church. They claimed to be "servants of Christ" (2 Cor. 11:23) and professed to be apostles (2 Cor. 11:5, 13). They came armed with written testimonials to the success of their preaching elsewhere (2 Cor. 3:1). These "superlative apostles" drew unflattering comparisons between their works and those of Paul. They said Paul lacked charisma, that he was an ineffective preacher. He was frail and hypocritical—a bully in his letters but harmless in person (2 Cor. 10:10). When Paul was in Corinth he had refused money, these men alleged, either because he was insecure in his apostolate (2 Cor. 11:7, 9) or because he planned to cream off some of the Jerusalem offering for himself (12:16–18). For their part, these Jewish-Christian missionaries boasted of their exploits in service of the gospel. By signs and wonders they demonstrated the power of their message; through visions they gained access to heavenly secrets; and for these divine gifts they demanded support from the church and thus undermined Paul's efforts to collect an offering for the "poor" in Jerusalem.[10]

6. Paul's Painful Visit to Corinth

Upon hearing the bad news, Paul made a brief, "painful" visit to Corinth (2 Cor. 2:1). Once there he was insulted publicly by a Corinthian Christian (2 Cor. 2:5–8; 7:12) and frustrated in his efforts to reclaim the church for his gospel. So he returned to Ephesus in humiliation (2 Cor. 12:21). His disastrous visit played into the hands of his critics. Didn't his swift departure give substance to the charge that he was a coward? His position in the Corinthian church seemed more insecure than ever.

7. Paul's Third Letter to the Corinthians (2 Corinthians 10–13)[11]

In a last-ditch effort, Paul now wrote his third letter "out of much affliction and anguish of heart" (2 Cor. 2:3–4, 9; 7:8–12) and dispatched Titus with it. Paul arranged to meet Titus in Troas to receive his report. Although we cannot be certain that any part of this letter exists, it is commonly suggested that 2 Corinthians 10–13 contains the heart of this severe letter. Certainly the subject matter qualifies as severe. Here we see Pauline sarcasm at its best, and it contrasts rather sharply with Paul's mood in 2 Corinthians 1–9.

8. Titus Delivers Letter and Returns with Report

So anxious was Paul about the effect of his "severe" letter that he found it impossible to wait for Titus in Troas. Instead, Paul set out to meet him (2 Cor. 2:12–13), finally linking up in Macedonia, perhaps in Neapolis, the port of Philippi. Titus brought encouraging news. The Corinthians mourned their wrongs; they longed to see Paul (7:6–7). They had reprimanded the troublemakers and restored order. After hearing the good news, Paul sent Titus and two others bearing his fourth letter (8:16–24) which may have comprised 2 Corinthians 1–9 (minus 6:14–7:1, an insertion).

9. Paul's Fourth Letter to the Corinthians (2 Corinthians 1–9)

It seems clear that the crisis had passed. Paul reveals that he had earlier canceled plans to come to Corinth again to spare the church "another painful visit." He seems happy that the adversary has been disciplined and is now restored; he seems both apologetic and pleased by the work of the "severe" letter—sorry that it caused pain but relieved that it effected a positive change. Now Paul announces his plans to visit Corinth once more to receive the offering for the Jerusalem church.

OUTLINE OF 1 CORINTHIANS (Paul's Second Letter)

OUTLINE OF 2 CORINTHIANS 10:1–13:14 (Paul's Third Letter)[13]

OUTLINE OF 2 CORINTHIANS 10:1–13:14 *(cont.)*

3.	Concerning Justifiable Boasting	11:1–12:13
	a. Reason for this foolish indulgence	11:1–6
	b. Response to the charge of refusing money	11:7–15
	c. Plea to accept the folly of his boasting	11:16–21
	d. Paul's boasting rooted in suffering and weakness	11:22–12:10
	e. Conclusion	12:11–13
4.	Concerning Paul's Imminent Visit	12:14–13:10
	a. Announcement of visit	12:14–18
	b. Paul's fear of finding Corinthians unrepentant	12:19–21
	c. Sharp apostolic warning	13:1–10
5.	Conclusion	13:11–14

OUTLINE OF 2 CORINTHIANS 1–9 (minus 6:14–7:1) (Paul's Fourth Letter)

1.	Address, Salutation, and Thanksgiving	1:1–11
2.	Autobiographical Report and Apology	1:12–2:17
	a. Sincerity of the apostle	1:12–14
	b. Reason for postponement of apostolic visit	1:15–2:4
	c. Treatment of the offender	2:5–11
	d. Report on his ministry from Troas to Macedonia	2:12–17
3.	Defense of Paul's Apostolic Ministry	3:1–6:10
	a. Others need letters of recommendation but "you are our letter of recommendation"	3:1–3
	b. Others claim sufficiency but our sufficiency is from God who appointed "us" as ministers of the new covenant	3:4–11
	c. Truth of scripture veiled to others; for "us" Christ lifts the veil from the scriptures	3:12–18
	d. Others preach themselves; "we" preach Christ	4:1–6
	e. Others validate preaching with manifestations of glory; we validate ours through suffering	4:7–5:10
	f. Others pride themselves on their "position" but the "love of Christ controls us"	5:11–6:2
	g. Final appeal to recognize the manifestation of God in his suffering, weakness, etc.	6:3–10
4.	Invitation to Reconciliation	6:11–7:16
	a. Plea to restore relationship	6:11–13; 7:2–4
	b. Report of Titus on Corinthian visit with a parenthesis on the severe letter	7:5–16
5.	The Collection for the "Poor" in Jerusalem	8–9
	a. Example of the churches in Macedonia	8:1–6

Galatians (c. 50–55 C.E.)[14]

Paul founded the Galatian church[15] from a sickbed. When illness overtook him on his way through Galatia, the local people took him in and nursed him back to health (4:13–16). During his recuperation, and perhaps after, Paul spoke to the Galatian Gentiles of their adoption as children of God. No longer, he said, need they be slaves of this world's hostile, demonic powers (4:8–9). Through the crucified one and the gift of the Holy Spirit, they could be liberated from their pagan gods. After hearing this "good news" and witnessing the mighty deeds of Paul (3:5), the Galatians received his gospel with enthusiasm and revered the apostle himself. Their patient had become their savior; an "angel of God," even Jesus Christ himself they called him (4:14). Their devotion was so extreme that they would, if possible, have given him their eyes (4:15).

1. Opposition Develops

At Paul's departure all was well. Some time later, however, he learned that the Galatians were adopting another version of the gospel. His apostleship was under attack, and the church was in turmoil. Whether the opposition to Paul was inspired by outsiders or led by insiders is hotly debated. In any case, the nature of the opposition is clear. Since Paul had left Galatia, his converts there had learned from Jewish scriptures that the promises of God belong to the children of Abraham and that one becomes a son of Abraham through circumcision. Abraham, the father of many Gentiles (Gen. 17:5), received circumcision when ninety-nine years old after having received God's promise. Likewise, the Galatians might well have reasoned, it was necessary for them, the spiritual descendants of Abraham, to receive circumcision. Such a conclusion would have been natural in light of Genesis 17:10, which reads, "This is my covenant, which you shall keep, between me and you and your descendants after you: Every male among you shall be circumcised." Later in Genesis 17:14 divine proscription is placed on those who disobey the command: "Any uncircumcised male who is not circumcised . . . shall be cut off from his people." Word of the observance of circumcision by the Jewish Christians in Jerusalem may have strengthened the belief of the Galatians that they, too, should be circumcised. For whatever reason, by the time Paul writes our letter, the Galatians are requiring all baptized males to be circumcised (5:2, 11; 6:12–13). Their zeal for God and the scriptures led them to keep other parts of the law as well (3:2; 4:21; 5:4, 18).

The Galatians thus attempted to revise Paul's gospel by adding the Hebrew rite of circumcision. They also incorporated much from the local folk religion. They continued worshiping certain "elemental spirits" (4:9) and observing their sacred pagan festivals—"days, and months, and seasons, and years" (4:10).

Of a piece with the modification of Paul's gospel were the questions raised about Paul himself. It was impossible to separate the credibility of the message from the integrity of the messenger. The Galatians began to wonder if Paul were not simply an interloper into the apostolic circle? Jesus' original followers, even Jesus' brother James, were leaders in the Jerusalem church. Their link with the Lord was personal and the authority for their leadership was unquestioned. Paul, however, was a johnny-come-lately, for it was only after Jesus' death that Paul learned of Jesus and his followers, and then only as their adversary. How could Paul claim to be the Lord's apostle when he had not known Jesus? Paul's tradition had come from followers of Jesus, not from Jesus himself. Thus, in the Galatian view, Paul's gospel was secondhand and deficient. However good his intentions or impressive his preaching, Paul's gospel required an additive. It was necessary to supplement the Apostle's message with a version of the gospel wider in scope, stricter in discipline, more firmly grounded on scripture and apostolic tradition. It is possible that their appeal to the law was developed partly in opposition to certain religious enthusiastic tendencies in the church that had resulted from Paul's preaching of salvation by grace alone. Note, however, Galatians 5:13ff., where Paul himself warns against "freedom in the Spirit," i.e., insensitivity to any distinction between moral and immoral behavior.

2. Who Were Paul's Opponents?

(a) Scholars hold three views on the identity of Paul's opponents. One view is that Jewish Christians from Jerusalem, possibly from Peter's or James's circle, trailed Paul from place to place seeking to correct his misrepresentation of the gospel. The theory is that the Jewish Christian church in Jerusalem kept the law and sought to impose it on Paul's congregations that believed in justification by grace apart from the law. This view suffers from the lack of any reference or allusion to such opposition in Paul's letter. Although Paul was eager to show his independence of "the pillars" in Jerusalem, he nevertheless reports their endorsement of his gospel (2:9–10). If the pillars endorsed Paul's gospel, it is unlikely that they would then actively oppose it. Moreover, the Galatian charge that Paul was dependent on the Jerusalem church for his gospel makes no sense at all if the Jerusalem leaders were opposing him. And if Paul's opponents were Jewish Christians from Jerusalem, it is puzzling he should have to remind them that one who submits to circumcision is obligated to keep the whole law. Any Jewish Christian from Jerusalem would have known that—it was an ancient Pharisaic principle, and it is not likely they would have neglected it. Finally, the reversion of the Galatians to the service of "elemental spirits" (4:9) and their tendency to turn Christian freedom into libertinism (5:13) could hardly have been the result of a campaign by Jewish Christians to bring all of Paul's converts into obedience to the law.

(b) Followers of Johannes Munck, a distinguished Danish scholar, hold that Paul's opponents were members of the Galatian congregation.[16] Munck pointed out that Paul refers to the troublemakers as "those who are being circumcised" (6:13, my translation), which would be singularly inappropriate if it were meant to refer to Jews from Jerusalem—who, of course, had been circumcised long ago. On Munck's side also is the absence of a single reference to the opponents as "outsiders" (unlike 2 Corinthians 10–13). In support of Munck's view, Lloyd Gaston has shown that, oddly enough, there were Gentile Judaizers in Asia Minor, although in a somewhat later period.[17] We must allow Ignatius (*Letter to the Philadelphians* 6:1) to speak in his own words: "If anyone interpret Judaism to you do not listen to him; for it is better to hear Christianity from the circumcised [such as Paul] than Judaism from the uncircumcised [Gentile Judaizers]."[18]

It would be natural enough for Gentile converts to conclude from reading Jewish scripture that circumcision was required of all believers (see Gen. 17:11, 14). Inevitably, this practice would cause some to wonder why Paul had not required circumcision. Paul's silence on this issue would have been especially perplexing in light of the practice of circumcision in the Jewish Christian church in Jerusalem. Had Paul deliberately misrepresented the gospel he got from Jerusalem by omitting the circumcision requirement? The issue is complicated by the fact that Paul, unlike Peter and James, had not known the earthly Jesus. Could it be, the Galatians may have asked, that the gospel of the pillars is more authentic than Paul's gospel?

Although Munck has raised important questions about the identity of Paul's opponents, many scholars feel his thesis does not account for the references to behavior having nothing to do with Jewish faith and practice. It is especially difficult to square Munck's thesis with the references to worship of elemental spirits, to observance of days, months, seasons, and years, and to libertine behavior.

(c) Walter Schmithals, a noted German scholar, argues that Paul's Galatian converts were syncretists. Combining certain features from

Jewish practice (like circumcision) with items drawn from their own folk religion, they tried to accommodate Paul's gospel to their own religious and social context. Such a thesis allows for the amateurism that characterized the Galatian observance of circumcision. One is struck by their unawareness of the principle that this cultic act obligated them to keep the entire law. But it seems strange, if it was syncretism that threatened the integrity of Paul's gospel, that he should give so little space to the threat of the local folk religion and so much to the Judaizing menace. In our discussion we have adopted a variation on this third option.

3. *Paul's Response*

The attempts to undermine Paul's apostleship and supplement his gospel evoked a fiery rejoinder. In place of the usual warm, friendly thanksgiving, Paul opens with an angry outburst: "I am astonished that you are so quickly deserting him who called you in the grace of Christ" (1:6). He then proceeds to call down a curse from heaven on the heads of his rivals preaching another gospel (1:7–9). And later he excoriates those who take delight in circumcising others and suggests in disgust that they mutilate themselves (5:12). He even tells those who receive circumcision that they are severed from Christ (5:4). Finally, he warns those who attack him that it is really Christ they oppose (6:17).

It may seem strange to the modern reader that Paul would link the defense of his apostleship with the defense of his gospel. But for Paul and his readers the integrity of his apostolic commission and the truth of his gospel were inseparable. It is clear then why the letter opens with Paul's defense of his apostleship. The Galatians charge that Paul's gospel came from a human source, that is, from the leaders of the Jerusalem church (1:11). Paul, however, insists that since the time of his call he has been independent of the Jerusalem church. For three years after his call he did not so much as visit Jerusalem, and when he finally did, it was only for fifteen days. And he did not return to Jerusalem again for fourteen years. Moreover, he insists, even during his brief time in Jerusalem, he maintained his independence, gained acceptance for his gospel, and on one occasion publicly rebuked Peter for his duplicity on the issue of eating with unclean Gentiles. By arguing that Christ, not the Jerusalem leaders, commissioned him directly, Paul wants to break free of the charge that he is dependent on the Jerusalem "pillars" for his gospel (see 1:18–2:21).

Paul begins his defense of his gospel by appealing to scripture. His discussion centers on Abraham, a figure important to both the apostle and the Galatians. As a Jew, Paul was a son of Abraham according to the flesh (Rom. 4:1; 11:1). Abraham was also the patron of all proselytes, since God's promise was that through Abraham all the world's peoples (i.e., Gentiles) would be blessed. It is likely that the Galatians shared Paul's interest in the Abraham narrative, for in it they would have found grounds for requiring circumcision. After receiving the covenant, Abraham and all of his descendants were commanded to undergo circumcision (Gen. 17:9–11). Any male who remained uncircumcised would "be cut off from his people" (Gen. 17:14). Against this interpretation of the Abraham narrative, Paul appeals to Genesis 15:6, which says Abraham *"believed* the LORD; and he [i.e., Yahweh] reckoned it to him as righteousness" (italics added). Therefore, Paul concluded, since Abraham was counted righteous on account of his faith before he was circumcised, it is faith, not circumcision, that links the children of promise with Abraham.

In Galatians 3:16 Paul employs a method of scripture interpretation that some might think grotesque. There he says,

> Now the promises were made to Abraham and to his offspring. It does not say, "And to offsprings," referring to many; but, referring to one, "And to your offspring," which is Christ.

Given the benefit of modern exegetical methods, we know, of course, that Paul is unfaithful here to the original intent of the Genesis material. But it is unfair to expect him to use modern, sophisticated techniques in his interpretation of scripture. His rabbinic methods were second nature and automatically came into play here to support his conviction that on the last day God will gather people from all quarters of the world, Jew and Gentile, to form the new holy community. Significantly, Paul argues that since the promise is to Abraham's seed (*zera',* sing.; i.e., Christ), it is through faith in Christ, not observance of law, that Gentiles become true children of Abraham.

In light of his more positive statements about the law elsewhere, Paul's almost totally negative picture of it in Galatians is disturbing. The statements here must be read as exaggerations for effect—a polemical attempt to confute the Galatian revisionists. Paul opposes their effort to supplement his gospel with observance of law for two reasons: (1) It reveals a fundamental distrust in the adequacy of his gospel and the God who gave it. In Jerusalem Paul had successfully defended his right to offer full salvation to Gentiles. He believes in the full right of Gentiles as Gentiles to be equal members of the people of God. Now Paul's critics are suggesting that Gentiles who enter the church through grace instead of the law are second-class citizens. If they are to become full members of the elect community, they must receive circumcision. To Paul this addition is no mere minor change but a fundamental repudiation of the gospel of salvation by grace. (2) In Paul's view the Galatian experiment with the Law is amateurish. One senses Paul's disdain, if not contempt, for those who think they can keep selected portions of the law. Paul reminds the Galatians of a basic Pharisaic principle that evidently they have overlooked: "Every man who receives circumcision . . . is bound to keep the *whole* law" (5:3, emphasis added). Paul says this, however, not to urge those who are keeping only a part of the law to keep all 613 commandments, but to encourage his listeners to claim full membership in God's kingdom by grace and not as righteous proselytes via Judaism.[19] Since the Galatians came to enjoy life in the Spirit through "hearing with faith" free from "works of the law," Paul would have them continue in the way of responsible freedom (ch. 5).

OUTLINE OF GALATIANS

Romans (c. 55–57 C.E.)

1. Integrity of the Letter

There are, or once were, three different manuscript versions of Romans—one ending with chapter 14, one with chapter 15, and one with chapter 16. But which one went to the church of Rome? The scholarly consensus is that it was not the bobtailed edition (chs. 1–14 and the benediction in 16:25–27). This short version was used if not created by Marcion, a second-century heretic. Given his tendency to take the knife to disagreeable texts and given his distaste for the Old Testament,

Marcion may have been inspired by Paul's praise of the Old Testament in 15:4 and his positive use of it in 15:9–12, 21 to amputate the entire chapter and add his own benediction (16:25–27). Since short versions of the letter do surface, however, in a few late Latin manuscripts, it is possible that Marcion adopted but did not father the short form of the letter.

Arguments that the long version (chs. 1–16) went to Rome raise a host of questions. Would Paul have known twenty-six Christians in Rome whom he could greet by name (16:3–15)? Since in the other letters he greets no addressee by name, one might wonder whether, even had he known twenty-six Christians in Rome, he would have greeted them. Prisca and Aquila were working with Paul in Ephesus when 1 Corinthians 16:19 was written. Had they now returned to Rome? Paul greets Andronicus and Junia (Rom. 16:7), who were in prison with him, presumably in Ephesus. Had they also moved to Rome? Paul calls Epaenetus "the first convert in *Asia*" (16:5; emphasis added), but now he also is in Rome—if chapter 16 is a part of the original letter. While such a mass movement of Paul's acquaintances to Rome is not impossible, it is not likely. More important than the greetings, however, is Paul's stern warning against false doctrine in 16:17–19. From all that we know, such an injunction squares less with the Roman milieu than with the situation in the eastern church (e.g., see 2 Corinthians and Philippians).[21]

More tenable is the view that Paul's original letter to Rome contained only chapters 1–15 plus a concluding benediction that was removed to make way for chapter 16. Chapter 16 is a later work, perhaps by Paul himself, and was probably sent to a church in the East. Ephesus is the leading candidate for that honor. Even if chapter 16 were written at the same time as chapters 1–15, it was not a part of the same letter and should not be used to ascertain anything about the Roman situation. We will assume here that the original letter contained only chapters 1–15.

2. Background of the Roman Church

We do not know who founded the Roman church or when. We know only that it had already been in existence "for many years" before Paul wrote Romans (15:23), and that there was a church in Rome in the forties C.E. when the Emperor Claudius "expelled from Rome the Jews who were constantly stirring up a tumult under the leadership of Chrestus" (Suetonius, "Claudius," 25, in *The Lives of the Twelve Caesars*).

Although Suetonius's report is vague, it probably refers to heated or even violent arguments in the Jewish community concerning Christ. Aquila and Prisca, Paul's co-workers in Corinth (1 Cor. 16:19), conceivably were among those expelled by Claudius. Meanwhile the Gentile Christians remained in Rome, unmolested by the ban of Claudius. After the death of Claudius, the ban was lifted (54 C.E.), and Jewish Christians were free to return to Rome once more. But the return of these Jewish Christians brought new tensions to the Roman church.

3. Problem Within the Church

Scholars disagree over the purpose of Romans. Perhaps no single reason is sufficient to explain its existence. In chapter 14 at least, Paul is aware of conflict between Jewish and Gentile Christians and seeks to address that problem. Apparently the Gentile emphasis on justification by grace apart from works of the law had encouraged certain licentious tendencies in the church. Moreover, returning Jewish Christians or Jewish converts would have been offended by the suggestion that the observance of dietary rules and the Christian gospel were incompatible. Some Gentile Christians may have argued that the church had replaced Israel and therefore Jewish Christians were obligated to quit their hallowed traditions (see 9–11).

In all likelihood Jewish Christians were offended that Gentiles would think observance of Jewish dietary laws was a refusal of salvation apart from works of the law (see ch. 14). In spite of the disdain of their Gentile brothers and sisters, these Jewish Christians preferred eating no meat at all (14:2) to eating what was not kosher. Jewish Christians would also have abstained from the wine that was routinely offered to pagan gods before its sale (14:21). Eating the food of the pagan gods or drinking their wine was in the Jewish tradition to be guilty of idolatry (14:3). Naturally, in their view, it was better to be a Jewish Christian— obedient to Torah, even at the risk of being overly scrupulous—than to be led into immorality through a gospel of justification by grace alone. Abraham, in their view, had shown that faith and the observance of law are compatible for he kept the whole law even before it was written. Moreover, enough immorality existed among Gentile Christians to cause these Jewish Christians to wonder if rejection of the law had encouraged lawlessness.

In Romans Paul answers a number of Jewish objections to his gospel. "Are we to continue in sin that grace may abound?" (6:1). "Are we to sin because we are not under law but under grace?" (6:15). Is the law sin (7:7)? If God has turned to the Gentiles away from his chosen people, have God's promises failed (9:6)? Paul was in a unique position to answer these questions because they had all been hurled at him before. Most Jewish Christians, like Paul, were active in both synagogue and church and were thus continually exposed to ridicule and harassment from non-Christian Jews. Thus, the same Jewish Christians who were accused by Gentile Christians of being overly scrupulous in the observance of law were charged by the synagogue leaders with abandoning it. Why, these leaders might ask, do not the Gentiles first become proselyte Jews if they wish to become heirs of the promise? Moreover, some Jewish Christians had abandoned the synagogue altogether, claiming to be "not under law but under grace" (6:15). What kind of gospel was this that caused believers to jettison the law and begin the gradual slide into immorality? Incredulously they asked, how could anyone keep God's law and also accept a gospel that rejected the law as unnecessary?

4. Paul's Response

Unlike Paul's other letters, Romans was written to a church he had neither founded nor visited. In Romans Paul names no adversary and attacks no opponent. Yet, like his other epistles, Romans is a genuine letter, not a treatise in systematic theology. Although its depth of insight is great—some would say unsurpassed—it nevertheless has the structure of a letter, conveys the warmth of a truly personal correspondence, and addresses a particular situation.

Written on the heels of Paul's heated exchanges with the Corinthian and Galatian churches, Romans echoes many of the concerns in those letters. But Romans is also quite definitely distinct from them and is by no means, as several have suggested, simply a calm, reflective summary of the wisdom Paul gained in his turbulent dealings with the Corinthian and Galatian churches. In this letter Paul mentions neither Judaizers (Galatians) nor Gnostic enthusiasts (Corinthians and Philippians). The Roman church is troubled, but it is not heretical. As Paul says, "I myself am satisfied about you, my brethren, that you yourselves are full of goodness, filled with all knowledge, and able to instruct one another" (15:14). About some things, however, Paul wants to strengthen them and be strengthened by them (1:11–12). He hopes to reconcile a divided church and build a base from which to launch his mission to Spain (15:24, 28). Since he has never visited the church, the situation is delicate. The Gentile majority might resent his intrusion in their affairs. The Jewish Christian minority, after hearing that Paul was a dangerous innovator, might be less than overjoyed at the prospect of a visit from him. In the discussion below we see how carefully Paul addresses the Roman situation.

After the long introduction (1:1–17) Paul reminds his audience that the coming of Christ exposed the historical failure of both Jews and Gentiles either to do the will of God or to render the thanks due. Therefore, Paul asserts, boasting by the Jew and arrogance by the Gentile are both excluded: "all have sinned and fall short of the glory of God" (3:23), and all stand in equal need of God's grace (3:24). Paul's gospel appeared to some Jews to be a pernicious provocation. If sin elicits God's grace, why not do more evil that more good may come

(3:8)? Paul's gospel was suspect on two counts: (1) His mission to the Gentiles raised questions about God's credibility. Had God now reneged on his promise to Abraham and his seed (i.e., the Jews) by going to someone else? (2) The gospel of grace outside the law encouraged immorality by suggesting that morality did not matter.

Paul defends himself against both charges. He first argues that Gentiles who believe are the real children of Abraham, who also was counted righteous because of his faith. Before turning to the charge of libertinism, Paul uses the analogy of Adam to show how one person's act can affect the destiny of all. Just as through one person, Adam, sin was introduced into the human context to the detriment of all, so now through one man, Jesus, acquittal and life are offered to all (Jew and Gentile).

In chapter 6 Paul returns to the question raised in 3:8. If human sin elicits God's grace, then why not sin in order that grace may be multiplied? Paul was especially touchy over the charge that his gospel encouraged immorality as a means of receiving grace. In Corinth and Philippi at least, some had understood salvation by grace outside the law to mean that all things were lawful. In those cities certain libertines seemed to anticipate Herod's caricature of grace found in W. H. Auden's "For the Time Being": "I like committing crimes. God likes forgiving them. Really the world is admirably arranged."[22] Drawing on three images—baptism, slavery, and marriage—Paul asks how anyone who shares in the life of the new age can still act like a member of the old. In baptism, Paul argues, the Christian dies to sin. How, therefore, can anyone continue to live in it (6:1–14)? How can those freed from sin to become slaves of righteousness revert to the old slavery (6:15–23)? A woman is freed after the death of her husband to remarry. So Christians who have died to the law through Christ now belong to another. How, therefore, can they still act as if the old marriage was in effect (7:1–6)? Drawing on these images, Paul wants to correct the impression that his gospel encourages immorality by pointing to the new obedience effected in Christ.

Upon broaching the subject of the law, Paul hears the Jewish Christian (7:1) asking if the law is sinful (7:7). The Jews had called the law God's gift to Israel. To call the gift "evil" would raise questions about the very nature of God. Is the divine will so dark and nature so sinister that God gives malevolent gifts to God's children? Paul submits that it is the creature's crooked heart that twists the law into a grotesque caricature, not the law that is evil. The law may forbid one to "covet" (7:7), but it is human nature to covet most what is forbidden. The fault is not in the law or God who gave it, but in the creature himself or herself. Paul says it is the misuse of the law, not the law itself, that will "bring death" (7:13). Two problems face us in 7:13–25: (1) the ambiguity of the term "flesh" *(sarx)*, and (2) uncertainty about how Paul is using the term "I." As a faithful Jew, Paul would have been unable to attribute evil to the flesh per se. Flesh, for the Jew, was morally neutral, but it was, nevertheless, humankind's Achilles heel. Through the flesh and the desires associated with it, humanity was vulnerable to sin's attack. After gaining a foothold, the evil impulse *(yetzer)* takes up residence in the flesh and corrupts the whole person. It is possible for the flesh to be corrupted, but the flesh is not in and of itself a corrupting element. Paul does mean his "flesh" when he refers to the corrupted element ("nothing good dwells within me," 7:18), but when he does so, he is not saying that the physical is inherently perverse but that the person has fallen victim to the power of sin. When Paul speaks of those who live "according to the flesh" (8:12), he is referring to those whose flesh has been taken captive by the diabolical force in the world, but in the strictest sense the term "flesh" carries no negative charge.

The second problem concerns Paul's use of the term "I" in 7:7–25. His use of the first person singular coupled with the past tense and the apparent parallel Paul draws between his own development and that of Adam (man) in the Genesis narrative suggest that Paul may be referring to his own personal experience in this section. It is more likely, however, that Paul, here as in 1 Corinthians 13, uses the first person singular to speak not just of his own experience but representatively of all human experience. Therefore, the passage probably should not be read as an autobiographical statement about the anxiety and depression Paul suffered trying to keep the law. In Philippians 3:4ff. he suggests, on the contrary, that he was blameless before the Law. It is simply that the coming of Christ has fundamentally altered Paul's former view that salvation came through the law.

In chapters 9–11 Paul answers a barrage of questions raised by his mission to the Gentiles: Does this mission undermine the promises God made to Israel? If God made promises to Israel but has now turned to the Gentiles, has his plan failed? Has he reneged on the promises (9:6)? One might reply: Paul says that God has always chosen to bless some and not others. For example, God preferred the younger son Joseph over his older brothers. He chose Jacob over Esau, and so on. Could he not do the same by turning to the Gentiles instead of Israel? If such a natural selection process is operative, then the question arises, is it fair for God arbitrarily to reject the chosen and choose the rejected (9:14)? Furthermore, if it is God who hardens hearts or makes them receptive, how can fault be found with the Jews for rejecting Jesus (9:19)? Finally, if the Gentiles who did not pursue righteousness receive it through faith, will the Jews who did pursue righteousness be excluded from God's plan of salvation? If so, is God just? In answer to these questions, Paul argues for the validity of his Gentile mission. At the same time he insists that God has not forsaken Israel. It is Paul's conviction that both the Gentiles and Israel will be brought together in God's final eschatological community (11:29–32). In an aside found in 11:13–24, Paul warns his Gentile converts against presumption: "For if God did not spare the natural branches [i.e., Jews], neither will he spare you" (11:21).

Paul was alive to the charge that his gospel of salvation apart from the law encouraged immorality. By means of analogy he has already argued that license is inconsistent with his gospel of freedom (Romans 6). Now in Romans 12–15 he deals with the issue more directly. Throughout this section Paul develops an ethical imperative consistent with the gospel he preaches.[23] He admonishes all who have special gifts—prophets, teachers, leaders, administrators, etc.—to use their gifts for the nurture and the reconciliation of the church. He urges believers to love outsiders—"Bless those who persecute you . . . associate with the lowly . . . repay no one evil for evil . . . never avenge yourselves . . . ; if your enemies are hungry, feed them" (12:14–21). This preoccupation with the outsider flows into Paul's discussion of the believers' relationship to "governing authorities" in 13:1–10.

An additional word is necessary because of the influence this passage has had on the Christian view of the state throughout the centuries. At the beginning we should ask if or how the discussion in 13:1–10 is related to Paul's wider epistolary purposes. Already Paul has stated that Jesus is the head of a new humanity (5:18) and is the new Lord *(Kyrios)* for the believer (5:15–16 and 10:9). Paul was painfully aware that their membership in the arriving kingdom of God had led believers elsewhere to disregard the claims of this world (see 1 Thessalonians and 1 Corinthians). Perhaps believers in Rome had also abandoned the present, provisional order in favor of the new divine order soon to come. By withholding support (taxes, civil service, etc.) from the "earthly" kingdom, they could testify to their loyalty to a kingdom not of this world. On the other hand, Paul may have been responding to the indictment that his gospel encouraged irresponsible if not immoral behavior.

Paul answers by reaffirming the otherworldly character of his gospel along with its worldly imperative. He tells the believers in Rome, "Do not be conformed to this world" (12:2), but at the same time he says, "Let every person be subject to the governing authorities" (13:1) and pay "taxes to whom taxes are due" (13:7). He reasserts his conviction that the day of the Lord is at hand (13:12), but the nearness of the hour does not cancel civic duty. It gives it cosmic significance. As the divine denouement nears, the opportunity for witness becomes more limited and the necessity for it becomes more urgent; the Christian is to seize whatever opportunities are available to witness. The fact that the state provides an orderly society in which travel and witness can go on unimpeded is not Paul's main point. More likely he is urging the Christian to use the civic realm as an arena in which the eschatological fruit of love receives concrete expression. This love of the neighbor (13:10) is to be expressed partly by support for "authorities," for such institutions reward the good (13:3) and punish evil (13:4) and thereby protect the neighbor.

Paul also argues that the "governing authorities" are ministers of God (13:4). Implicit in this statement is Paul's view that in the cross and resurrection God has not canceled divine action in history. Instead, the final stage of Lordship over events has begun. Loyalty to Jesus as Lord, therefore, is allegiance to one whose realm includes rather than excludes historical agents such as "the authorities." Hence, to abandon responsibility in this world, in Paul's view, means to retreat from the arena of God's activity. This hardly implies, however, that Paul espoused blind allegiance to the state. The primary claim in his view always belongs to God. But allegiance to God, Paul says, does not preclude giving to the state what properly belongs to it (taxes, honor to magistrates, and so on). One might wonder what Paul would have said had he lived to see the persecution by Nero ten years later.

In 14:1–15:13 Paul deals at great length with peace within the community of the faithful: "Welcome one another . . . as Christ has welcomed you" (15:7), etc. Gentiles are urged to respect the dietary scruples of Jewish Christians, and Jewish Christians are urged to refrain from harsh polemic against Gentile Christians.

In the close of the letter, the western horizon of Paul's mission breaks into view. Paul writes, "I shall go on by way of you to Spain" (15:28; see also 1:13). With his eastern mission complete between Jerusalem and Illyricum (15:19), and the offering for the "poor among the saints" ready for delivery to Jerusalem (15:25–27), Paul's mind races to Rome and beyond to Spain. Paul obviously hopes that a strong, united church in Rome will share his vision of God's eschatological community and will include representatives of all peoples on earth: Jew and Greek, Galatian and Spaniard, slave and free, male and female. If they share this vision, his hope is that they will also share in his mission, as the Macedonian church had done for the mission in Greece (2 Cor. 11:9). But even while these hopes burned in his breast, Paul seemed to suspect what was to happen in Jerusalem. "The unbelievers in Judea" (Rom. 15:31), Paul feared, might cause trouble. If Luke's account is correct (Acts 21:27ff.), Paul's intuition was sound. Arrested while on his visit to Jerusalem to deliver the offering, Paul, as a Roman citizen, appealed to and was granted a trial in Rome. There his ship moored for the last time. There was no launching of the great western mission to Spain.

OUTLINE OF ROMANS

Since the conclusion of Romans has been tampered with, we no longer have the heavily stereotyped conclusion of the other letters. The doxology in 16:25–27 is almost universally recognized as a non-Pauline addition.

Philippians (c. 55–56 C.E.)

Paul wrote to the Philippian church from a jail either in Ephesus (winter of 55–56) or in Rome (c. 58–60).[24] From the time of its founding, the Philippian church had a turbulent history. Paul spoke of his shameful treatment and the fierce opposition he ran into there (1 Thess. 2:2). The church was hounded by outsiders (Phil. 1:29–30) and fractured by the pettiness and jealousy of insiders (3:2ff.; 4:2–3). Some there preached the gospel out of love and respect for Paul; others preached it out of partisanship (1:15–17).

But throughout these strains and stresses, the relationship between Paul and the Philippian church remained warm and deeply affectionate. The Philippians gave money to support Paul's mission in Thessalonica (4:16) and possibly also in Corinth (2 Cor. 11:9). They gave generously to the Jerusalem collection (2 Cor. 8:1–5), and they sent Epaphroditus to care for Paul in prison (Phil. 2:25). Paul was to return to Philippi on his way to Corinth (2 Cor. 2:13), and possibly again on his final visit to Jerusalem with the offering. And when in prison, Paul writes movingly of his love and longing for the Philippian Christians (4:1).

When Paul wrote the letter from prison, one judicial hearing had already been held, and either Paul's condemnation (1:20; 2:17) or his release (1:25; 2:24) seemed imminent. His mission continued, however, in spite of the chains. Some, both inside and outside the praetorian guard, were touched by Paul's witness (1:13). Some of the slaves and freedmen from Caesar's household were converted (4:22). Through the courageous example of the apostle, some believers who were timid had become fearless (1:14). Word of Paul's imprisonment eventually leaked out to the congregation at Philippi, and considering their special reverence for Paul, the response was predictable. The exchanges that ensued may be reconstructed as follows:

1. Having learned that Paul was a prisoner in Ephesus, the Philippians sent Epaphroditus with money for his support and with instructions for his care.
2. Paul sent a letter of thanks (now lost?), and the bearer of this letter reported to the Philippians that Epaphroditus was very ill.
3. The Philippians wrote to Paul expressing:
   a. Their distress over Epaphroditus's critical condition — 2:26
   b. A request for the return of Epaphroditus and perhaps an expression of regret that his illness prevented him from serving Paul as they intended — 2:25–30
   c. Report of a quarrel between two women in the congregation, Euodia and Syntyche — 4:2–3
   d. Concern over the efforts of local Jews to win (back?) converts that the church had gained from the God-fearers — 3:2–16
   e. Concern about libertines in the congregation — 3:17–20
4. Paul sent the present letter (in whole or in part) with Epaphroditus — 2:25[25]
5. A visit by Timothy to Philippi was planned. He was to report back to Paul — 2:19–23
6. Paul planned a visit to Philippi if or when he was released — 2:24

1. Opposition at Philippi

Do not be afraid of your "opponents," Paul tells his readers in 1:28. Who were these "opponents"? What were they doing? What were they saying about Paul? Where did they come from? Although no precise description of the outlook of the opponents is possible, the general contours of their thought can be seen. They nag Gentile Christians to accept circumcision (3:2); they preach a partisan gospel deliberately designed to torment the imprisoned apostle (1:17). They reject the importance of the cross (3:18) in favor of the glorious resurrected life. And they make a fetish of self-indulgence—"their god is the belly" (3:19). Owing to the absence of any sustained discussion of the law, it is unlikely that the opponents were Judaizers of the Galatian type. Given their proclamation of Christ (1:17), they could not be from the synagogue, although Jewish opposition did exist in another form. The "opponents" were probably a type of religious syncretist. To them Paul's gospel was just one ingredient among many in a religious potpourri. Circumcision was a Jewish sign and seal of the covenant. Initiation into the local mystery religion was also adopted to allow the neophyte to pass directly and completely from death to immortal life. These, when added to Paul's gospel of grace and freedom in Christ, led to a very peculiar, not to say grotesque, configuration.[26]

An alternative view is that Paul addresses several types of opponents in this letter—Jews bent on winning back Gentile God-fearers, those who had slipped into morally lax habits, and Christians critical of his gospel. Another suggestion is that Paul was slow to recognize the character of the opposition and is thus somewhat confused in his response. Although both of these alternative views are tenable, they seem less persuasive than the first view. Given the range of Paul's opposition elsewhere, it is hardly likely that he would have misjudged his opponents here. Moreover, if several types of opponents exist, it is strange that the groupings are so indistinct in the letter itself.

2. Paul's Response

To those who claim total salvation in the present, Paul speaks of "full salvation" as only a future possibility. Paul underscores the provisional nature of present salvation when he writes of sharing Christ's "sufferings, becoming like him in his death" in order to "attain the resurrection" in the future (3:10–11). To reinforce this point Paul adds, "Not that I have already obtained this [resurrection], or am already perfect; but I press on to make it my own. . . . I press on toward the goal for the prize of the upward call of God" (3:12–14). Paul then calls on the Philippians to imitate him, and thus by implication he rejects the view of those who claim too much here and now (3:15–17). His emphasis on the future not only undercuts the smug, it also reassures those now suffering humiliation and loss. They, like their Lord, obedient in service, can look forward to exaltation and triumph (see Paul's use of the ancient Christian hymn in 2:6–11).

In 3:4–9 many think Paul is rejecting his Jewish past: "Whatever gain I had [as a Jew], I counted as loss for the sake of Christ" (v. 7). This statement, however, is really just part of Paul's polemic against the "dogs" who seek to modify his gospel and discredit him by appealing to circumcision as the gateway to the new life for Gentiles. Paul responds in total disgust at such an eclectic view. In Romans 9:1–5, on the other hand, Paul speaks most positively of his Jewish heritage (vs. 4–5):

> They are Israelites, and to them belong the sonship, the glory, the covenants, the giving of the law, the worship, and the promises; to them belong the patriarchs, and of their race, according to the flesh, is the Christ.

In spite of the competing claims, internal strife, and external threats, there is a genuine warmth and human tenderness in Philippians that is refreshing compared to the sharp clashes in Galatians and Corinthians. Paul, we see, was not always the stormy combatant or divine warrior. He is also a towering figure whose confidence in the outcome of history enabled him to look past the immediate disturbances and irritations with confidence.

OUTLINE OF PHILIPPIANS

1. Introduction, Salutation, and Thanksgiving   1:1–11
2. Paul's Situation
    The effect of his imprisonment on the local
    church, and his own attitude toward the
    imprisonment.   1:12–26
3. Exhortation to Stand Firm Against
    Opponents, Following the Model of Christ
    (Note especially 2:6–11, a pre-Pauline hymn
    that gives important information on the devel-
    opment of Christology in the early church.)   1:27–2:18
4. Announcement of Travel Plans   2:19–30
5. Beginning of Conclusion to Letter   3:1
6. Exhortation to Persevere in the Struggle
    Against Judaizing Propaganda and Libertinism   3:2–4:1
7. Continuation of Conclusion   4:2–23
    a. Appeal for harmony   4:2–6, 8–9
    b. Thanks for gifts
        (Possibly a fragment of a separate letter)   4:10–20
    c. Closing greetings and benediction   4:7, 21–23

Philemon (c. 55–56 C.E.)

Perhaps after stealing money (v. 18), Onesimus, a slave, ran away from his rich Christian master, Philemon (v. 5), and Apphia. By coincidence he met Paul in prison and was converted to Christ (v. 10). Paul wanted to keep Onesimus with him, and, on the strength of his apostolic office, he felt entitled to do so. Instead, he returned Onesimus to his master along with this brief letter. Paul urges Philemon to restore Onesimus to his household and treat him like a "beloved brother" (v. 16). He pleads with Philemon not to mete out the harsh punishment to which Onesimus was liable as a runaway slave and possible thief.[27]

Paul looks forward to his own imminent release from prison and a visit with Philemon. "Prepare a guest room for me," he says (v. 22).

Colossians 4:9 refers to Onesimus traveling with Tychicus to Colossae. If Colossians was written by Paul, then Philemon must have lived in the neighborhood of Colossae, the destination of the travelers Onesimus and Tychicus. This assumes that the letters to the Colossian church and to Philemon were written about the same time, and that the trip of Onesimus referred to in Colossians was the same one Paul speaks of in Philemon, the return of Onesimus to his owner. If Colossians is a genuine Pauline letter, then the date of Philemon and the location of the addressee would be the same as that of Colossians.

On the other side, the Pauline authorship of Colossians is questioned by many scholars. Indeed, it is possible that the references to Onesimus in Colossians may have been put there under influence from Philemon. It is better to plead ignorance and say we simply do not know where Philemon lived or where Paul was imprisoned when he wrote the letter. From our discussion of Philippians, we see that Ephesus is a strong contender, but by his own admission Paul was in prison many times in many places. If, however, Ephesus is taken as the place of the imprisonment mentioned here, then the date 55–56 is plausible. If Rome is taken, then 56–61 would be a safe guess.

OUTLINE OF PHILEMON

1.	Salutation		1–3
	a.	Sender—Paul	1a
	b.	Recipients—Philemon, Apphia, Archippus, and the church	1b–2
	c.	Greeting	3
2.	Thanksgiving		4–7
3.	Body of Letter		8–22
	a.	Return of Onesimus	8–20
	b.	Anticipated apostolic visit *(parousia)*	21–22
4.	Conclusion		23–25
	a.	Final greetings	23–24
	b.	Grace and benediction	25

We have come to the end of our discussion of the letters as conversations. We confined our treatment to letters whose authenticity is not seriously questioned, for in those it is easier to see that we are dealing with real letters, highly personal in nature, intensely particular in their discussion of problems, and essentially conversational (a talking *with* not *at* others). It is hoped that reading the letters as conversations will help us appreciate them as dynamic exchanges rather than static deposits of eternal truth waiting passively to be mined for their treasure.

5. Paul and His Myths

To THE PERSON on the street the term "myth" is synonymous with "fiction" or "untruth." Because the old stories about gods, devils, witches, and talking snakes seem quaint, they are shelved, assigned a place with other relics from humanity's infancy. But could it be that myths from the archaic past do not reflect primeval ignorance and superstition so much as they reveal the heights and depths the human spirit can reach when it wrestles with questions about life and death, love and hate, fate and freedom, truth and falsehood? Could it be that myth and legend mirror not what happened in the ancestral period but rather the response in the soul to what happened? Even if unhistorical, could myth be, like art for Picasso, "a lie that makes us realize the truth"? As important as it is to know "what happened" in the ancient past, do we not also need to know how men and women responded to those happenings? Increasingly, anthropologists, historians of religion, and biblical scholars are turning their scrutiny upon myth and legend because mythological materials provide a living window on men and women of an earlier time expressing their inmost imaginings. Such expressions often sensitize us to the profundity and high originality of these people of old.

To avoid misunderstanding, we must distinguish myth from metaphor. The term "pig" is a graphic expression when applied to a male chauvinist, but it is hardly myth. When Paul calls himself a boxer who pummels his body into submission, he is using metaphor; when he recites the eucharistic formula, "This is my body," he is drawing on myth. Metaphor is descriptive language about an event, whereas mythological language is an event itself, transporting the participants into a zone of sacred time or space. The breaking of the bread is more than picture language about Jesus' execution; it is an avenue through which one enters the presence of the Redeemer figure and becomes "a contemporary disciple."[1]

No definition of myth will do entirely. Myth has been called a means of comprehending reality and of being apprehended by it, but this description is vague and too general. Frankfort describes myth as

a form of poetry which transcends poetry in that it proclaims a truth; a
form of reasoning which transcends reasoning in that it wants to bring
about the truth it proclaims; a form of action, of ritual behavior, which
does not find its fulfillment in the act but must proclaim and elaborate
a poetic form of truth.[2]

Although Frankfort's statement is helpful and evocative, it is more a
poem about a poem than it is a useful definition of myth. Gerardus van
der Leeuw calls myth "a spoken word, possessing decisive power in its
repetition."[3] Although myth, like all forms of communication, is tied
to the word, can its power be restricted to the word? The three statements above are sufficient to show the difficulty of forging a satisfactory
definition of myth. Because of this difficulty, most writers discuss instead myth's character and function. It is that approach which we will
follow here.

1. The World Viewed Mythologically

In the first century, the relationship of both peasant and philosopher
to the natural world was closely personal. Where we see a landscape
stiff and mute, they saw a world sparkling with life. Where we see things
passively waiting for our hands to put them to use, they saw "Thous"
actively forcing themselves on the human consciousness. Where we see
an order defined by abstract laws, they saw both order and chaos as
vehicles of will and intent. When the cloud rumbled or the wind roared,
they did so because they decided to, or because their master said,
"Rumble!" or "Roar!"

Paul's experience of the nonhuman world was likewise a personal
one. In Romans 8:22 he speaks of the world's participation in the final
apocalyptic woes attending the birth of the new age. The earth's share
of this wretchedness goes back to the dawn of creation when as an
innocent bystander it was forced to bear a part of the pain that followed
Adam's disobedience. Earthquakes and storms, plagues and drought,
snakes and disease are signs of the futility and decay that nature suffered because its destiny was linked from the very beginning with the
destiny of humankind. The natural world, however, shares not only the
agony but also the ecstasy of humanity. For God is now acting not only
to redeem the wayward creature but also the burdened creation. Now
that its redemption is near, the creation stands on tiptoe waiting to
share in the liberation of the human and nonhuman world (8:19–21).

All through the ages the creation has worn an image of its Creator.
In spite of its distorted nature, the image of God's power and deity has
remained recognizable. Notwithstanding humankind's efforts to deface
the image, the marks of God's power and deity have never been com-

pletely erased (Rom. 1:20). The Gentiles have always been able to recognize the fingerprints of the Creator on creation. Thus the creation, like the creature, suffers from the alienation and dislocation that reach back to the primeval period; and nature, like human beings, continues to bear the image of its Maker even if in a twisted form. We see that the alienation and hope that creature and creation share make them kin.

In spite of this feeling of kinship, however, the world also seemed alien to Paul. He spoke of breaking through the barriers that restrict his existence either by ascending to the third heaven (2 Cor. 12:2) or by being delivered from the struggles that attend life in the world (2 Cor. 5:8). He saw his life unfolding in a world under the dominance of Satan (2 Cor. 4:4), and he perceived the unsteady footing of that world—"the form of this world," he says, "is passing away" (1 Cor. 7:31). So Paul did not feel at home in the world as it was but looked forward to the time when the original order would be restored and all fear and dread between humanity and the world would be removed. As Paul says, "When anyone is united to Christ, there is a new world; the old order has gone, and a new order has already begun" (2 Cor. 5:17, NEB).

2. Myth and Cult

In the West we view time as an everflowing stream that bears its sons and daughters away. But in the cult, time stands still. Time stops and is even reversed as the celebrant repeats the acts of God or shares in the sacred deeds of an earlier day.

In the celebration of the Passover today, for example, one sees Jewish families who are indistinguishable from their neighbors in the clothes they wear, the jobs they hold, or the cars they drive. Yet in recalling the deliverance of the Hebrews from Egypt thousands of years ago, they speak as if they lived in the second millennium B.C.E. Drinking the wine and eating the unleavened bread, they see themselves as slaves in Egypt liberated from the Pharaoh's bondage.

> We were Pharaoh's bondsmen in Egypt: and the Lord our God brought us out therefrom with a mighty hand and an outstretched arm. Now, if the Holy One, blessed be He, had not brought our fathers forth from Egypt, then we, and our children, and our children's children, would be servants to Pharaoh in Egypt.[4]

While to the outsider it may sound strange for an American Jew to speak solemnly of sweating in Pharaoh's quarry long ago, to the insider who views that bondage through the eyes of faith, the liberation that was effected then is experienced once more.

Through the cultic act, the worshiper participates in what is real for all time. While the key occurrences of both Judaism and Christianity are historical, for those within the traditions these events possess a vitality that goes beyond the facts of the events themselves. As Jacob Neusner says, "If 'we, too, the living, have been redeemed,' then the observer no longer witnesses only historical men in historical time, but an eternal return to sacred time."[5] The great events that happened "once upon a time" continue to direct the course of the world and are experienced as current. Through the cult, the worshiper not only shares in the benefits of the primeval time but also finds an organizing center there for the disordered world.

The old shepherd ritualistically jumps over his staff three times; Mary regularly calls for her four "friends" (stuffed animals) and her drink before going to sleep; the Eskimo Emma Willoiya routinely bows her head to offer thanks both before and after eating her diet of raw fish. All are celebrating a tiny slice of life, and for each one, these gestures provide a structure for what otherwise would be an incoherent mass of activity. In myth also an order is imposed. The order is not just any order but the true order, the only order that is fundamentally real. In the Hebrew experience of the exile we see how even the terrors of history were integrated into a divine order and were thus bearable because meaningful.

In 597 B.C.E. the Hebrews were uprooted from Palestine and deported to Mesopotamia. Eventually the temple was destroyed, the daily sacrifice interrupted, and Jerusalem left in shambles. Babylonian troops were garrisoned in the "promised land" while the Hebrew people raised the poignant cry, "How can we sing the Lord's song in a foreign land?" Yahweh had promised "the holy land" to his people Israel. Now Babylon had robbed Israel of its possession. Was Yahweh credible any more? Had God forsaken the people? Since Israel's whole existence had been defined in relation to Yahweh, what would happen if there was a break in that relationship? Would Israel languish and die at the feet of its captors, or would it survive to stand at their grave? The Hebrews found strength to face those hard times in worship, especially in the celebration of the Sabbath. The Babylonians could occupy the land, destroy the city, reduce the temple to dust, but they could not burn or destroy the Sabbath. On the Sabbath the Hebrews recalled how God had created the world out of formlessness and void, and how he had crowned his creation with the Sabbath itself (Gen. 1:1–2:4a). Thus, on each Sabbath the Hebrews celebrated an order that was real for all time, an order as old and fundamental as the creation itself. Empires might come and go, but this order always remained. Moreover, in each celebration of the Sabbath the Jews affirmed their faith that the God who in the beginning had brought order out of chaos would conquer the present historical chaos as well.

In Paul's letters also we see how the liturgy of the church serves as a bridge between the past and the present. In all of the early Christian churches baptism was used as the rite of initiation, and a sacred communal meal was eaten regularly—how regularly we do not know. In both these sacred rites the church shared in God's redemption of the world. Strangely enough, for Paul the death and resurrection of Jesus rather than his teachings formed the glowing center of God's work. In passing through the water and in eating the bread and wine, the believer established a continuity between himself or herself and the death that happened "once upon a time." In baptism the identification with Jesus is so complete that Paul can speak of being united with Christ in a death like his, of being baptized into his death (Rom. 6:3, 5), or even of being crucified with Christ (6:6). The immersion of the initiate in water simulated the burial of Jesus; the emergence of the initiate from the water imitated Christ's resurrection. Through this rite the saving significance of the death and resurrection of Jesus was experienced within the community, and the believer was linked with that which is real for all time. As the spiritual says, in baptism the initiate was "there when they crucified my Lord."

Eliade's observation that "every ritual has a divine model"[6] applies to the Eucharist as well as to baptism. Throughout Paul's letters the eating of the bread and the drinking of the wine commemorate Jesus' last meal with his disciples. And the connection of this commemorative meal with the cross is so close that repetition of it spontaneously brings to mind Jesus' death. In 1 Corinthians 11:23ff., for example, Paul recites the eucharistic tradition that he has received. Throughout the passage the emphasis is on death. Betrayal is mentioned. Bread is broken, simulating the breaking of Jesus' body, and the red wine is offered as the "new covenant in my blood." And finally to underscore the death motif, Paul adds the exhortation, "as often as you eat this bread and drink the cup you proclaim the Lord's *death* until he comes" (11:26, emphasis added). To "proclaim the Lord's death" obviously extends beyond verbal announcement and means a mythic (or "spiritual") *participation* in the death as well.

Nevertheless, in 1 Corinthians 10:1–13 Paul counters the Corinthian belief that the Eucharist is a magic potion automatically guaranteeing salvation. He reminds the church that just as its life as the sacramental community was prefigured in Israel's wilderness wandering, so also its punishment for any abuse of its status was anticipated in the judgment of Israel. Israel's role as the sacramental family of God did not exempt it from the retribution of its Lord. Its murmuring brought capital punishment. Immorality and idolatry brought the fall of 23,000 in a single day. Tempting the Lord brought destruction by snakes. Likewise, Paul warns, being in the community of the saved exempts no one from God's judgment or condemnation. Believing their place in the sacramental community was absolutely sure, some Corinthians attended pagan feasts, perhaps with friends or relatives, assuming that they could do so without harm to themselves or the church. Appealing to their saved condition, the Corinthians felt they could participate in such pagan feasts and yet avoid fellowship with demons. Why, they might ask, should those who are already in the messianic age be intimidated by warnings of apostasy? Paul, however, thought flirtation with paganism arrogant and foolhardy. While to the modern reader Paul appears unnecessarily harsh in his remarks here, it is useful to remember that Paul saw the world as an arena of competing spheres of power. Understandably, then, Paul was worried when a Christian blithely entered the realm of demonic domination and participated: To do so was always to risk being attracted in a deeply interpersonal way.

After citing the example of Israel and warning the Corinthians to "shun the worship of idols" (1 Cor. 10:14), Paul introduces a reference to the Eucharist: "The cup of blessing which we bless, is it not a participation [koinōnia] in the blood of Christ? The bread which we break, is it not a participation [koinōnia] in the body of Christ?" (1 Cor. 10:16). The word koinōnia is at present an "in" word, being used for everything from sensitivity groups to church campgrounds. When translated "fellowship," as is common, koinōnia is taken to mean a spirit of jovial camaraderie. Ernst Käsemann has proposed a more accurate reading. He suggests that the word be rendered "falling into a sphere of domination."[7] And because this eating of the bread (flesh) and drinking of the wine (blood) places the Christian in the zone of the sacred, i.e., in the presence of the dead and risen Lord, Paul must urge the Corinthians to purify themselves lest they profane the "body" (1 Cor. 11:27–32). Even perfunctory obeisance to demonic powers, as in the pagan sacrificial meals, was incompatible with participation in the body and blood of Christ. Because some believers persisted in attending the pagan sacrificial meals, however, and neglected to rid themselves of the taint of such unholy alliances, illness and even death had entered the community. This sickness and death, according to Paul, was not from natural causes but from the judging presence of the Lord in the cultic meal. In the solidarity with Christ effected in the Eucharist, the believer even now had a foretaste of the salvation or condemnation that would come in full at the end of the age.

The radicality of Paul is most obvious in the way he fixes on the death of Jesus as the locus of God's redeeming activity. In mythic participation in this death and resurrection, the believer already senses victory over the destructive, negative, and sinister elements in the world and already shares in the reconciliation, love, and newness of the new creation. Intimations of the promise come through participation mythically in an event in the past. But the promise contained in that past event waits on the future for its full maturing. Thus, the past, brought mythologically into the present, becomes the basis of the future hope.

3. Death as Model

Jesus' death functions in Paul's writings not only as an earnest of God's plan but also as a model for action in the world. In other words, Jesus' death is experienced not only in the cult but also in the daily round of work and play, eating and drinking, buying and selling, making love and social conversation. Paul frequently connects his own activity with the death of Jesus. Shipwreck, beatings, imprisonments, conflict, and strife all serve as imitations of that death. Looking at the scars left by the "slings and arrows of outrageous fortune," Paul speaks of "carrying in . . . [his] body the death of Jesus" (2 Cor. 4:10). Injuries suffered in the service of the Lord are called "marks of Jesus" (Gal. 6:17)—an obvious allusion from his injuries to the wounds of crucifixion. Since the hunger, thirst, nakedness, homelessness, persecution, and slander Paul endured duplicated the suffering of Jesus, and since it was received in service to the Lord, Paul felt that his suffering shared in God's redemptive work. Even his hurt and pain inflicted by the world was shouldered for the sake of that same world.

Drawing on his own experience, Paul urged the Corinthians to follow him and share "in Christ's sufferings" (2 Cor. 1:5). The Corinthian Christians, however, believed that they had already overcome the world, that they were "rich," "filled," and already ruling (1 Cor. 4:8) and therefore had no need to share the world's incompleteness. Believing themselves already saved, they celebrated their liberation from, not their participation in, suffering. By citing his own humiliation and deprivation and calling on his converts to "be imitators of me," Paul undermined the claims of the Corinthians. He reminded them that neither their redemption nor the redemption of the world was complete. When Paul says, "I decided to know nothing among you except Jesus Christ and him crucified" (1 Cor. 2:2), he is trying to strip pretensions from the Corinthians and bring them down to earth, so that they will see the reality of the world's hurt and the power of the cross (see 1 Cor. 1:17–25). As in 1 Thessalonians, so also in the Corinthian letter, Paul says suffering can be a symbol of honor, for it proclaims the affliction of the Lord: "You became imitators of us and of the Lord, for you received the word in much affliction" (1 Thess. 1:6). In contrast, those who reject Paul's example and indulge themselves are called "enemies of the cross of Christ" (Phil. 3:17–18). It is not that sex or food are evil, but that preoccupation with them renders believers incapable of accepting either the suffering or the power that accompanies the way of the cross. It is possible that the sexual excesses and the gluttony at Philippi came of accommodating the gospel to old pagan ways, but most scholars believe they sprang from a perversion of Christian freedom. In Paul's view, God had been revealed in the cross. Now the transforming power of that moment was to be apprehended anew as it was remembered in both liturgy and the commonplace.

4. The Powers That Be

Although science has ostensibly freed us, superstition and fear, demons, monsters, wormlike and larval beasts live on in our collective fantasy. Goblins and witches come out on All Hallow E'en (Halloween); crepe paper dragons snake their way down city streets in popular parades; monster movies punctuate weekly television calendars; and bizarre mutant creatures stalk the pages of science fiction. Despite our scientific better judgment, our fascination with these mythological beings persists. That fascination, however, surfaces only sporadically, mostly in our moments of corporate play or our personal dreams. For Paul, however, contact with such powers was real, insistent, and dreadful. The Devil, the superhuman rulers of this world-age, the elemental spirits of the universe, the principalities and powers, the beasts at Ephesus, Death, Sin, and pagan deities all lived, and contended for dominion of the world and the loyalty of humankind.

The Devil, for example, was an uncanny force, preying on the unsuspecting (1 Cor. 7:5), seeking to gain advantage over Paul (2 Cor. 2:11), and putting to death those excommunicated from the church, the realm of the rule of Christ (1 Cor. 5:5). Likewise, Death for Paul was a personalized power threatening God's purpose, wages paid by sin to its recruits and the host of an army that would be defeated only at the end of the world (1 Cor. 15:26, 54–55). The rulers of this age are also hostile to the Creator, having crucified Christ and made false claims for their wisdom (1 Cor. 2:6–8). Moreover, in pagan cultic feasts, demons offer food and drink to the partakers, weaning them from the table of Christ (1 Cor. 10:20–22). Both angels (which may be evil) and principalities (which include but also transcend political power structures) vie for the loyalty of the believer in Jesus as the Christ (Rom. 8:38–39).

In Paul's view, therefore, the Christian lives on a battlefield. In this world of competing forces there are no fire-free zones in which the uncommitted may live; there is no arena free from the claim or dominion of some power. We see, therefore, why the term "Lord" *(Kyrios)* is such a pregnant term for Paul. Informing the term is the belief that in the death and resurrection of Jesus, God has begun the final conquest of the hostile powers; the final victory is imminent when God will place all things in subjection (1 Cor. 15:24–25). In the meantime, the conflict between God and the hostile powers goes on. Those once held captive are now being released from the clutches of the "powers that be," but they still look forward to the final triumph of God's righteousness when Jesus' lordship will be complete.

The modern reader may find such views of personalized evil strange or even offensive. However, our memory of Nazism and our continuing witness of racial hatred make references to demonic forces at least not incomprehensible. And though Paul's references to apocalyptic terrors may appear to us surrealistic, we shall miss the power of individual passages and misunderstand the letters as a whole if we cannot be sensitive to the way these mythological images inform Paul's thought and that of his readers. Life for some was simply empty; for the others, it was absurdly oppressed—they felt helpless in the grip of forces too great for anyone to resist or even to comprehend. Paul's gospel spoke to the first of help and to the second of salvation from their ugly web, and thus he nerved men and women for their daily lives and for the final struggle.

5. The Last Adam

Richard Rubenstein, discussing Paul's use of the Adam symbol, writes,

> Almost two thousand years before the depth psychology that his religious imagination helped to make possible, Paul of Tarsus gave expression to mankind's yearning for a new and flawless beginning that could finally end the cycle of anxiety, repression, desire, and craving—the inevitable concomitants of the human pilgrimage.[8]

Whatever one thinks of Rubenstein's effort to link Paul with depth psychology, his observation is correct that the Adamic myth plays a major role in Paul's thought.

Paul could have joined Hamlet in saying, "The time is out of joint." In the apostle's view, this disjointed state represents degeneration from a flawless beginning. The cosmic decline began when Adam revolted against the Creator's prohibition: "You shall not eat of the fruit of the tree which is in the midst of the garden, . . . lest you die" (Gen. 3:3, also 2:17). Before the Fall man and woman lived in a state of innocence, unshamed by nakedness, strangers to want, freely taking from nature's abundance without sweat or toil, and untroubled by anxiety over death. A friend of the animals, Adam was neither hunter nor hunted. Barely inferior to God, he shared in the creation by naming the animals and ruling the world without enmity or strife. Eve had the capacity to bear children without pain. But because of their disobedience, Adam and Eve were exiled from the garden to a life marked by toil and want, fratricide and fear, death and pain. Ever since that time creature and creation have shared Adam's frustration and futility, and have suffered under the dominion of demonic powers. Even though Paul nowhere fully articulates this scenario, he seems to take it for granted. For although the Old Testament and the Gospels rarely mention the

Adamic myth, it occupies a prominent place in Paul's letters. Three passages will receive our attention here: Romans 5:12–21; 1 Corinthians 15; and Philippians 2:6–11.

a. Romans 5:12–21

The belief was widespread in first-century rabbinic and apocalyptic thought that the original state which the world enjoyed would be restored at the end of the age. Paul obviously shared this view, but for him the agent of this restoration was the Christ whom he alternately called the "second Adam," "the last Adam," and "the Adam who is to come." In Romans 5:12–21 Paul contrasts this last Adam with the first. The two Adams were alike in that the action of each influenced the destiny of all humankind; they were different in that through the act of righteousness of the last Adam came "acquittal" for all, whereas through the disobedience of the first Adam "many were made sinners" (Rom. 5:19). Through the last Adam came life (5:18), whereas through the first Adam came death (5:21).

Although Paul speaks of Jesus as the antitype of Adam, he is uncomfortable with the comparison, for in Jesus, he adds, grace has abounded "much more" to humanity's good than did the sin of Adam redound to the hurt and loss of all people. While Paul does say that sin entered the human context through Adam, he does not create or endorse the doctrine of original sin as it came to be known later. He did believe, as did every rabbi, that sin was universal and that its existence originated with Adam, but it is perpetuated through repeated acts of disobedience, not by seminal transmission. Since the beginning of time, with few exceptions (e.g., Enoch and Elijah, who were sinless and therefore did not die), each person has become his or her own Adam. Paul here addresses those who wonder how it is possible for Jesus' acts of obedience and righteousness to benefit other persons. Those who comprehend what it is to be one with the first Adam, Paul argues, should have no difficulty in understanding how one can be united with the last Adam.

b. 1 Corinthians 15

In 1 Corinthians 15 Paul answers those who are skeptical about the resurrection of the dead by appealing to the solidarity of the believer with the last Adam. Evidently it was unclear to the Corinthians how the resurrection of Jesus applied to them; his triumph over death appeared to be nothing more than the private victory of one individual. Paul argues instead that Christ's resurrection is only the first instance of the general resurrection (1 Cor. 15:20). Jesus' rising signals the arrival of the kingdom of God and thus anticipates the imminent resur-

rection of those who are in him. Paul responds (in 15:21–22) to those
who wonder how a believer can be "in Christ" with an example that
would have been familiar to any convert having the most casual acquaintance with synagogue discussions or Hebrew scriptures:

> For as by [*dia*] a man came death,
> by [*dia*] a man has come also the resurrection of the dead.
> For as in [*en*] Adam all die,
>   so also in [*en*] Christ shall all be made alive.

To be "in Adam" meant to participate in the destiny of the old
Adamic humanity, whereas to be "in Christ" meant to share in the
power and glory of the new creation. As Robin Scroggs puts it, Christ
for Paul is not just an example of but the medium through which one
shares in the resurrected life.[9]

The resurrection for Paul was a bodily resurrection. In 1 Corinthians
15:35–38 Paul probably addresses Greek Christians who find the idea
of a resurrection of the body crude and perhaps ridiculous. Conventional Greek piety and the major philosophical movements denigrated
the importance of the body. Salvation to them meant release from, not
perpetuation of, the body. In the rhetorical questions of 15:35 we may
have an echo of their scorn: "How are the dead raised? With what kind
of body do they come?" Paul responds first by distinguishing between
different kinds of bodies—human bodies and animal bodies, fish bodies
and bird bodies, heavenly bodies and earthly bodies (15:39–40). Body
for Paul was a synonym for the complete self, or all that made the self
an "I." Thus, Paul here contrasts the form that the self now enjoys with
the form it will take in the world to come. The form and substance that
the self now has will perish, but the heavenly body will last forever (1
Cor. 15:42). Likewise, the two Adams belong to very different spheres:
"The first man was from the earth, a man of dust; the second man is
from heaven" (1 Cor. 15:47). This statement contrasts the first Adam—
created from the ground and thus perishable—with the last Adam, who
as the heavenly man is "a life-giving spirit" (15:45). By implication both
are bodies—one earthly, the other heavenly. Paul ends his somewhat
tortuous, if not circular, argument with the affirmation that "Just as we
have borne the image of the man of dust [Adam], we shall also bear the
image of the man of heaven [Jesus]" (15:49).

c. Philippians 2:6–11

In Philippians 2:6–11 Paul quotes a Christian hymn in which many
scholars see a contrast of Jesus with Adam. Although the hymn makes
no direct mention of Adam, a contrast between Jesus and Adam seems
implicit. The first strophe of the hymn refers to Jesus, who, "though
he was in the form of God, did not count equality with God a thing

to be grasped." The mention of "form" *(morphē)* evidently refers to the image of God, which both Jesus and Adam (Gen. 1:26) bore. Unlike the first Adam, however, the last did not try to usurp the place of God (see Gen. 3:5) but instead took the role of a slave, becoming "obedient unto death." Where Adam sought to exalt himself, Christ humbled himself; whereas Adam rebelled against the Father, Jesus was obedient unto death. The conduct of the last Adam was a model of selflessness, obedience, innocence, and sacrifice that Paul exhorts his converts to emulate: "Let this mind be in you, which was also in Christ Jesus" (2:5, KJV). We see, therefore, that the second Adam is not only the agent of redemption, reversing the decline of the cosmos, redefining hardship and death, but also the model of the true Adam before the Fall. Christ retains untarnished the image of God (2 Cor. 4:4), and he will rule as Adam was meant to rule until all things are placed under him (1 Cor. 15:24–28). The last Adam serves as both the medium and the model of a restored humanity.

Our discussion of the function of myth in Paul is far from exhaustive. This treatment of representative passages aims to show (1) how, for Paul, the past was not dead nor the future unreal, but both met and clasped hands in the present, and (2) how mythological materials grow and change. The way myth and symbol receive energetic and creative use in the letters provides a clue to certain of Paul's primary concerns. (3) Our purpose has also been to go beyond investigation of what happened ("external history") and learn how Paul and his converts experienced those happenings ("internal history"). H. Richard Niebuhr, who first used this distinction between internal and external history, writes:

> To speak of history in this fashion is to try to think with poets rather than with scientists. That is what we mean, for poets think of persons, purposes and destinies. It is just their Jobs and Hamlets that are not dreamt of in philosophies which rule out from the company of true being whatever cannot be numbered or included in an impersonal pattern. . . . Hence we may call internal history dramatic and its truth dramatic truth, though drama in this case does not mean fiction.[10]

I hope that we are in agreement when I use myth where he uses drama, for through myth also we see how events are apprehended from within the community, how history is lived, and how persons interpret the way events shape their destiny. In the cult the believer was in Christ and Christ was in the believer. In the daily life of the Christian the sacrifice of Christ was replicated. In the attack on the demonic powers, the paradise once lost was being regained.

In his ascent to the third heaven, Paul was breaking the confines of this world and experiencing what defied articulation (see 2 Cor. 12:1–6). The only way to speak of it would be mythically. And since the church frequently spoke of such events, it had to be careful. In speaking mythically, the church constantly risked being called (and indeed becoming) a lunatic fringe interested only in subjective, individualistic experiences. It avoided that by insisting that any experience of what happened always be judged by the church's memory of what indeed did happen. Moreover, recollection had to be corporate, to weed out the faulty or the fanciful in memory. In this sense the mythological experience of the tradition is different from the private experience of a mystic, and thus Paul speaks not just of his own experience of history but of the experience he shares in and with the Christian community.

6. The First Interpreters of Paul

WITHIN THE NEW TESTAMENT itself there are almost as many disputed as genuine letters of Paul (six vs. seven). That persons would write under the name of a famous person from the past shocked no one in the ancient world. Within the Old Testament itself pseudonymous writings appear (e.g., Daniel and the books of Moses). And in the period between the Testaments they flourished.[1] In the New Testament as well, the use of pseudonyms was a common literary device (e.g., in the epistles of Peter, James, and John). While such a practice opened the door to extreme forgeries in the second and third centuries of the Common Era, the possibility of abuse did little to discredit or discourage writing under a pseudonym in the late first century. While many complex factors influenced the adoption and use of a pseudonym, at least two things are clear: (1) The author writing under an assumed name claimed to stand within the tradition associated with that name (whether Peter, John, Paul, or James). Thus, those who wrote letters in Paul's name served as interpreters or defenders of Paul's theology for a later time when the existence of the church was threatened. (2) The writer appealed to the name of some outstanding figure from the past to gain credibility and to claim authority for and compliance with views expressed. As the earliest writings for the instruction of the Christian church, Paul's letters established a precedent that was easily adaptable to an endless variety of situations. The later collection of those letters also suggests that within a generation of his death the work of Paul had become standard and, therefore, could be used like the measurements at the Bureau of Standards to test the accuracy of other traditions. Moreover, since Paul was the founder of such a significant part of the Gentile church, the selection of his letters to nurture it was a natural choice. Thus, the appeal to Paul's name and the use of ideas or phraseology from his letters served to guarantee "the truth" or authenticity of traditions.

Colossians

1. The Question of Authorship

Of the deutero-Pauline letters, Colossians and 2 Thessalonians make the strongest claim to be genuine Pauline epistles. But as far back as 1839 a German scholar, Mayerhoff, questioned the authenticity of Colossians. Reservations about its authenticity have persisted into our own time. The unusual language, style, and theology of the letter are the principal reasons for this skepticism about its genuineness. While none is decisive by itself, these reasons when taken together make the case against Pauline authorship more convincing.

a. In the linguistic evidence, one can cite the appearance of language that is unusual for Paul, the absence of favorite Pauline words and expressions, and the presence of certain stylistic features that are rare or missing altogether in the undisputed letters. In Colossians one finds thirty-three words that occur nowhere else in the New Testament and fifteen words that are used by other New Testament writers but fail to appear in the recognized letters of Paul.

In addition we see a number of unusual expressions in Colossians that Paul never used elsewhere. References to "blood of his cross" (1:20), "evil deeds" (1:21), "forgiveness of sins" (1:14), and "*the* faith" (2:7, italics added) are made in Colossians but go unmentioned in the undisputed letters. Likewise, the contrast of the visible and invisible in 1:16 is made nowhere else by Paul. While an argument from silence is hardly decisive, it is strange that the author of Colossians does not use such characteristic Pauline words as "salvation," "righteousness," and "justification." Such an omission is rather telling in light of the legalistic tendencies of the addressees. Moreover, the absence of such favorite Pauline words as "brothers [and sisters]" or "my brothers [and sisters]" seems peculiar.

b. If the presence of non-Pauline language and the absence of favorite Pauline expressions raise questions about the Pauline authorship of Colossians, its style causes further doubt. Even a casual reading of the letter will uncover its redundant style. Expressions like "to *pray . . . asking*" (1:9), "all *endurance* and *patience*" (1:11), "firmly *established* and *steadfast*" (1:23, my translation), "for *ages* and *generations*" (1:26), "*teach* and *admonish*" (3:16), and "*psalms* and *hymns* and spiritual *songs*" (3:16; emphasis added) are common in Colossians but less pronounced in the undisputed letters. Moreover, there is in Colossians a greater tendency to string together dependent clauses and phrases into long, rambling sentences. Note, for example, that the thanksgiving which begins in 1:3 continues without interruption for five verses.

In assessing the evidence cited here, few would quarrel with the observation that significant differences exist between Colossians and the undisputed Pauline letters. The disagreement arises over the assessment of this evidence. Those inclined toward assigning the letter to Paul would argue that the differences can be explained by factors unique to the composition of Colossians itself. The peculiarities of language and style can be attributed to the hymnic style of the letter,[2] evoked by circumstances unique to Colossians, created by an aging, mellow, contemplative apostle waiting in prison for his trial, or caused by a secretary taking liberties with the apostle's words. But it is difficult to understand how a hymnic style would account for the omissions noted earlier, or how an altered context could effect the stylistic changes seen above. Moreover, there is no evidence in Paul's other letters of a mellowing process. And, finally, if the secretary is responsible for the significant shifts in style and language in the letter, then he has in some sense become the author. In any case, while it is important, linguistic evidence alone is less than decisive when considering the question of authorship. So usually, as here, the linguistic argument is linked with theological evidence.

c. At many points the theology of Colossians agrees with that of the undisputed letters, but in its concept of apostleship, Christology, and eschatology we see significant departures.[3] In Colossians Paul appears as the apostle who through his preaching *and suffering* takes the gospel "to every creature under heaven" (1:23). Although in the undisputed letters Paul does represent himself as the apostle to the Gentiles who shares in the suffering of Christ, nowhere in the recognized letters does Paul speak of the vicarious character of his suffering. In Colossians, on the other hand, the apostle gladly suffers, he tells his hearers, "for your sake" (1:24). Thus, the suffering of the apostle for others complements the suffering of Christ, which also was for others.

Paul, in the undisputed letters, seeks to elicit and nurture faith in Jesus as the Messiah, but the apprehension of the new life is always partial in nature. In 1 Corinthians especially, Paul scoffs at those who claim to be mature (3:1–4). In Colossians, on the other hand, Paul appears as the apostle to the nations, whose message given "in all wisdom" (1:28) serves to make everyone "perfect" *(teleios)* in Christ. In the Hellenistic world such "perfect ones" *(teleioi)* were those deemed worthy of divine illumination and truth.

Finally, in Colossians the sense of urgency so characteristic of the apostolic mission in the undisputed letters is missing altogether. No longer is the apostle driven to complete his work before time runs out. No longer does the apostle write under the shadow of the world's denouement. No longer is apostleship itself seen as a gift of the end time. So, while in some respects the understanding of apostleship in Colossians resembles that of the undisputed letters (e.g., as a mission to the Gentiles), in its view of the suffering of the apostle, its understanding of the apostolic preaching as wisdom for the perfect, and its diminished sense of apostolic urgency, this epistle differs significantly from the letters we know to be genuine.

The Colossian view of Christ, like that of apostleship, is unusual for a Pauline letter. Instead of the body of Christ, as in 1 Corinthians 12:12–27, the church is viewed as the trunk of the body of which Christ is the head. This Christ who is the head is seen as a cosmic figure whose universal rule is already expressed within the church. Such a view, which most scholars feel comes from Hellenistic philosophy, is surely unusual if not unique among the undisputed letters of Paul.

The above emphases clearly distinguish Colossians from Paul's letters elsewhere. However, the most radical difference between this letter and the undisputed letters is the understanding here of eschatology. In other letters, the apostle's belief in the imminent return of Christ profoundly influences his thinking. He views the harassment, beatings, misfortunes, and imprisonment that he has suffered for the gospel as apocalyptic "woes," which like birth pains announce the imminent arrival of a new creation. Normal, wholesome human attachments to a marriage partner and children are discouraged in light of the imminent trauma. Support for civil authority is encouraged because it will restrain the evil powers loosed in the last days. The believers who now experience salvation partially are promised its full realization soon. The offering taken to the Jerusalem church symbolizes the inclusion of Gentiles in the people of God that the prophets promised would take place in the end time. The apostle prosecutes his mission with feverish intensity in order to complete it before the final hour of history. We see, therefore, that Paul's view of the end was central to his understanding of the church, his instruction for believers, and his personal sense of mission.

In Colossians, on the other hand, the mood of expectation is subdued. No longer does the prospect of the imminent end of the age influence the perception of all human relationships. Rather than the full experience of salvation being a future prospect, the author believes that already God *"has delivered* us from the dominion of darkness" (1:13). The mystery hidden for ages is "now *made manifest* to his saints" (1:26). Readers are reminded: "You *were buried* with him in baptism, in which you *were also raised* with him . . ." (2:12), and "you, who *were dead* in trespasses . . . God *made* alive . . ." (2:13). Those "once estranged" are assured that they are *"now* reconciled" (1:22; emphasis added). In these quotations the emphasized words show a dramatic shift in the understanding of salvation that we usually associate with Paul. The full experience of salvation, reserved for the future in the undisputed letters, now moves into the present or even the past. The future dimension almost disappears.

In this shift of emphasis from the future to the present, the concept of hope also changes. Where hope springs from faith in the Pauline letters and is linked with the anticipation of the end of the age (a temporal category), hope in Colossians is stored in the heavenly realms (a spatial category). Hope as a symbol of anticipation is thus replaced by hope as a symbol of assurance.

While it is possible that these theological departures from the outlook of the undisputed letters can be explained by changes in the thinking of Paul, the context, sources, or a new secretary, it seems improbable. It is more reasonable to assume that the alterations in language, style, and theology were due to the work of a later interpreter or school of interpreters who sought to bring the Pauline tradition to bear on a new situation. By the way the author integrates major theological motifs and literary devices from the undisputed letters, we know he was acquainted with the tradition and/or letters of Paul.[4] But the deviation in language, style, and outlook suggests the author belongs to a time perhaps twenty years after Paul's death.

2. The Context of the Letter

Like the undisputed letters of Paul, Colossians gives the impression of being a real letter, that is, a conversation between its author and a concrete situation. And as in the undisputed letters, we search the letter itself for clues to the content of this conversation. We learn from the letter that "false teachers" are present in the congregation. Their identity is much debated, but the letter does reveal something about their "philosophy" (2:8). The word "philosophy" here hardly refers to clear, logical thought or speculation, but rather to special religious traditions, rites, revealed knowledge, or way of life through which the ultimate ground and secret meaning of the universe was known.

a. *The "Philosophy" of the Heresy*

Concerned with the cosmic powers or "elemental spirits of the universe" (2:8), the scope of this teaching is breathtaking. Rather than merely material elements like air, earth, fire, and water, these "elemental spirits" were divine beings who, it was believed, exercised control over the world and as such were worthy of special veneration and service. The "worship of angels" (2:18) was probably linked in some way with the obeisance given the "elemental spirits" or the "principalities and powers" mentioned in 2:15. Through one's proper relationship with these cosmic powers, it was believed, came the experience of divine fullness *(plērōma)*. As possessors of this divine fullness or cosmic mystery, these mystagogues claimed special "visions" (2:18) of divine things and became overly proud of their religious knowledge. It could be that these people who are offensive to the writer of Colossians were revered as the perfect ones *(teleioi)* by the rank and file. The *teleioi* (a code word meaning those fully possessed by divine power and wisdom) are graphically described by our author as "vainly puffed up by the mind of the flesh" (2:18, my translation).

The teaching of this "heretical" philosophy was also world-denying or ascetic in nature. "Self-abasement" was an integral part of its outlook (2:18). Certain judgments were passed on the basis of "food and drink or with regard to a festival or a new moon or a sabbath" (2:16). Their religious devotion meant that believers were to shun the world. The commands, "Do not handle, Do not taste, Do not touch" (2:21) promoted a certain "rigor of devotion and self-abasement and severity to the body" (2:23). At the same time, if we may judge from the ethical instruction, overindulgence was also practiced (3:5). Is it possible that through their asceticism, these believers hoped to strip "off the body of the flesh," a mystical form of circumcision (2:11ff.)? And was their prodigal indulgence a way to demonstrate their defiance of the world and the values of the culture?

The background of this Colossian "heresy" has been much disputed. The cosmic speculation linked with world-denial suggests a Gnostic background to many. The reference to the observance of new moons, Sabbaths, and the submission to regulations (*dogmata,* 2:20)—when coupled with the worship of cosmic forces, an appeal to visions, and the simultaneous practice of asceticism and indulgence—led Bornkamm to say there is "no doubt that the heresy was a variety of Jewish gnosticism."[5] Others, however, see the "heresy" as an expression of Hellenistic Jewish piety or even Neo-Pythagorean spirituality.[6] There seems to be a consensus emerging that the "heresy" represents a form of Hellenistic Judaism that was receptive to the popular religious piety of the day.[7] Certain features of this piety (like cosmic speculation and asceticism) tend toward Gnostic speculation that later receives a bewildering array of expressions. Whatever this heresy may finally be called, it is significant for our study that the main contours of the "heresy" are not in dispute.[8]

b. *Response to the Heresy*

In the face of this "heresy," it is important to note that the author invoked Paul's name to refute his opponents. Paul appears in the letter as a powerful figure whose ministry is worldwide in scope. This one who brings the gospel "to every creature under heaven" (1:23), this apostle to the nations (1:5–8, 24–29), this world-renowned figure, as he is described, attends to this little church in the remote Lycus River valley in Asia Minor. This towering figure shares the limelight with none of the inner circle in Jerusalem, and, moreover, he is said to suffer on behalf of the churches and to minister with "divine" credentials (1:25).

By appealing to the apostle's name, our author hoped to secure a hearing for his teaching and to certify the correctness of his gospel. This attempt to establish the validity of his teaching was especially important if he was to refute the false teaching of the "heretics."

In response to the emphasis of the "heresy" on cosmic speculation and the veneration of the "elemental spirits," our author simply subordinated all powers to Christ. This Christ, who is head of the church, exercises cosmic dominion over all principalities and powers. He, and no other, is Lord over the *stoicheia* or cosmic forces worshiped by the Colossians. The creation worshiped by Colossians had its origin in Christ and is sustained by him (1:16, 17). Christ is the "head of all rule and authority," and in him, not in the cosmic powers, is the *plēroma* or divine fullness realized (2:10). He disarms and subjugates the celestial powers worshiped by the Colossians (2:15). Thus through the reconciliation of Christ, the whole cosmos is brought back into the divine order.

The author, thus at least implicitly, drew a contrast between that which is found *in Christ* and that realized through cosmic speculation and worship. *In Christ,* they were told, "the fullness of deity dwells bodily" (1:19). *In Christ* reside "treasures of wisdom and knowledge" (2:3). *In Christ* is found a circumcision "made without hands" (2:11). *In Christ* is the resurrection realized here and now (2:12). *Through Christ* the estranged are reconciled (1:22). And so in this way our author set the teaching of Paul about Christ over against the Colossian "philosophy and empty deceit" (2:8) and contradicted those who delude and beguile innocent people (2:4). Their ascetic commands are called "human precepts and doctrines" (2:22). Moreover, from a practical point of view, these regulations, our author said, are ineffective in restraining indulgence (2:23). In contrast to those who are "puffed up" (2:18), or arrogant, and assertive, he admonished the believers to "put on love" for the sake of church unity and to teach each other "in all wisdom" (3:14, 16). In contrast to the regulations that are essentially world-denying ("Do not handle, Do not touch," etc.), our author juxtaposed a set of rules adopted from Hellenistic Jewish circles that are world-affirming: "Husbands, love your wives. . . . Children, obey your parents. . . . Fathers, do not provoke your children . . ." etc. (the so-called household rules or *Haustafeln,* 3:18–4:1).

Unfortunately, we have no further word to or from the church at Colossae. It was eclipsed in importance by the church at Laodicea and ultimately failed to survive one of the many earthquakes that regularly devastated the area. So we are left, as is the case so often in New Testament writings, not knowing how the story ended. While we do not know what happened to the church, we do know that the letter to it survived, and very soon this letter exerted a profound influence on another New Testament writing—the Epistle to the Ephesians.

OUTLINE OF COLOSSIANS

Ephesians

Ephesians and Colossians are literary siblings. Almost one-third of
Colossians appears in Ephesians, and approximately one-half of the
sentences in Ephesians include some language from Colossians. Although Ephesians borrows more from the Pauline epistles than does
any other New Testament epistle (except 2 Thessalonians), the literary
relationship to Colossians is so close as to suggest a direct dependence.
In the "household rules" taken from Colossians 3:18–4:1, for example,
the author of Ephesians changes, expands, and sharpens his Colossian
source to fit a new situation. Where wives are asked to "be subject to
your husbands, as is *fitting in the Lord*" in Colossians (3:18, italics
added), Ephesians has the more demanding, *"as to the Lord"* (5:22).
Given the completely different understanding of such key words as
"mystery" and "stewardship" in these two letters (cf. Col. 1:25–28; 2:2;
and Eph. 3:3–6; 1:9; and 5:32), it is unlikely that they came from the
same hand. What is more probable is that the author knew a collection
of Pauline letters and had Colossians before him when he wrote Ephesians.

1. The Question of Authorship

If Colossians is judged to be deutero-Pauline and the author of
Ephesians relies on Colossians, then it follows that Ephesians is also
deutero-Pauline. It is important, however, to decide the question of

authorship of Ephesians on its own merits without regard to its dependency on Colossians. As in other cases this judgment must be made using linguistic and theological criteria.

a. The language and style of Ephesians are unusual for a Pauline letter. Nowhere else in the New Testament is there such an interest in the saintliness of an apostle (thirteen references). Instead of the "least of the *apostles*" (1 Cor. 15:9), Paul is now called "the very least of all the *saints*" (Eph. 3:8). References to "the heavens" (five occurrences), "the Beloved" (referring to Christ, 1:6), "flesh and blood" (6:12), "commonwealth" (2:12), "piety" (*hosiotēs,* 4:24), "incorrigibility" (*asōtia,* 5:18), "compassionate" or "tenderhearted" (*eusplagchnos,* 4:32), and "favor one with" (*charitoō,* 1:6), occur in Ephesians but nowhere in the genuine letters. The absence of this language in the undisputed letters of Paul plus its presence in later post-Pauline writings both within and outside the New Testament argues for placing Ephesians in the post-apostolic period, 80–100 C.E.

Stylistically Ephesians also shows certain idiosyncratic tendencies. Long, complex sentences abound in the Greek (e.g., 1:3–10; 1:15–23; 3:14–19). Synonyms pile up to the point of redundancy. We see the frequent use of such expressions as the "energy of his great strength" (1:19, my translation), the "aeon of this world" (2:12, my translation), and "prayer and supplication" (6:18). While Paul also builds long, convoluted sentences and multiplies synonyms, a casual reading of Ephesians will detect certain excesses that are uncharacteristic of Paul.

b. The theology of the letter more than the vocabulary and style suggests that the author was someone other than Paul. In at least three important areas the outlook of Ephesians differs from that of the undisputed letters: its eschatology, its view of the church, and its understanding of apostleship.

As we noted in our discussion of Colossians, the eager expectation of the imminent end of the age is a major motif of the undisputed letters. The tension between the "now" and the "not yet" characteristic of the genuine letters is muted in Ephesians. The approaching end and impending judgment are alluded to only in the most general way (1:4). The sense of urgency that informs the apostolic mission is gone, and no interest in the Parousia (or coming) of Christ is expressed. The temporal dimension, as expressed in Paul's statements about the past (or salvation history, Romans 9–11) or the future expectation, are displaced by spatial categories. Christ appears in Ephesians as the head of the cosmos "far above all rule and authority and power and dominion" (1:21). Those "far off" have been "brought near" (2:13). Believers are given the power to comprehend "the breadth and length and height and depth" (3:18). In these three statements about Christ, salvation of the Gentiles, and the understanding of the believers, space rather than time is the controlling category.

The author's view of the church provides the integrating center of the letter. Whereas in 1 Corinthians the church is seen as the body of Christ, in Ephesians the church is viewed as the sphere of activity of the cosmic Christ. The presence of this cosmic Christ expands the horizons of the church enormously. It is the universal church now rather than the local congregation that is emphasized. In fact, the mystery of Christ is no longer God's gracious work through the cross but the way both Jew and Gentile are embraced by the universal church. This worldwide community, founded on "the apostles and prophets" (Eph. 2:20), which serves as the seat of the cosmic Christ, differs markedly from the struggling local congregations we know from the undisputed letters. While it is true that the term *ekklēsia* can refer to the wider community in the genuine letters, a subtle shift has now occurred. Whereas in the undisputed letters the church is understood in light of Paul's Christology, Käsemann was quite correct in noting that in Ephesians "Christology . . . is interpreted almost exclusively by ecclesiology" (i.e., the author's view of the church).[9]

Finally, the understanding of apostleship in Ephesians differs significantly from that of the recognized Pauline letters. The apostles provide the foundation of the church (2:20), a statement that would have made Paul wince. Thirteen times the apostle Paul is referred to as a saint. According to the undisputed letters, the mission of the apostle is to proclaim the gospel to the Gentiles (Gal. 1:16; 2:7, etc.). The horizon of the mission stretches from Syria to Spain (Gal. 2:11; Rom. 15:24), and Paul consistently defends this gospel for the Gentiles. In Ephesians, on the other hand, Paul's apostolic task is to proclaim the unity in the church of Jews and Gentiles (3:2–6). This shift of emphasis reflects a situation that developed after the time of Paul and, therefore, argues for a post-Pauline date for this letter. We see, therefore, that the language, style, eschatology, view of the church, and understanding of apostleship separate Ephesians from the undisputed letters of Paul.

2. The Context of the Letter

As we saw in chapter 4, the recognized epistles of Paul are real letters addressing real situations. In each letter we could recognize a concrete situation evoking the letter. Ephesians, on the other hand, yields clues to its purpose grudgingly, and thus the attempts to reconstruct the setting of the letter have been disappointing. Paul Sampley, a respected American scholar, believes the "purposes of its author are hidden from the modern reader."[10]

a. *The Problems Evoking the Letter*

Ephesians resembles a religious tract more than a letter, and the general nature of the instruction has invited a number of theses about its purpose. More than a generation ago Goodspeed argued that Ephesians was written as a summary of Pauline theology to serve as a cover letter for a collection of the Pauline epistles.[11] While such a thesis would explain the general nature of the letter, it does not explain the absence of references to prominent motifs that appear in the undisputed letters (e.g., the Parousia and the cross). Moreover, if Ephesians ever stood at the head of a collection of Pauline letters, all evidence for such a position has been lost. Nils Dahl, a distinguished Pauline scholar, once suggested that Ephesians was written to instruct new Gentile converts on the meaning of baptism.[12] With some plausibility Chadwick thinks the letter addressed the crisis created by the success of Gentile Christianity and its drift away from its moorings in the Jewish tradition.[13] Others have seen an attempt to counter the influence of Gnosticism or a popular religion of the day. A very old thesis that enjoys little favor today is that Ephesians was a defense of Paul against competitors from Johannine and Petrine circles. From this short list of hypotheses it is easy to see the confusion that persists about the purpose of this letter. Perhaps the difficulty lies in the attempt of scholars to find a single purpose behind the writing, when in a postapostolic work, no less than in a writing of our own, a letter, an essay, or a tract may serve many purposes simultaneously.

Adaptations of two of the proposals mentioned above continue to be attractive to scholars: (1) that our author writes to urge the Gentile Christian majority to accept a Jewish Christian minority and to retain its ties with the ancient Hebrew traditions, and (2) that in the ethical admonition the author corrects libertine tendencies stemming from Gnostic influence or from the popular religion of the day (mystery cults, Neo-Pythagorean philosophy, folk religion, etc.). Let us now look at each in turn.

1. During and after the Roman-Jewish War (66–70 C.E.) that left Jerusalem in ruins, tensions increased between Jews and Christians. Before the war, we know from Paul's letters, it was possible to believe that Jesus was the Messiah and remain active in the synagogue. But after the war, tensions between church and synagogue increased. By the time Matthew's Gospel appeared, harsh exchanges were taking place (c. 85 C.E.), and when the Fourth Gospel was written a decade later, belief in Jesus as the Messiah meant expulsion from the synagogue, at least for the Evangelist's community. Such developments were especially hard on Jewish Christians.

One can easily construct a scenario leading to this break. In the war Jewish Christians who refuse to support the revolutionaries are called traitors and cowards. Gentile Christians, who are seen as Jewish Messianists until the time of the war, want to dissociate themselves from the nationalistic cause of the Zealots, if for no other reason than to avoid Roman reprisals. Thus, there would be in both Jewish Christian and Gentile Christian circles an emphasis on their particularity apart from a Jewish tradition dominated by a radical, revolutionary posture. While understandable, such a posture would have made it increasingly difficult to confess Jesus as the Messiah and continue living as a Jew. The pressure, whether subtle or overt from the Gentile majority, would be to encourage either assimilation or withdrawal into a Jewish Christian sect. The threat of a rupture between Jewish and Gentile Christians was real. The danger then of isolation from or even repudiation of the Jewish tradition in the Gentile Christian church was ever present. Our author attempts to speak to this crisis.[14]

2. More than a decade ago, scholars observed that both the language of the author and the outlook of the addressees showed some Gnostic coloration. Given the Gnostic desire to escape the prison of the body to ascend to a higher realm, the command of our author to "put off your old nature . . . and put on the new nature" (4:22, 24) rings true to the Gnostic outlook. The libertine inclinations of the audience or the temptation "to practice every kind of uncleanness" (4:19) likewise parallel Gnostic inclinations. But, whether the ideology ("every wind of doctrine," 4:14) that informed these tendencies came from Gnostic circles as such, or from the mysteries, popular religion, or folk piety that displayed Gnostic tendencies, it is difficult to say. It does appear that a concrete situation evoked the letter, although the exact contours of that conceptual landscape are clouded.

b. *The Response to the Problems*

In this response to the concrete situation the author tapped many traditions. Certain undisputed letters of Paul and Colossians were known by the author. Paraenetic material, or ethical instruction resembling that of the Essenes at Qumran, influenced his thinking as well. The instructions for members of the household derive from Hellenistic Judaism via Colossians, and his perception of Christ as the head of the cosmos and of the sexual union of Christ and the church may go back to Hellenistic circles with a Gnostic tinge.

In the undisputed letters Paul repeatedly argues for the right of Gentiles to be included in the church *as Gentiles* without first converting to Judaism (see Romans 9–11 and Galatians 1–3). In spite of his protestation, the Jerusalem church continued until the end to exert a powerful influence on Paul. But with the war and the dramatic growth of the Gentile church, the symbiotic relationship between Gentile and Jewish Christians or even between the Christian proclamation and the

Jewish traditions could no longer be taken for granted. Since Paul had argued for the inclusiveness of the church and since he had come to a position of respect and honor (at least in some circles), the use of his name and teaching seemed entirely apt. Under these altered circumstances, the author of Ephesians uses Paul's name to argue for the inclusion of Jewish Christians in the community without assimilation to the views of the Gentile majority. While Paul had argued for the inclusion of Gentiles *qua* Gentiles, the author of Ephesians argues for the inclusion of Jewish Christians *qua* Jewish Christians.

The appeal to the suffering of the apostle for the church is intended to arouse within the community a willingness to follow the instruction in the letter out of gratitude to the "apostle." Paul appears as "a prisoner for Christ Jesus on behalf of you Gentiles" (3:1) and as a "prisoner for the Lord" who encourages the recipients "to lead a life worthy of the calling to which you have been called" (4:1). In 3:13 the hearers are asked "not to lose heart over what I am suffering for you." While in the undisputed letter the emphasis on suffering is stronger, only in the deutero-Pauline letters does the suffering have a vicarious dimension. One can easily imagine how reverence for Paul and careful observance of instructions from him would be fostered by the awareness that the Apostle was suffering for the readers.[15]

In the undisputed letters Paul argues that his call and apostolic commission legitimize his gospel to the Gentiles (Gal. 1:15–16; Rom. 1:5). Although the apostolic call remains as an important part of Ephesians, the mission is understood differently. The apostle's task is now described as the communication of a mystery. This mystery is no longer seen as the puzzling or even bizarre way God reveals his grace through the cross, or even as the unspeakable, numinous presence of God, but rather as the inclusion of both Jews and Gentiles in the *one church.*

Since this unity derives from Christ, in whom the whole cosmos finds its unity and purpose, in a faintly Platonic sense the mystery of the unity of the church shares in the divine, cosmic mystery. Thus in Christ's reconciliation of the cosmos, the author found the model for the reconciliation of Jew and Gentile in one community.

Finally, only Ephesians presents the apostle as the "least of all the *saints*" (3:8). Paul, it is said, belongs to the "holy apostles" of God through whom Gentiles become fellow heirs (3:5). The apostles and Christian prophets form the foundation of the church (2:20), a view that is nowhere shared by Paul.

In this elevated view of Paul that borders on reverence, our author interpreted Paul's message for his day and invoked the authority of this suffering, holy, apostolic figure to deal with a crisis that threatened to fracture the church and to cut it loose from its Jewish moorings. Quite appropriately he appealed to Paul in order to encourage tolerance of and respect for Jewish Christians *as Jews,* and to discourage participation in the popular religions of the day. He urged the church to resist erroneous doctrine (4:14) and to shun immorality or libertine behavior. Most scholars agree that the paraenetic material comes from many sources. But, our author fashioned that material to emphasize the importance of unity, order, and mutual respect. In a characteristic Pauline fashion, the closing reaffirms the major concern of the letter. There the church is urged to reaffirm its support for Paul (through prayer) *and* the mystery (the unity of the church) (6:18–20).

OUTLINE OF EPHESIANS

2 Thessalonians

1. The Question of Authorship

Although 2 Thessalonians is short on pages, it is long on problems. The question of authorship, the identity of the *katechōn* ("restrainer" or "oppressor") in 2:7, the literary relationship to 1 Thessalonians, the sequence of the two Thessalonian letters, and the purpose of 2 Thessalonians are just some of the problems facing the interpreter of this letter. Although included here in our discussion of deutero-Pauline letters, 2 Thessalonians receives strong support for inclusion among the authentic letters. Persuasive arguments can be marshaled both for and against Pauline authorship, but it is included here because its authenticity is in doubt.

The case against Pauline authorship includes linguistic, literary, and theological arguments. First, the language and style of this letter differ from the undisputed letters. Nowhere else does Paul speak of being "made worthy of the kingdom of God" through suffering (1:5), or of the "restrainer" (or "oppressor") (2:7), or of "good hope" (2:16), "eternal comfort" (2:16), "good resolve" (1:11), or of being "shaken in mind" (2:2). Nowhere else does he speak of his readers as those whom God chose to "believe the truth" (2:12; cf. 2:13).[16] On the other hand, we find many places where 2 Thessalonians agrees with the wording of 1 Thessalonians. The salutation of each letter is nearly identical, and the thanksgiving in 2 Thessalonians 1:3–4 closely parallels that of 1 Thessalonians 1:2–3. Similarly, the expression, "brothers [and sisters], we beseech and exhort you" in the first letter (4:1) is echoed in "we beg you, brothers [and sisters]" of the second (2:1). The expression, the "heathen [Gentiles] who do not know God" (1 Thess. 4:5) becomes "those [unbelievers] who do not know God" (2 Thess. 1:8), and "Finally, brothers [and sisters]" (1 Thess. 4:1) is repeated exactly in 2 Thessalonians 3:1. The reference to the "labor and toil" of Paul and his co-workers and the statement that they worked "night and day" (1 Thess. 2:9) is almost exactly duplicated in 2 Thessalonians 3:8.

While the language in 2 Thessalonians agrees rather closely with that of 1 Thessalonians in places, the significance of these parallels is disputed. Some argue that Paul wrote 2 Thessalonians either shortly before or after 1 Thessalonians and naturally uses the same language to address a situation that has changed little. Others notice that most of the parallels appear in the letter opening and closing, traditionally the most stereotyped parts of the letter. It would be these sections that would be easiest to duplicate. So, we see that the linguistic arguments tend to cancel each other out. The issue of authorship must be decided on other grounds.

Second, taking up the literary question, the unusual form of the letter poses more of a problem for Pauline authorship. The thanksgiving especially has been singled out for scrutiny. All of the undisputed letters have one thanksgiving, except for 1 Thessalonians, which has two. Now we have learned that the second thanksgiving (2:13–16) was added later.[17] The break in the material, the unusual language, and a veiled allusion to the destruction of Jerusalem in 70 C.E. support the argument that the second thanksgiving was added after Paul's death. The second thanksgiving was inserted to reflect the developing tensions between non-Christian Jews and Christians after the war. Now 2 Thessalonians, duplicating the unusual form of 1 Thessalonians, also has two thanksgivings (1:3–12 and 2:13–17). It is possible then, if not likely, that a later writer using the edited version of 1 Thessalonians with two thanksgivings imitates the version before him. It follows, obviously, if such were the case, that Paul could not have written 2 Thessalonians.

One other small clue seems to point toward some author other than Paul. In 2:2 the author urges his hearers not to be disturbed by letters "purporting to be from us." Given the fact that Paul was *persona non grata* in many regions, it seems strange to have pseudonymous letters circulating in his name. From what we know of pseudepigraphy[18] elsewhere, most often the names used belong to some venerated figure from the past (e.g., Moses, Enoch, Abraham, or in the New Testament, Peter, Paul, James). We know of no instance of a pseudonymous letter being written in the name of a living person. From a practical point of view we can see why. It would seem contrary to reason for a person to adopt the name of a contemporary figure when the risk of being exposed would be rather high; it would be very easy to check the authenticity of the letter with the person in whose name it was written. Moreover, a special problem intrudes when one argues, as many do, that Paul wrote 1 Thessalonians only a few weeks before 2 Thessalonians. While such an argument explains the similarity of the letters, it is difficult to see how in only a few weeks after the writing of the first letter a pseudonymous letter could appear bearing Paul's name. The conclusion of the letter, "I, Paul, write this greeting with my own hand" (3:17), may be an attempt to establish the credibility of this letter against the claim of rivals in a post-Pauline period when other deutero-Pauline letters were appearing. In any case the conclusion is not proof of Pauline authorship.

Third, the theological outlook of 2 Thessalonians differs from that of 1 Thessalonians. In the first letter Paul expects that some of his readers will still be alive at the Parousia of Jesus (4:17). We have seen above that this emphasis on the imminent return of Christ persists throughout the undisputed letters of Paul. Even in Romans, one of his last letters, Paul suggests that salvation (or the end) "is nearer to us now than when we first believed; the night is far gone, the day is at hand" (13:11–12). It seems strange, therefore, in 2 Thessalonians to see an apocalyptic timetable that postpones the end. Before the "day of the Lord" (2:2) the believers will witness the appearance of the "restrainer" (2:7), the "man of lawlessness" (2:3), and a period of apostasy from the faith (2:2–12). Although the end of the age still lingers on the horizon in 2 Thessalonians, the delay effected by the apocalyptic timetable is unique in Paul's letters. Gerhard Krodel has noted how the use of the apocalyptic timetable here functions in a way quite different from that of the eschatological allusions in the Corinthian letters. Before the *parousia* of Jesus there must come first the apostasy of believers, the arrival of the Rebel, and the disappearance of the Restrainer. Presupposed by this timetable is a delay. In 1 Thessalonians, on the other hand, Paul uses an imminent eschatology to counter the discouragement of his addressees.[19]

In addition to the altered eschatological strategy in 2 Thessalonians, other prominent Pauline emphases are subdued. The Pauline view of the cross, resurrection, and Spirit play an insignificant role. Instead of asking his hearers to imitate his suffering as their share of the cross, "Paul" invites his addressees to copy his work ethic, that is, to earn their bread by sweat and toil as he does (3:7–13). For these reasons, we incline toward including this letter among the deutero-Paulines written in the first generation after Paul's death. However, no scholarly consensus exists on this question. Fortunately, however, the problem the epistle addresses is much clearer than the identity of the author. It is to that issue that we now turn.

2. The Context of the Letter

Second Thessalonians addresses two problems: apocalyptic enthusiasm and persecution. The suffering that some endure (1:5) is understood as a sign that the end has already come. Some are disturbed and others alarmed by a bogus Pauline letter announcing that "the day of the Lord has come" (2:2). Moreover, "wicked" people prey on this anxious congregation, deceiving some and exploiting others (3:2). In this period of feverish expectation of the world's denouement created by the letter and by false teachers, some have quit work to wait for the end (3:6). They idle away their time, sponging off those who work (3:11–12), and these busybodies disturb and disrupt the church (3:11).

In response our author promises relief (or rest) to the victims of terror and harassment. He offers the tortured souls consolation and hope, confidently predicting the demise of the oppressors (whoever they are). Recalling the ancient principle of "an eye for an eye," he forecasts affliction for those who afflict the church (1:6) and vengeance for those rejecting the gospel and its obedient subjects (1:8). The oppressed are assured that the "apostle" prays for them and they are urged to persist in their good resolve (1:11) in order that "Jesus may be glorified in you" (1:12). They are reminded that he solicits God's comfort for the persecuted (2:17) and that they should remain calm and resolute, steadfastly holding "to the traditions" (2:15). And finally, he promises them that the Lord will strengthen them for their struggle, guarding them from evil (3:3).

By establishing an apocalyptic timetable, the author seeks to modify the intense apocalyptic enthusiasm threatening the church. Those who insist that "the day of the Lord has come" (2:2) are told that the "day" will arrive only after the apocalyptic rebellion, a period of apostasy, the judgment of "the man of lawlessness" (2:3), and the exposure of his "signs and wonders" as false (2:9). The identity of the *katechōn* or one "who now restrains" (2:7, RSV) is concealed from us. His identity and function were probably known to the readers but are hidden from us. This figure plays some role in the final apocalyptic drama, but we cannot be sure what it is. The background for this concept is probably in a Jewish apocalyptic tradition, but we know of no exact parallel.

Through his skillful use of the Jewish apocalyptic traditions in 2:3–12, the author modifies the enthusiastic eschatology of his readers. By speaking of the delay of the "end" and the apocalyptic reversal of the position of the oppressor and oppressed, he seeks to encourage the persecuted and prod the idle to return to work. The apostle who toils and labors, even while he preaches the gospel, is held up as a model to be imitated (3:7–12). Members of the community are commanded to shun all idle busybodies and thus by shaming them reclaim them for the church (3:6, 11, 14–15).

We see, therefore, how our author drew on 1 Thessalonians and the Jewish apocalyptic tradition to address both persecuted persons and enthusiasts. Relying heavily on both the form and content of 1 Thessalonians[20] and the apostle's example and name, he offers comfort and correction to the church. Although his strategy differs from that employed by Paul (use of the timetable), our author stands squarely in the Pauline tradition. He correctly understands the Pauline resistance to religious enthusiasm, the apostle's emphasis on the tension between "the now and the not yet," and Paul's stress on the implications of the gospel for such human concerns as bread and nurturing relationships.

OUTLINE OF 2 THESSALONIANS

1.	Address, Salutation, and First Thanksgiving	1:1–12
2.	Encouragement ("Do not be shaken") in the Face of the Coming Eschatological Trauma	2:1–12
3.	Prayers and Exhortations	2:13–3:5
	a. Second thanksgiving, exhortation, and prayer of intercession	2:13–17
	b. Prayer request, exhortation, and prayer of intercession	3:1–5
4.	Paraenesis (Ethical Instruction)	3:6–16
	a. Word to the workers: Avoid the idle	3:6–7
	b. Paul's example	3:8–10
	c. Word to the idle: Earn your own living	3:10–13
	d. Advice to all: Ostracize those who refuse to obey	3:14–15
5.	Letter Closing	3:16–18

1 and 2 Timothy and Titus (The Pastorals)

1. The Question of Authorship

Written from a "pastor" to "pastors," these letters have been called the Pastorals, or the pastoral letters, for 350 years. It was simply taken for granted that these letters were by Paul until the early nineteenth century, when biblical critics noticed that the language, style, and content of these letters differed markedly from the undisputed letters of Paul. With few exceptions, modern scholars agree that Paul did not write the Pastorals. While their absence from an early manuscript (Chester Beatty papyrus number 46) can be discounted because part of the papyrus appears to be missing, it is more difficult to explain why Marcion omits the Pastorals from his collection of Paul's letters c. 160 C.E. One could object that the anti-Gnostic polemic in the Pastorals was offensive to Marcion and thus led to their rejection. But it is harder to explain why they were assigned a subordinate position as a kind of addendum to the body of the letters of Paul in the church's first canon of scriptures. This subordinate position suggests that though they were included, their acceptance was somewhat tentative. The church could not say "no" to the Pastorals, but it was unable to utter a resounding "yes."

The more compelling arguments against Pauline authorship are linguistic and theological. Excluding proper names, about twenty percent of the vocabulary appears nowhere else in the New Testament, and approximately thirty percent of the language of the Pastorals is absent from the undisputed letters. More decisive than the quantity of unusual words, however, is their character. The distinctive vocabulary of the Pastorals reminds one more of a Hellenistic-Jewish philosophical treatise than a Pauline letter. Such words as "piety" (*eusebeia,* 2 Tim. 3:5), "irreligious" (*anosios,* 2 Tim. 3:2), "way of life" (*agōgē,* 2 Tim. 3:10), "truth" (*alētheia,* 2 Tim. 2:15), "in accordance with piety" (*eusebeian,* Titus 1:1), "loving good" (*philagathos,* Titus 1:8), "temperate" (*sōphrōn,* Titus 1:8), "self-controlled" (*egkratēs,* Titus 1:8; all are my translations) are more characteristic of the popular Hellenistic writings of the day than the letters of Paul.

Moreover, some of the vocabulary that is integral to the undisputed letters appears nowhere in the Pastorals. Such words as "uncircumcised" (14 times), "to die" (35 times), "to proclaim the good news" (*euaggelizesthai,* 18 times), "spiritual" (18 times), and "body" (59 times) are absent. Also, an important theological word like "righteousness" (45 times) appears in the Pastorals only five times with an altered theological meaning. While an argument from silence is suspect if used alone, when taken with the other positive evidence cited above it raises insurmountable objections to Pauline authorship.

Statistical evidence, while valuable, seldom is decisive by itself in deciding questions of authorship. A comparison of the outlook of the Pastorals with that of the genuine letters is more instructive. First, the understanding of the church in the Pastorals is markedly different from that of the recognized Pauline letters. The institutional forms we see in the Pastorals are clearly more developed. Through the laying on of hands, we are told, "Paul" ordained Timothy to a ministerial task (2 Tim. 1:6), and Timothy is in turn to pass on the apostolic charisma to others (2 Tim. 2:1–2). Thus the church receives an ordained clergy that claims apostolic authority and with that authority the responsibility to maintain "sound teaching" in the church. Timothy and Titus, who stand in the apostolic chain, also appoint "elders"[21] who govern the church and proclaim the word. They choose deacons who are sober, unselfish, married only once, and good managers (1 Tim. 3:8–13). The deacons manage the church and administer charity; the elders govern and preach. The leaders are also charged with protecting "sound teaching" from false interpretation or compromise to assure the survival of the institution.

Both internal and external threats to the church are met in the genuine letters with vigorous and often heated debate. In the Pastorals, however, there is little independent argumentation. For Paul the mission of the church is expansive; the posture of the Pastorals is essentially defensive. For Paul church leadership is charismatic or Spirit-endowed; for the Pastor the leadership is institutional. For Paul "faith" is usually understood in an active sense (e.g., trust in God, belief in Jesus as the Messiah, confidence), but for the Pastor faith is a body of Christian truth to be defended. For Paul the church is the body of Christ; for the Pastorals the church is a fortress that defends the "deposit" (1 Tim. 6:20; 2 Tim. 1:12, 14). For Paul error is corrected by forceful debate; for the Pastor contradiction of error comes through a calm comparison of truth and error. For Paul the imminent return of Christ colors all of his thought; for the Pastor the Parousia or return of Christ plays little if any role in the order and mission of the church. We see, therefore, that in their understanding of the church, its organization, purpose, and function, Paul and the Pastor are poles apart.

The paraenetic materials in the Pastorals are vastly different from those of the Pauline letters. Martin Dibelius, an influential German scholar, once referred to the paraenesis of the Pastorals as a bourgeois ethic.[22] By that he meant the deeds and rules prescribed in the Pastorals encourage a type of piety that is indistinguishable from the popular religion of the day. When Paul borrowed ethical material from Hellenized circles, he normally placed his own stamp on it. The Pastor, on the other hand, is hardly such a master of his material.

In at least one instance, the Pastorals depart significantly from their Pauline model. In describing the role women exercise in the church,

Paul speaks approvingly of the ministry of women. He notes with appreciation the contribution of his co-worker Prisca, the female prophets, and Junia, the female apostle (Rom. 16:7; not Junias as in the RSV), and Paul asserts that in Christ there is "neither Jew nor Greek, there is neither slave nor free, there is *neither male nor female*" (Gal. 3:28, italics added). In the Pastorals, on the other hand, the accepted cultural norms prevail.[23] Although the Pastor assigns some role to widows *over sixty,* he forbids women to teach or "to have authority over men"; rather, the woman "is to keep silent." She will earn salvation by "bearing children, *if* she continues in faith and love and holiness, with modesty" (1 Tim. 2:12, 15, italics added). It is hardly possible to harmonize the Pastor's view of the role of women in the church with that seen in Paul's letters.[24]

We see, therefore, why the Pastorals cannot be ascribed to Paul, but this negative judgment on Pauline authorship hardly means that the Pastorals played no significant role in the church in the late first century or early second. Given the delay of the Parousia, the Gnostic threat, and episodic persecution or harassment, some development of Pauline theology was required. It is to that development that we now turn.

2. Context of the Pastorals

a. *The Problem Within the Community*

Although the Pastor refrained from aggressive confrontation with the false teacher, his contrast of sound doctrine with erroneous teaching gives us a good picture of the "heresy" he opposed. Subscribing to Jewish "myths," "genealogies," and "commands of men" (1 Tim. 1:4; Titus 1:14), the Pastor's opponents also engaged in certain ascetic practices. They repudiated marriage and avoided certain foods (1 Tim. 4:3). In claiming that they had already experienced the resurrection (2 Tim. 2:11), they effectively removed the eschatological reservation from Paul's theology[25] (2 Tim. 2:18). They claimed "knowledge" *(gnōsis)* (1 Tim. 6:20; Titus 1:16), and it is at least possible that they emphasized the total freedom of expression by men and women in the service of worship. This emphasis on asceticism, mythology or aeon speculation, realized eschatology, higher knowledge, and libertine behavior linked with law observance, shows that the heresy was a form of Jewish Gnosticism. The "false teachers" had enjoyed some success with naive and "unstable" persons (2 Tim. 3:6f. and Titus 1:11), enriching themselves at the expense of the credulous. It was against this threat that the Pastor struggled.

b. *The Pastor's Response*

The Pastor appealed to Paul in two ways. First, he sought authority for and acceptance of his "teaching" against the Gnostic "heresy" by invoking the name of the now-revered apostle. He wrote in Paul's name, interweaving appropriate Pauline traditions into his epistle. By writing in Paul's name, he was able to appeal to a patriarchal figure whose ministry was linked with the church's origin. By using the Pauline traditions, he sought support in a body of writings now accepted as the standard for Christian truth.[26] Second, through those who learned from Paul and were chosen and ordained by the divinely ordained Apostle (namely Timothy and Titus), the Pastor claimed authority for the deacons and elders of his church. In the Pastorals, "Paul" is said to write to Timothy, a co-worker and "true child in the faith" (1 Tim. 1:2), and Titus "my true child in a common faith" (Titus 1:4). He authorized Timothy and Titus to "appoint elders" (Titus 1:5) and deacons (1 Tim. 3:8–13). Thus, through Paul's "students" in ministry, the Pastor forged a link between the ordained clergy and Paul, which gave the emerging church organization legitimacy and credibility. In the dispute with the Gnostics this organization proved useful. Although the link with the Apostle was forced, there is a certain aptness in the appeal because the real Paul had opposed Gnostic tendencies in Corinth. Though his strategy was different, Paul would have agreed with the Pastor on the seriousness of the Gnostic threat.

In addition to his appeal to authority through Paul, the Pastor also offered a substantive alternative to the Gnostic emphasis on asceticism, aeon speculation ("myths"), realized eschatology, and superior knowledge *(gnōsis)*. Instead of seeking to discredit these views and the "false teachers" through direct confrontation, the Pastor simply contrasted their "silly myths" with his "sound doctrine." A "knowledge of the truth" (Titus 1:1), "sound doctrine" (Titus 1:9), what is "sound in the faith" (Titus 1:13), or "teaching" (1 Tim. 4:16) was contrasted with the *"gnōsis"* of the adversaries. The "sound words of our Lord Jesus Christ and the teaching which accords with godliness" (1 Tim. 6:3) were compared to the claims of those swollen "with conceit" (1 Tim. 6:4). The "good confession" (1 Tim. 6:12) belonged to those who "rightly [handle] the word of truth" (2 Tim. 2:15) and confuted those who are mere "word chasers" (2 Tim. 2:14) or who engage in "godless chatter" (2 Tim. 2:16). Not only did the Pastor avoid a pitched battle with his adversaries, he also advised his addressees to refrain from any direct challenge to the "false teachers." He urged them instead to abstain from "stupid, senseless controversies" (2 Tim. 2:23) and to correct their "opponents with gentleness" (2 Tim. 2:25), hoping for their repentance. One feature that shines through all of his response is the Pastor's remarkable confidence that through this gentle approach the errors of those "of corrupt mind" (2 Tim. 3:8) would be recognized by all.

In his attempt to counter the ascetic tendencies of the Gnostics, the Pastor suggested that all foods were to be received with thanksgiving (1 Tim. 4:3). Against those who forbade marriage, the Pastor recommended it for young widows and presumably for the unmarried as well. Against those who claimed to have already experienced the resurrection, a pale copy of traditional Pauline eschatology was held up that assigned "the last days" and the resurrection to the future. Appealing to Pauline teaching, the Pastor said, "If we have died with him, we *shall also live with him*" (2 Tim. 2:11, emphasis added).

Finally, it seems possible, if not probable, that the traditionally subordinate position assigned to women in the Pastorals was a reaction against Gnostic practice. We saw in our discussion of the Corinthian correspondence that religious enthusiasts promised an existence transcending sexuality to those fully experiencing salvation in the present. In their glorified state some Corinthians held that all distinctions between men and women were erased. Agreeing with Paul, they could say that in Christ "there is neither male nor female." A similar viewpoint was likely shared by the Gnostics of the Pastor's community. The Pastor attempted to refute such claims by reimposing on women the traditional social restrictions that the Gnostics had abandoned. They were commanded to avoid alluring attire and to "learn in silence with all submissiveness" (1 Tim. 2:11). They were forbidden to teach (as they did in Corinth) or to exercise authority over men, and they were to earn their salvation by bearing children (1 Tim. 2:12–15).

It is tempting to say that these letters lack the vitality and interest of the undisputed Pauline letters. The Pastor's static view of faith and demeaning view of women offends our modern sensibilities. He could be faulted for his bourgeois ethic, which has had a significant impact on Pauline interpretation over the centuries. One could easily point to his lack of intellectual vigor and imagination. But however harshly we judge his strategy, in retrospect we know that the ideology that he opposed was formidable. Had Gnosticism dictated the institutional form and theology of the church, the history of the whole Western world would have been very different. It is possible that, had Gnosticism triumphed, the church as we know it would be unrecognizable.

In our survey of the deutero-Pauline letters, we have seen various interpretations of the Pauline tradition for a new context. The Gentile mission had succeeded so well that the Gentile church was in a position to determine its own agenda, to create its own theological idiom, and to chart its own course, heedless of the views of the Jerusalem circle or the sensibilities of a shrinking Jewish Christian membership. The Roman-Jewish War had exacerbated tensions between Jews and Gentiles, which further threatened the relationship between Jewish and

Gentile Christians. The growing theological disputes and animosity between synagogue and church were waving them steadily toward a decisive rupture. The loss of confidence in traditional religious forms, combined with a growing disenchantment with social institutions, was to spark off a vast array of world-denying movements (Gnosticism was, of course, the most notable among them). The Parousia, or return of Jesus, so eagerly expected by Paul, had not come even though Jerusalem lay in ruins and Roman Christians had suffered severe persecution. None of these conditions was foreseen or addressed by Paul. It is a tribute to him, nevertheless, that in his teaching, personality, and example, others in a vastly different age have found instruction and encouragement, consolation and hope. Given the benefit of our perspective, we can see certain differences or even contradictions when comparing the deutero-Pauline letters with the undisputed epistles of Paul. But their very use of the Pauline tradition is proof that the deutero-Pauline authors chose to associate themselves with the tradition in order to complement it, not to contradict it.

OUTLINE OF 1 TIMOTHY

OUTLINE OF 2 TIMOTHY

OUTLINE OF TITUS

7. Currents and Crosscurrents

IN DEATH as in life controversy swirled around Paul. During his Gentile mission heated exchanges with believers punctuated his letters. Conflict with public officials, arrest, and incarceration interrupted his ministry. Harassment and beatings at the hands of his synagogue critics sapped his energies and grieved his spirit. But even after his mission was cut short by death, Paul's power to provoke continued. More than a century after his burial, his interpretation of the gospel still raised the hackles of some Jewish Christians. In one circle of believers he was tagged with the unflattering epithet "Simon Magus," a demonic magician of some notoriety in Christian apocryphal materials.[1] More recently Paul stands accused of diverting Christianity out of its source in the teachings of Jesus and into the stagnant backwater of church dogma.[2] Even now Paul's name is anathema to some who see him as a male chauvinist.

Although Paul has always had his detractors, he has also had his disciples. If the test of profound and seminal thinking is its ability to generate speculation, certainly Paul's thought qualifies as profound and seminal. In the first place his letters meant enough to merit their collection and preservation. The vigorous and imaginative understanding of gospel present in that collection spawned a whole family of imitations, the pseudo-Pauline letters. The writers of these deutero-Paulines (Hebrews, 1 and 2 Timothy, Titus, etc.) were so impressed by Paul that they adopted his name to legitimate their interpretations. Paul's shadow also falls across various types of noncanonical Christian writings in later centuries. Among these extrabiblical materials we find the Acts of Paul, an apocalypse of Paul, and more deutero-Pauline letters.[3] Allusions to Paul and quotations from his letters abound in writings of the early church. Pivotal exegetes like Augustine and Luther found in Paul the prism through which they could see the rich colors of all scripture. We see, therefore, Paul's power to provoke and excite has continued through the centuries. In the following pages we shall sketch the high points of that dialogue with Paul. In viewing currents and crosscurrents in the history of Pauline interpretation, we gain a better appreciation of the subtlety of Paul's thought and the difficulty that certain prickly passages pose for the interpreter. Although such an appreciation is no magic formula for easy mastery of these ancient documents, it is none-theless helpful for any reader seeking an accurate assessment of Paul's thought.

We shall focus on five of the issues that have dominated Pauline interpretation over the centuries. In chronological order, they are (1) Gnosticism: the problem of evil in the world, (2) Pelagianism: the problem of sin, (3) the relationship of Paul to Jesus, (4) the relationship of Paul to his background, and (5) Paul and women.

1. Gnosticism: The Problem of Evil in the World

The feud over the proper relationship of the Christian to the world smoldered for almost a century and then erupted into blazing fury about 150 C.E. Even as early as Colossians, written before the end of the first century, an author was attacking those in the early church who scorned the world below in favor of the world above. The worship of angels (Col. 2:18), the elevation of visionary experiences, and the prom-ise of apotheosis for those who acquire special cosmic knowledge (2:18, 20), all reflect the otherworldly preoccupation of the writer's oppo-nents. Their special disdain for the world also manifested itself in such prohibitions as "Do not handle, Do not taste, Do not touch" (2:21). Strangely enough, a wild and reckless abandon accompanied this as-cetic mentality. Those condemned for treating the world with disgust were also accused of "immorality, impurity, passion, evil desire, and covetousness" (3:5). Although world denial and physical indulgence appear to us to be mutually exclusive, a peculiar form of logic held them together for the author's opponents. Rejection of the world, they be-lieved, demonstrated one's deliverance from the world, and indulgence in the world showed one's superiority to it. In fact, some Christian Gnostics felt obligated to break all of the moral strictures that earth-lings consider important in order to demonstrate their loyalty to an-other, higher order. The important thing to see, however, is that Paul's name is invoked to refute these Gnostic innovators.

Around 100 C.E., 1 and 2 Timothy and Titus were written under Paul's name. They are called the Pastoral epistles because they instruct in the performance of pastoral offices. In these epistles the authority of Paul is likewise summoned against what the author believes are danger-ous interpretations of the Christian message. But in them the profile of the opponents is sharper than in Colossians. In 1 Timothy those who have "missed the mark as regards the faith" (6:21) claim knowledge (the Greek is *gnōsis*, from which the term "Gnosticism" is derived). These "heretics"[4] believe that through *gnōsis* they have already experi-enced the resurrection (2 Tim. 2:18), and thus they have overcome the world. Although they are Jews (Titus 1:10), they reject the Jewish belief in the fundamental goodness of the creation (see 1 Tim. 4:4, which opposes them by vigorously insisting on the creation's goodness). Their adherence to "godless and silly myths" (1 Tim. 4:7) and their use of "endless genealogies" (1 Tim. 1:4) reflect their belief that a hierarchy of angelic mediators separated the good God from the evil world. It would appear that the Gnostics had found support in Paul's letters for their position and our author is attempting to rescue Paul from them. The writer of the Pastorals wants to show that Paul in fact repudiated the position for which the Gnostics claim his support.

Second-century Gnosticism came and almost conquered under the banner of Paul. Although Gnosticism was multifarious, the diverse expressions of the movement held certain themes and emphases in common. Gnostic sects everywhere displayed hatred for the world and things of the flesh. Their disdain for the creation spilled over onto its creator; they reasoned that if the earth is evil its architect must also be evil. Christian Gnosticism, therefore, often contrasted the creator God of the Old Testament with the God revealed in Christ. One was seen as the "god of the world" and, therefore, diabolical; the other was viewed as the God of the highest heaven and, therefore, gracious and good. Salvation, naturally enough, was understood as liberation from this wretched earth and rescue from corrupted flesh. According to the Gnostic myth, through some tragic failure a spark of the divine was planted in some (but not all) persons and the memory of its divine origin erased. Humankind continued in its ignorant stupor until the high God had mercy and sent Christ to remind humanity of its true origin. Salvation, therefore, comes through knowledge *(gnōsis)*, but this *gnōsis* is more than just intellectual awareness of the divine origin of one's true self. Knowing for the Gnostic went beyond mental recall; it meant active reunion with one's divine source through all kinds of ecstatic experience—dreams, visions, speaking in tongues, etc. In this return to the divine source, one is liberated from the bodily prison. It was hardly surprising, therefore, that the Gnostics equated this moment of liberation with the resurrection. As the *Gospel of Philip* (56:15–19) says,

> Those who say that the Lord died first and (then) rose up are in error, for he rose up first (then) died. If one does not first attain the resurrection, will he not die?[5]

Moreover, since the body shared the taint of this evil world, the whole concept of the resurrection of the body was repugnant to Gnostics. Their contempt for the world was matched by preoccupation with heavenly things—divine mysteries, esoteric wisdom, manifestations of the power of the Spirit, and so on. As "spiritual" beings they worshiped the spiritual person, Christ, but they conveniently ignored or even cursed the earthly Jesus.

Marcion was one of the key figures in the second-century controversy about Paul. Whether he was a Gnostic, strictly speaking, is debatable; his outlook shared enough features of the Gnostic vision to cause him to be associated with them, perhaps mistakenly. Although he was excommunicated by the church at Rome in 144 C.E., he and his disciples dominated Syria until the beginning of the fifth century. Orthodoxy prevailed over Marcionism only after Bishop Rabbula (411–435) managed to have Marcionite meeting places destroyed and their property transferred to the Great Church, and after the zealous bishop "gently" persuaded Marcionites to give up their "error," be "baptized," and submit to the "truth."[6]

Interestingly enough, Paul's letters formed the heart of Marcion's Bible. And none of the Old Testament books was included. It may seem strange that the Gnostics were so fond of Paul unless one notices that certain statements of Paul, isolated from their immediate and broader context, do seem to buttress Gnostic claims. In 1 Corinthians 9:26–27 Paul speaks of the body as if it were an enemy that must be beaten into submission ("I pommel my body and subdue it"). Elsewhere Paul appears to speak pejoratively of the flesh ("nothing good dwells . . . in my flesh," Rom. 7:18). In Romans 7:24 Paul begs for deliverance from "this body of death." Romans 8:23 was a crucial passage for the Gnostics. Paul says, "we ourselves, who have the first fruits of the Spirit, groan inwardly as we wait for adoption as children, the redemption *of* our bodies," but the Gnostics read, "redemption *from* our bodies." Since they despised the body, the Gnostics could easily join Paul in saying, "flesh and blood cannot inherit the kingdom of God" (1 Cor. 15:50).

In other passages, too, the Gnostics found Paul advocating views they cherished. They were preoccupied with "spiritual things" and with divine mysteries. Paul also, they discovered, spoke of "what no eye has seen, nor ear heard, nor the heart . . . conceived" (1 Cor. 2:9). Moreover, Paul boasted of a vision in which he was "caught up into Paradise . . . [and] heard things that cannot be told, which no mortal may utter" (2 Cor. 12:3–4). They too aspired to fly to the third heaven (or higher) to receive special visions and to taste the ambrosial food and drink.

The Gnostics also found support in Paul for the radical dualism between the world above and the world below. In 2 Corinthians 4:4 Paul says the "god of this world has blinded the minds of the unbelievers." No doubt Paul was referring to the Devil as "god of this world," but the Gnostics interpreted the passage as referring to the creator of this world, i.e., Yahweh of Genesis. They concluded from this that it was the evil God, Yahweh, who "blinded the minds" of humanity so that mortals could no longer remember the true, extramundane, changeless God.

The stubborn insistence of the Gnostics that Yahweh was the evil "god of this [evil] world" clashed with the classic Hebrew view that

Yahweh was just and merciful and that the creation was good. The Jew delighted in the pride that Yahweh took in his handiwork—"and God saw everything that he had made, and behold, it was very good" (Gen. 1:31). The Gnostic rejection of the Old Testament as the revelation of a base, pretender God in favor of certain Christian writings threatened to drive a wedge between Hebrew scripture and Christian revelation. This threat posed in the sharpest way the question of the relationship between Jewish and Christian tradition.

Early in the second century the church fathers[7] took up the cudgels against the Gnostic position. Central to their attack was the conviction that the Hebraic scriptures and Christian writings belonged together. They denounced as a grotesque caricature the Gnostic teaching that Yahweh was wicked. They argued instead that the God of the creation and Israel was the same God revealed in Jesus Christ. They tirelessly maintained that there was no basis in Paul for the dualism of the Gnostics. Origen persistently objected that there was no evidence in Paul's letters to support the view that matter per se is evil.[8] Irenaeus, a second-century bishop of Lugdunum (Lyons), attempted to rob the Gnostics of their base of support in Paul. He knew of the Gnostic use of Paul's statement that "flesh and blood cannot inherit the kingdom of God" (1 Cor. 15:50) to bolster their dualistic position. Against them Irenaeus submitted four reasons for belief in the resurrection of the physical body, all of them drawn from Paul's letters.[9]

Causing the greatest difficulty for the Fathers was Paul's interpretation of the law. The Gnostics had gathered grist for their mill from passages like Romans 3:21, where Paul seems to do away with the law: "Now the righteousness of God has been manifested apart from law." The Gnostics had read this and similar passages as evidence that Paul also rejected the Hebrew scriptures. The Fathers were justifiably puzzled by the ambiguity and shifting emphases in many of Paul's statements about the law. Origen, for example, noted six different ways Paul used the term "law."[10] The Fathers admitted that Paul's characteristic emphasis on grace seemed to relegate law to a subordinate place if not cancel it out altogether. But the Fathers argued that while Paul does emphasize the superiority of Christ to the law, he nevertheless gives the law an important place in God's unfolding drama of redemption. Once the Fathers demonstrated convincingly Paul's positive use of law, they overcame the most serious objection to reading him in the light of, rather than as opposed to, his Jewish tradition. Their position prevailed and in time the Gnostic threat diminished. Nevertheless, it is important for us to see that the relationship of God to the world and the church to Judaism were such burning issues, not only because those questions are important for understanding Paul, but also because they are so near the heart of the life of faith itself. Humanity still wrestles with the problem of how to acclaim God's new acts without at least implicitly repudiating the Creator's old ones.

2. Pelagianism: The Problem of Sin

Even during the controversy between the Christian Gnostics and the Christian mainstream, other disputes were brewing over the proper interpretation of Paul. Whereas the Gnostics longed for deliverance from the evil world, other believers were preoccupied with the problem of sin and release from its burden. This concern over salvation from sin—how God can justify the unrighteous—has fascinated Western theologians from the fourth century to the present.

The principal figures in the early debate were Augustine and Pelagius, both churchmen of the late fourth and early fifth centuries. We know Augustine, of course, from his *Confessions* and from a history enriched by his theological profundity and powerful biblical exegesis. Pelagius, however, also a great intellect and a serious biblical exegete, did major commentaries on Romans and the two Corinthian letters,[11] and shorter ones on all of the other letters in the Pauline corpus.

At issue between Augustine and Pelagius was the correct understanding of the nature of sin, its origin and remedy. Long before the first ink flowed from his pen against Pelagius (in 412 C.E.), Augustine had already described humanity as a "lump of sin" who could do nothing toward its own salvation.[12] Meanwhile, in Rome, Pelagius was teaching that humanity had the ability within itself to live a sinless life. His exegesis of Romans led Pelagius to reject the idea that sin is transmitted like a pedigree from parent to offspring. The crucial passage in the dispute was Romans 5:12, where Paul says, "Therefore as sin came into the world through one man and death through sin, and so death spread to all because all sinned . . ." This passage, according to the British monk, says that the transmission of sin from Adam to all humankind is not by propagation but by imitation.[13] Human beings are sinners not by birth but by choice. Since Pelagius found no support in Paul for the seminal transmission of sin, he concluded that the doctrine of original sin was a false one. Moreover, he added, it was contradictory:

> If sin is natural, it is not voluntary; if it is voluntary it is not inborn. These two definitions are as mutually contrary as are necessity and [free] will.[14]

Not only did Pelagius raise questions about the scriptural authenticity of the doctrine of original sin and the anthropology implicit in it, he also argued that such a view undermined the Christian doctrine of God. How, he asked, could a just God create sinners and then condemn them for sinning? How could a righteous God command, "You shall be holy, for I the LORD your God am holy" (Lev. 19:2), after making the human being congenitally incapable of holiness? How could the Son of God command the believer to be "perfect, as your heavenly Father is perfect" (Matt. 5:48) if humanity is so stained by sin at birth that it is incapable of perfection?

Pelagius was quick to see the implications of this understanding of Paul for the practice of infant baptism. Since he rejected the doctrine of original sin, he denied that babies are in need of cleansing from the stain of sin. Although he endorsed infant baptism, he balked at the suggestion that it was necessary for the salvation of the child.

Seeing the position of Pelagius, it is easy to understand why he was infuriated by a line from one of Augustine's most famous prayers that reads: "Grant what You command, and command what You will."[15] Such an attitude, Pelagius argued, undermined genuine moral striving and sanctioned the moral indifference that he saw on every side in Rome.[16] Now that it was socially acceptable to become a Christian, Pelagius feared the gradual reduction of the high ethical imperative in Paul's gospel to the prevailing cultural low.

It was not long before Pelagius and Augustine collided. In 412 C.E. Augustine began writing to expose the errors of his rival. He attacked both Pelagius's understanding of sin and his doctrine of human nature. He disputed Pelagius's claim that God, not people, should be blamed for the existence of sin if human nature is sinful from birth. On the contrary, Augustine objected, God made Adam and Eve free and inno- cent. It was through their rebellion, not by God's design, that they and all after them became sinners. Adam was able to introduce sin into the human context, but he was unable to remove it. It was inconceivable to Augustine that Adam the sinner could produce innocent offspring. Consequently, in his view the whole human experiment begun by God was blighted by Adam's fatal error.

Augustine believed that Romans 5:12 supported his understanding of sin. Working from a Latin text, he read *in quo* as masculine even though *quo* could be read as neuter, changing the meaning entirely. Augustine understood Romans 5:12 to say that "death came to all, in whom [*in quo,* i.e., Adam] all sinned." Thus he assumed that he was faithfully transmitting the Pauline view. The Greek text, however, requires reading the Latin *in quo* as neuter, thus giving, "death came to all, *because* all sinned." Paul obviously is indebted to the Jewish tradition that holds that each person becomes his or her own Adam by choice ("because"), not by inheritance. The apostle did hold that social context puts strong pressure on people to act selfishly, but he hardly held the view of "original sin" as we know it.

Augustine further argued that Pelagius not only underestimated the power of sin but also overestimated human power to cope with it. For, once Adam introduced sin into the human framework, the trap was sprung. Humanity can neither remove sin from the world nor eradicate it from its own nature. Since creatures are powerless to help themselves, salvation has to come from a source outside the human world. This remedy is provided as a gracious act of God through Jesus Christ. Infants need baptism, Augustine contended, because from the very beginning they need redemption from the sin of Adam. To those who objected that such redemption could be effected only by faith, and therefore was not available to untutored infants, Augustine retorted that faith is not a human work but a gracious gift of the Creator. For their salvation all mortal creatures are totally dependent on God, and there is nothing they can do to effect their own redemption.

The charge by Pelagius that total reliance on God sanctioned moral indifference brought an angry reply from Augustine. Like the ancient rabbis, he placed statements about God's grace and human responsibility side by side without sensing any tension between them. Pelagius saw the Christian life as a cooperative affair: One half of the responsibility belongs to God, who gives people the ability to do right; the other half of the responsibility belongs to individuals, who exercise that ability. Appealing to Paul, Augustine on the other hand viewed the work of divine grace and human response in paradoxical and total terms: all is given by God, yet all is required of human beings.

In the opinion of Augustine, Pelagius's confidence in human achievement took the power to direct history out of the hands of God and placed it in mortal hands. For if the creature is the maker of its own destiny and has the ability to direct the course of history, the doctrine of the sovereignty of God is needless, or worse. Pelagius's emphasis on human freedom and responsibility virtually eclipsed the traditional stress on divine providence. Augustine, on the other side, resorted to the use of the paradox once again to hold the two motifs in balance. Drawing on Paul's discussion of predestination in Romans 9:14ff., he coupled opposing statements in an attempt to state a profound truth: All things are predestined by God; the human is totally free and responsible.

The debate between Pelagius and Augustine raged for six years. Finally, in 418 Pelagius was officially condemned by the Synod of Carthage and dropped out of sight. The debate continued, however, in spite of the official condemnation because "it was a real debate on central issues of Christian faith."[17]

More than a thousand years later Martin Luther felt that the anti-Pelagian tracts of Augustine still addressed the most urgent question of his time. Augustine and Luther clearly are brothers in their assessment of human depravity and divine grace. Both came to their understanding of the gospel after searing personal struggles, and both found their way out of their distress through Paul's letters. It is not surprising that Luther, with his history of personal struggle, should regard as nonsense Pelagius's belief that all are capable of keeping God's commandments. With great poignancy Luther describes his collision with Romans 1:17 and its obstinate refusal to surrender its meaning. He was galled by Paul's statement that "the justice of God is being revealed from heaven against all ungodliness and wickedness" (my translation), and he was angry at God for exacting justice even through the gospel. For no matter how hard Luther tried, he still failed to fulfill God's just demand. If salvation depends on performing the impossible, how could one ever be saved? Near despair, Luther noticed the context of Romans 1:17. With astonishment he read the words, "the just shall live by faith" (KJV). He was relieved to learn that it was through faith, not works, that one was placed in a proper relationship with God. This emphasis on God's justification of the sinner held enormous implications for the interpretation of scripture and gave the interpretation of Paul a critical significance in the theological debates that followed.

In assessing these men and the implications of their thought for our understanding of Paul, we should remember that Pelagius, as well as Augustine or Luther, was a committed Christian eager to discern and propagate the faith. He raised questions about troublesome passages that we cannot avoid in a close reading of Paul's letters. Augustine misreads Romans 5:17, but Pelagius fails to appreciate fully either the power or the mystery of human sin. So which is more faithful to Paul? Whether they realize it or not, most American Protestants come to the letters with spectacles provided either by Luther or Augustine. For justification by faith, which was central to the thought of both men, has traditionally assumed a dominant place in American Protestantism. No doubt the motif is critical to Paul's argument in Romans and Galatians. But it is mentioned infrequently or not at all in the other letters. We need to be careful in reading these other letters lest our preoccupation with the guilt of the individual and God's grace blind us to the great variety and scope of Paul's concern. Some scholars feel that Paul's thought should be viewed in a broader cosmic frame that includes but transcends the emphasis on individual salvation. Others argue that justification by faith is the center of gravity of the whole body of Pauline letters. It is these unresolved issues that continue to make the reading of Paul an exciting and challenging experience for inquiring minds.

3. The Relationship of Paul and Jesus

"Jesus was not a Christian, he was a Jew." So spoke Wellhausen in 1905. Many would still heartily agree. They image Jesus as a charismatic Galilean who had an uncanny feel for the essence of true religion. Trusting completely in God, he lived a life free of anxiety and devoid of pretense. He cared little for religious rules or rituals, and he stepped across social barriers to befriend criminals, prostitutes, the poor, and little children. But somehow the primitive and beautiful religion of this

Jewish peasant has been spoiled by the professionals, obscured by theological overlay, cluttered by dogmatic assertion, and robbed of vitality by institutional forms. Usually in this scenario it is Paul who is seen as the initial corrupter of a vital, true religion. According to this view, Paul's insistence on the Jesus of the cross totally eclipsed Jesus the teacher in parables. Paul pushed aside the "gentle Jesus meek and mild" in favor of the vindictive Judge coming with God's angels in flaming fire. He forced Jesus' simple announcement "your sins are forgiven" (Mark 2:5) to give way to theological speculation about guilt and redemption. This interpretation holds that the history of Christianity would have been entirely different had Paul influenced only a small circle of disciples. Paul's interpretation was decisive, however, because his influence was so far-flung. As the Johnny Appleseed of early Christianity, he planted the seeds of the gospel from Antioch to Rome. As the founder of churches, he locked the religion of Jesus in an institutional case. It was Paul, many feel, who cut Christianity off from its roots in the life and teachings of Jesus, the Galilean holy man.

This contemporary juxtaposition of Jesus and Paul has a long history. As early as the seventeenth century, John Locke, an English Deist, saw such a cleavage. He reached this conclusion after beginning a search for a "reasonable Christianity" free from the "shackles of dogma." He wanted to make a fresh appraisal of the New Testament independent of the bias of a Christian orthodoxy. This independent study convinced him that a great chasm ran through the New Testament between the simple gospel of Jesus and the complicated, obscure theology of Paul. The gospel of Jesus, according to Locke, came from the lips of Jesus himself, but the gospel about Jesus was the invention of later interpreters like Paul. The implications of Locke's study were clear. If one is to recover the message of Jesus in its pristine purity, one must strip off all dogmatic distortions whether of the Church of England or of the apostle Paul himself. It is the four Gospels that must be used as the primary and even exclusive source if the simple gospel of Jesus is to be reclaimed.

This tendency to divorce the teaching of Jesus from the theology of Paul reached its apogee in the thought of William Wrede (1859–1906), a brilliant German biblical scholar. In his view, Jesus was a simple, pious Jewish peasant whose prophetic insight, moral sensitivity, empathy for the oppressed, and strong sense of the presence of God meant nothing to Paul. Although Jesus was remembered by the apostle as a real historical figure, the particulars of his earthly life meant little to Paul. Before Paul came, Wrede argued, Christianity was only "an inner Jewish sect," but after Paul we have "a Christian Church."[18] According to Wrede, the religion of Jesus is true Christianity, but the religion of Paul is a fabricated and institutionalized dogma.

More recently Geza Vermes, an Oxford Reader in Jewish Studies, has tried once again to untangle the Jesus of history from the Christ of dogma, in his *Jesus the Jew* (London: William Collins Sons & Co., 1973). Vermes's study of the Dead Sea Scrolls and the Talmud persuades him that Jesus is fully understandable only within the framework of first-century Judaism in Galilee. He finds in northern Palestine strong interest in the Elijah miracle tradition and in meditation, which would explain Jesus' acceptance there and his mixed reception in Jerusalem. Presumably religious enthusiasm and ignorance of rabbinic tradition were viewed differently in Galilee and in Jerusalem. Placing Jesus in this Galilean setting, Vermes contends that Jesus probably did not claim to be the Messiah, that he certainly did not claim to be divine, and that he would have been outraged by the incarnation formula "true God from true God, . . . and was made man," as the Nicene Creed affirms. Vermes believes that it was Hellenistic paganism, not Paul, that led Gentile Christianity into error; nevertheless, it was church doctrine that spoiled the simple religion of this pious Galilean peasant and his Jewish followers. It is hard to understand why Paul should escape the blame since he enjoyed the greatest success in interpreting the Christian gospel for the Hellenistic mind. Vermes's approach avoids some of the mistakes of the earlier scholars, but the jury is still out on his case. It would seem, however, that the challenge his thesis poses has already been met by two earlier developments in this century: (1) the advent of form criticism, and (2) the studies of Albert Schweitzer.

Rudolf Bultmann and Martin Dibelius first taught us that the traditions of Jesus circulated orally in certain forms (parables, sayings, miracle stories, etc.) long before they were assembled and edited by the Gospel writers. Through his careful study of the forms, Bultmann was able to show that the church not only kept alive the Jesus materials by oral tradition, it also shaped and interpreted them to fit its changing needs. Gradually scholars saw that the Gospel writers further shaped, edited, and interpreted the materials that they got from the oral stream, in order to speak to their own times. Exegetes now realize that the Gospel writers were not composing objective biographies of Jesus but were writing their story of Jesus' life with a strong theological emphasis. Mark, for example, underscores the importance of Jesus as the suffering Son of God. Matthew emphasizes Jesus' role as the eschatological teacher. Luke speaks of Jesus as the bearer of the Holy Spirit, the friend of the poor, and the fulfillment of Israel's hopes. Through form criticism we have learned to appreciate the Gospel writers as creative authors who left their imprint on their work through their selection, arrangement, and interpretation of the oral tradition. Once it is realized that the Gospel writers as well as Paul had strong theological interests, the old view that the Jesus of the Gospels was free of dogmatic interpretation is no longer defensible. If any transformation had taken place, it clearly was not the work of Paul alone.

When Albert Schweitzer died in 1965, he was eulogized as one of the great human beings of our century, and he was. As a missionary doctor in French Equatorial Africa, an accomplished musician, the winner of the Nobel Peace Prize, and an Alsatian writer, he had captured the imagination of the Western world. But it was his biblical scholarship that led him in the first place to give up promising careers in music, theology, and philosophy to found a hospital in Africa. When Schweitzer went to Africa in 1913, he carried with him the rough draft of his book on Paul. Fifteen years later Schweitzer found time to prepare that manuscript for publication. When his book *The Mysticism of Paul the Apostle* did appear, it was revolutionary. Even today scholars consider acquaintance with Schweitzer's work to be an absolute requirement for discussion of Jesus and Paul. In 1906 Schweitzer had found his clue for understanding Jesus in Jewish apocalyptic thought. Now he argued that Paul, likewise, understood Jesus in the light of Jewish apocalypticism. In the first century, the view was commonplace in Jewish circles that God's eschatological rule would be ushered in by a period of intense suffering. Jesus, Schweitzer argued, identified his own rejection and death with the final trauma that would bring in God's rule. Paul likewise saw the cross as the pain accompanying the birth of the new age. Schweitzer concluded from this that in their common reliance on Jewish apocalyptic and in their understanding of the Passion, Paul and Jesus were in perfect agreement.

Some scholars correctly note flaws in Schweitzer's work.[19] Others even accuse him of making ground-level mistakes. His view that Jesus deliberately courted death to hasten God's final denouement is nowhere accepted, and the mystical solidarity with Christ effected in baptism is hardly the essence of Paul's thought. But all would agree that Schweitzer opened up new dimensions and raised profound questions concerning the relationship of Paul and Jesus. Whatever faults Schweitzer's work may have, there is no escaping his essential point—that both the character of Jesus' life and ministry and the proclamation of Paul were eschatological through and through, and both must be assessed in the full light of Jewish apocalyptic thought. Unquestionably, however, Paul's letters differ from the Gospels in style and emphasis. Long, involved discussions weave complicated patterns in the epistles. Short, pithy sayings dart from the lips of Jesus. Paul's letters are heavy with abstractions (e.g., the righteousness of God). Authentic Jesus materials such as the parables bear the unmistakable aroma of this earth. Paul's frequent allusions to the Parousia (the second coming of Christ) would sound unnatural on Jesus' lips. The postresurrection situation and Paul's worldwide mission summon forth themes in Paul that were muted or absent in Jesus' ministry. Paul has reflected long and deeply on the meaning of the Christ event. But even though Paul has modified the traditions and created new centers of meaning in

Christian thought, his theology does not contradict the proclamation of Jesus. His work is an extension and even a reformulation of the meaning of the Christ event, but he and Jesus are no more incompatible than are Bartok and Beethoven.

4. The Relationship of Paul to His Background

Paul's theology is often portrayed as the antithesis not only of the teachings of Jesus but also, paradoxically enough, of first-century Judaism. When Paul entered the Christian church, it is assumed that he repudiated his Jewish past, recalling it only in order to throw his Christian status into bold relief. In the conversion experienced by Augustine, Luther, and the Pietists, it is generally believed, we have a carbon copy of Paul's own spiritual biography.

"Pick it up, read it. Pick it up, read it," Augustine heard a child singing. So he took up the Bible before him and his eyes singled out Romans 13:13: ". . . not in reveling and drunkenness, not in debauchery and licentiousness, not in quarreling and jealousy. But put on the Lord Jesus Christ, and make no provision for the flesh, to gratify its desires." Augustine reported:

> Instantly, as the sentence ended, there was infused in my heart something like the light of full certainty and all of the gloom of doubt vanished away.[20]

So ended Augustine's long, dark night of the soul. His experiments with philosophy and Manicheanism had left him empty and restless. His excursion into hedonism was unsatisfying. But with his conversion to Christianity, Augustine felt that his period of blind groping had ended. The change in Augustine was dramatic. In a sensitive discussion of his pilgrimage of faith, he contrasted the dissatisfaction and aimless searching before his conversion with the peace and purpose he felt after baptism. Even the birds knew, he said, that he was a Christian.

In many ways Luther's experience paralleled that of Augustine. Restless and dissatisfied, Luther left the study of law at the university hoping to find peace in a monastery. But despite herculean efforts to live a blameless life, he felt condemned, empty, and wanting. Release came for this troubled, uneasy monk through his discovery of Paul's emphasis on salvation by grace alone. A total reorientation in his self-understanding and theological outlook occurred. Energies once sapped by anxiety and guilt burst forth anew in highly creative ways.

The Pietists of the late sixteenth and seventeenth centuries likewise found support in Paul for a strong emphasis on conversion. In Romans 7 and 8 they thought they found evidence that Paul divided life into two stages, one falling before, the other after conversion. They read the first-person singular references in Romans 7 as autobiographical statements that Paul made about his life as an unconverted, frustrated, guilt-ridden Pharisee. They pointed to verse 9 where Paul says, "I was once alive apart from the law, but when the commandment came, sin revived and I died." In verse 15 they witnessed Paul distracted, utterly confused: "I do not understand my own actions. For I do not do what I want, but I do the very thing I hate." This inward struggle, they believed, finally erupted in a cry of defeat, in verse 24: "Wretched man that I am! Who will deliver me from this body of death?"

In the view of the Pietists, chapter 8, on the other hand, speaks of Paul's Christian life after conversion. After the light of Christ had illumined his night, Paul can speak triumphantly: "Who shall separate us from the love of Christ? Shall tribulation, or distress, or persecution, or famine, or nakedness, or peril, or sword? . . . No, in all these things we are more than conquerors through him who loved us" (vs. 35, 37). The Pietist warmth over Paul's conversion was further supported by an appeal to his Damascus Road experience (Acts 9:1–9; 22:6–11; 26:12–18). Upon conversion Paul, the zealous Pharisee, finally acknowledged that his efforts to keep the law had failed. Now he openly admitted what he had tried to conceal by frenetic activity. Now the ethical crisis was overcome in a dramatic conversion by which he found release from enormous psychological tension.

The numerator in the experiences of Augustine, Luther, and the Pietists was in each case different, but the denominator was the same. All spoke poignantly of their rescue from a dreadful past. All viewed their life under grace as the exact reverse of their former life. And all found in the letters of Paul the inspiration and direction for their metamorphosis. Given the pattern of their experience, it was natural for them to see in Paul the same rupture as theirs between the way of unbelief and the life of faith. Paul the Jew was called the unbeliever; Paul the emissary of Christ was made the model of faith. Paul the devotee of law was cast as a wayward, guilt-ridden Pharisee; Paul the recipient of grace became the apostle of freedom. Understandably such an assessment of Paul tended to drive a wedge between his existence in Christ and his Jewish life under the law.

Without question, the idea that Jesus was the Messiah was flatly rejected by most Jews. Paul himself ran into conflict with the synagogue, and he dismisses as "dung" his considerable achievements under the law (*skybalon,* Phil. 3:8). He speaks with remorse of his persecution of the church before he reversed himself to become its foremost advocate. And finally, he speaks movingly of the revelation of God's righteousness "apart from law" (Rom. 3:21). All of this seems to argue for a radical discontinuity between Paul the Christian and Paul the Jew.

A growing number of scholars, however, question this interpretation. They point out that Paul nowhere suggests either that he found the law intolerable or that he felt conscience-stricken because his feverish attempts to keep it had failed. On the contrary, in Philippians 3:6 Paul says he was "under the law blameless." Even Romans 8:2 should not be read to mean that the two eras are incompatible. There he mentions two laws: "the law of the Spirit of life in Christ Jesus has set me free from the law of sin and death." Whatever life in the Spirit was for Paul, it was not lawlessness. Was Paul here, like Jeremiah, suggesting that the gap between God's requirement (Mosaic Law) and the human response had been overcome? If so, he may not be repudiating the law but rather announcing the day of the Lord when the gulf that existed in Torah between God's speaking and human hearing was overcome. Jeremiah heard God say, "I will put my law within them, and I will write it upon their hearts" (Jer. 31:33). Jeremiah did not mean that God's Torah would be repudiated, but that human resistance to the divine will would end. Evidently Paul believed that the time had arrived: God would etch the law of the Spirit on the human heart, and human stubbornness before God's will would vanish.

It is also misleading, if not erroneous, to suggest that Paul rejected his past when he became an apostle. Paul often speaks positively of his Jewish past (Rom. 9:4–5). And very often he speaks of the coming of the Messiah as the fulfillment of God's promise to the Jews. He quotes from the prophets who anticipated God's new day in Jesus, and he believes that salvation not only emerged from the Jews but will also embrace them at the end of history (Romans 11).

In addition, Paul's eschatology closely resembles that found in Jewish apocalyptic literature. In his eager waiting for God's final visitation as well as in the way he pictures the end, Paul is at one with much of first-century Judaism. The difference between them is found in Paul's belief that the end was already beginning—had been begun by Jesus. According to Jewish apocalypticism, God's cosmic clock read five minutes before midnight; for Paul the first bong of the midnight hour had sounded. We see, therefore, that although there were differences between the views of Paul and those of his Jewish contemporaries, the distinction was not total. Even Paul's reference to his achievements under the law as "refuse" (Phil. 3:8) was not a repudiation of his past but a revaluation of that past in light of his participation in the new age of Christ.

Almost daily we are made painfully aware of the separation of Judaism and Christianity. History books are replete with bitter and shameful strife between Jews and Christians. Synagogue members go to their worship on Friday night and Saturday; Christians gather on Sunday. Time and again ugly acts of anti-Semitism have stained human hands and aggravated the old divisions. All of our history and much of our present experience underscores the difference between these sister faiths. We should be careful, however, when we project patterns we take for granted back onto the time of Paul. Nowhere does Paul speak of

Christianity as an entity separate from Judaism. Everywhere he envisions his Gentile mission as a part of God's promise to Israel to include all peoples in a final redeemed human family. As we read the letters of Paul, therefore, let us guard against the too-common assumption that Paul rejected the tradition he once loved.

Not only does this dislocation of Paul from his background do violence to his thought, it also distorts our picture of first-century Jewish faith.

A rather poor likeness of first-century Judaism has often been drawn by merely reversing everything Paul says about his life in Christ. Paul's gospel was joyful so Judaism is depicted as joyless. Paul felt free from sin and death through grace; Jews, so it was said, were yoked by the law to sin, by sin to death. The God of Paul appears as a God of grace; the God of the Jews is cast as a severe taskmaster. Paul was self-giving; the Jews were self-seeking. As official warders of the law, the Jews became insufferable religious snobs. If they kept the law's letter, they ignored its spirit and were self-righteous hypocrites. And if they did not keep its letter, they were engulfed in a fog of guilt and anxiety. The more we know about first-century Judaism the better we realize that the reconstruction above is an absurd parody. Through the scrolls left by the Qumran community near the Dead Sea, we have gained a better understanding of both the variety and the nature of first-century Hebraic life and thought. The community attended to God's law, but it knew itself also as the beneficiary of God's grace. One faithful member says, "If I stagger, God's mercies are my salvation forever; and if I stumble because of the sin of the flesh, my justification is in the righteousness of God" (from *The Scroll of the Rule* 11:12).[21] The community opposed insincerity and hypocrisy. Their piety, moreover, although intense was hardly joyless. We see, therefore, that the Judaism invoked to show Paul to greatest advantage bears little resemblance to the Judaism that was.

Reading Paul by the light of the total reversals in Luther and Augustine at their conversion not only sets Paul adrift from his moorings in Judaism, but it also tends to focus our attention too narrowly on the salvation of the individual. With our attention riveted to this motif, as important as it is, we sometimes neglect other emphases in the letters. Most scholars would readily agree that Paul's theology is multidimensional. Disagreement exists, however, about what is the prevailing motif in that theology. Scholarly opinion has fluctuated from the view that Paul's message was individualistic to the core, to the belief his gospel was communal throughout. One focuses on the individual; the other encompasses the whole range of salvation history. Perhaps the works of Rudolf Bultmann and Johannes Munck best pose these alternatives for us.

Rudolf Bultmann, possibly the most influential biblical scholar of our century, found the key to Paul's theology in his understanding of the human.[22] In formulating Paul's anthropology, Bultmann relies for his insight and categories mainly on existentialist thought. Paul was aware, he believed, of the one question that forces itself on all humanity: Can a person be open to the future that stretches out ahead? Each person yearns to be free enough to be open and honest in each encounter. In spite of this longing for truth in the inward being, however, each person feels that his or her life lacks the integrity, authenticity, and fulfillment that belong to its true nature. The creature begins, therefore, with a deep sense of loss. Each person wants authentic existence, but each refuses to believe that such comes only as a gift from God—as a reprieve from self. Each tries to secure authentic life by human efforts, not realizing that self-assertiveness always ends in self-deception and doubt.

The self-reliant spirit manifests itself in many ways, religious as well as secular. To attain to oneness with the cosmos, some perform sedulous religious duties—only to become self-righteous and thus divided from all things. Others labor for recognition, cash, authority, children—only to find that in truth they are working solely against the suspicion of personal inadequacy. One's best efforts fail to secure what one wants, precisely because they are efforts—premeditated and self-conscious. The authentic existence one searches for is as elusive as the end of a rainbow. Yet each is also unable to accept life from God because God is out of one's control. To enjoy freedom the individual would have to surrender autonomy, but that risk is too great. Fear and anxiety attend this fruitless search. The more insecure a person is, the more one turns in on himself or herself; the more one turns in on the self, the more insecure one is. Humanity is trapped, unable to break out of this vicious circle.

This tangled web over the human is cut only through the proclamation of the word of God—or rather, the question of God. God's grace comes to the individual, but not to support efforts at regularizing the future; God's grace comes as a question: "Will you surrender, utterly surrender, to God's dealing?"[23] Through the acceptance of grace, one rests secure in the knowledge that one is loved. Thus he or she is released from self-preoccupation to be open to the future. Now one is free, risk is possible, anxiety is overcome. But this authentic existence is not realized once and for all; it must be continually re-presented in the question of God and the renewed acceptance by humanity.

It is clear from this summary that Bultmann sees salvation for the individual as the governing theme of Paul's theology. Understandably, therefore, Bultmann takes scant notice of the broad historical themes in Paul's letters (e.g., Romans 9–11). For this brilliant scholar, decisive history is not world history but the experience of each person.

Against Bultmann's understanding of Paul stands the work of Johannes Munck, *Paul and the Salvation of Mankind* (Richmond: John

Knox Press, 1959). The book opens with a study of Paul's Damascus Road experience. In the traditional view that experience is seen as a release from pent-up frustrations accumulated through Paul's repeated, unsuccessful attempts to keep the law and from guilt heaped up by his compulsive hatred and fanatical persecution of innocent Christians. Like a boil opening to release its poison, so this theory goes, through conversion Paul's life was cleansed of its gangrenous infection. Munck objects that neither in Acts nor in Paul's own letters is there a hint that Paul's preconversion history groaned under any such heavy psychological burden. Instead, Munck argues, Paul's Damascus experience conforms rather closely to the pattern of Old Testament prophetic calls. Paul, like Jeremiah and Isaiah, says that God "set me apart before I was born" (Gal. 1:15; see also Rom. 1:1; Isa. 49:1; Jer. 1:5). In Galatians 1:15–16, as also in Isaiah and Jeremiah, the call "from the womb" was linked with the mission to the Gentiles. Just as the prophets served under constraint, so Paul was under compulsion to fulfill Christ's commission. According to Munck, these similarities place Paul among the ranks of the prophets. And like those prophets, he had a peculiar role to play in the history of God's people. Unlike the Old Testament prophets, however, Paul's role was to be acted out during the final scene in God's historical drama. In fact, as the apostle to the Gentiles, Paul was assigned the lead role before the curtain was to fall. The end of the age was delayed, Paul believed, so that the Gentiles could be brought into the community of God's people. In other words, the end of the world stood waiting for the completion of Paul's mission.

Romans 9–11 assumes pivotal significance for Munck's thesis. In traditional Jewry the question was often asked, "What is holding back the coming of the Messiah?" The usual answer was that only when Israel is converted can the messianic age come. Paul's mission to the Gentiles enunciated in Romans 9–11, therefore, becomes essential for the success of God's plan. The strategy was to use the conversion of the Gentiles to arouse jealousy in the Jews and thus lead them to salvation. Paul's conviction that his role was crucial for the redemption of all humankind informed everything he did.

Even the offering that Paul collected for the "poor among the saints" in Jerusalem Munck fits neatly into this scheme. This act, like the prophetic signs of old, was pregnant with meaning. From Old Testament prophecy, Israel expected that in the messianic age Gentiles would stream to Jerusalem bearing tribute. Therefore, when Paul, along with a delegation from the Gentile churches, brought the offering up to Jerusalem, the act took on powerful eschatological significance. It was designed to announce the arrival of the messianic age to all Jews.

In this brief résumé of Munck's thesis we have passed over many stimulating features of his work. Even this short summary, however, shows where he and Bultmann differ. Where for Bultmann the domi-

nant theme in Paul is the salvation of the individual, for Munck everything in Paul is subordinated to the eschatological mission. The purpose
of this mission was not the conversion of the individual but the reas-
sertion of God's dominion over the entire creation. Whatever the
blemishes of his work (and there are many),[24] Munck has at least taught
us the hazard of melting Paul's thought down into a single element—a
singular preoccupation with the individual and his or her salvation.[25]
Perhaps a swing to the opposite extreme is equally unwise. Paul is
concerned for the salvation of the individual (1 Cor. 5:5) but never in
isolation from wider historical and corporate concerns. Paul's theology
does bracket themes as large as the cosmos itself (Rom. 8:19ff.), but the
individual is not thereby reduced to the status of an insect. Given our
emphasis today on the gospel as a resource for the "inner life," and
given our tendency to view matters of faith as private affairs, it is no
accident that we look for the individual emphasis in most things we
read. I do not wish to speak against the dignity or worth of the individual, but it must be said that such an emphasis if taken alone stands in
real tension with the outlook of Paul. God's call, for Paul, is more than
a summons to enjoy salvation; it is an invitation to participate in a
divine happening that is bigger than oneself—God's salvation of the
entire world—human and nonhuman. It is well to remember that for
the apostle there was simply no separation between individual fulfillment and group participation. To be in the community of God's people
was in and of itself fulfillment on the highest level. So although in a
certain sense Paul's message was personal, it was never private.

5. Paul and Women

Paul, according to George Bernard Shaw, is "the eternal enemy of
Woman."[26] In Shaw's view, Paul insisted that the wife "should be
rather a slave than a partner, her real function being, not to engage a
man's love and loyalty, but on the contrary to release them for God by
relieving the man of all preoccupation with sex just as in her capacity
of housekeeper and cook she relieves his preoccupation with hunger."[27]
The prevailing popular view of Paul suggests that his view of woman
was, to say the least, patronizing. For even while urging mutual love
and respect between husband and wife, he commanded the woman to
be submissive to her husband (Eph. 5:21ff.), and he officially endorsed
the subordination of women by forbidding them to exercise authority
over men (1 Tim. 2:12). Women are to fulfill the divine purpose by
having children (1 Tim. 2:15). And did not Paul relegate women to a
second-class citizenship when he called on them to be silent in the
churches (1 Cor. 14:34)? Paul's own decision for celibacy, and his
admonition to others to follow his example (1 Cor. 7:7), lend credibility
to this unflattering picture.

Robin Scroggs, a respected Pauline scholar, issued a caveat against this popular caricature.[28] He correctly noted that the primary support for the view of Paul as a male chauvinist comes from deutero-Pauline materials (1 and 2 Timothy, Ephesians, and Colossians). He joined other scholars in arguing that 1 Corinthians 14:33b–36 ("women should keep silence in the churches") was inserted by a later hand to bring 1 Corinthians into conformity with the outlook of the deutero-Paulines.[29] Indeed, Paul assumes elsewhere that women are to be vocal participants in church (1 Cor. 11:5). Moreover, as Scroggs is aware, 1 Corinthians 7:1 ("It is well for a man not to touch a woman") was probably not Paul's view but a slogan of the Corinthian church.[30] And even if it was Paul's view, it expresses his response to an emergency rather than his disdain for women. It was common in Jewish circles to suspend normal activities in times of great crisis (e.g., during holy war men gave up not only sex but also business dealings).

First Corinthians 11:2–16 poses more of a problem, however. There Paul seems to locate woman in an inferior position in the hierarchy of creation. God is the head of Christ, Christ is the head of man, man is the head of woman. Taking for granted that Christ was pre-existent and therefore active in the creation of the world, Paul speaks of Christ as the head (i.e., source) of man even as man was the source of woman (via the rib). Scroggs argues that Paul is here concerned with origins, not with superiority or inferiority. And Paul stresses different origins, says Scroggs, to show that it has been God's plan since the creation to keep men and women distinct, and that distinction must be maintained. In other words, the apostle is responding to what he judges as a scandalous view—that in Christ all distinctions disappear, even those between male and female.

Scroggs concludes that there is no substance to the charge that Paul was an "eternal enemy" of women. On the contrary, he finds support in the letters for an enlightened or even liberationist view. Scroggs argues that Paul "proclaimed the complete equality within the community of all people and groups. Distinctions between groups remain. Values and roles built upon such distinctions are destroyed. Every human being is equal before God in Christ and thus before each other."[31] Scroggs also notes that Paul lists women among his co-workers and alludes to a number of women who are active (presumably as leaders) in the church.[32]

Many scholars are delighted that Professor Scroggs was willing to step forward and challenge the popular and persistent notion of Paul's view of women. Few would quarrel with either the spirit or substance of his defense, for Paul is nowhere overtly hostile to women. Nevertheless, Scroggs's argument that Paul was a women's liberationist has raised some eyebrows.

Professor Elaine Pagels has expressed reservations about Scroggs's argument.[33] Although Paul can say that slaves are free in Christ, he quite obviously does not challenge the institution of slavery.[34] In a similar way, Paul's affirmation that women are equal does not mean he is challenging "the social structures that perpetuate their present subordination."[35] Professor Pagels remains unconvinced by Scroggs's interpretation of 1 Corinthians 11:2–16, an admittedly difficult passage. In his statement that Christ is the source of man and man the source of woman, Paul does seem to fall back on the natural order to argue for the subordination of women.[36] Especially troublesome is Paul's statement in 11:7 that man is the glory of God while woman is the glory of man. Pagels believes Paul views "certain incidents or practices in the Corinthian community—provoked by the presence of unveiled women believers—to be disorderly or even scandalous,"[37] and that by appealing to the primeval—i.e., divine—order, he hopes to restrict women's activity and thus restore order. Professor Pagels does not mention Paul's corrections of male conduct—these would seem to make men also responsible for the restoration of order (11:4, 7).

As the scholarly debate over Paul's view of women continues, much remains unresolved. But the discussion has produced some positive fruit. The conventional picture of Paul as a culture-bound male chauvinist has collapsed under close investigation. In many ways Paul's views contradict those of his Jewish background. He plainly expects that women will take an active role in the worship and witness of the church. Moreover, the evenhanded way that Paul addresses both men and women in 1 Corinthians 7 is instructive. This equal share of responsibility apportioned to each suggests at least approximate equality in the partnership. That in itself is somewhat revolutionary. And Professor David Daube has shown that Paul's expectation that a woman (in Christ) could consecrate her marriage with an unbelieving husband has no Jewish precedent (see 1 Cor. 7:14).[38] According to Jewish tradition, it was the male and only the male who consecrated the marriage. However murky 1 Corinthians 11:2–16 may appear, it seems clear that Paul lays a heavy burden on male and female to preserve the order of the church. Some degree of subordination of woman, however, may be taken for granted (especially in 11:7), but it is often overlooked that Paul's main point is the distinction between the sexes, not the dominance of one over the other.

In any case Scroggs and Pagels would agree that it is unfair to criticize Paul for not challenging the structures of discrimination against women. While it is true that Paul's gospel makes many structures seem unjust, it does not overtly call for their abolition. We cannot conclude from this that Paul either did or did not approve of such social practices. Paul may simply have found it unnecessary to challenge authoritarian structures because he thought they would soon be gone.

In 1 Corinthians 7:31 he expressly encourages his readers to "deal with the world as though they had no dealings with it. For the form of this world is passing away."

It is likely that Paul was neither a chauvinist nor a liberationist but something in between. The evidence is contradictory. One cannot dismiss Paul's evenhanded treatment of men and women, his references to women as his co-workers, or his assumption that women would actively participate in church worship. At the same time, some degree of subordination seems to be taken for granted in Paul's statement that man is "the image and glory of God; but woman is the glory of man" (1 Cor. 11:7). It would be remarkable indeed if Paul did not reflect some of the prejudice, superstition, and bias of his own time. The question is, how much should we worry about Paul's cultural views? Does his unconsidered prejudice against women vitiate his views on Jesus, and on other important questions of life? Theologians have long argued that the gospel is greater than any particular witness to it. (Perhaps that is why we retain the versions of Matthew, Mark, Luke, and John rather than one work entitled "The Gospel.") Moreover, Paul's letters address a rather limited set of circumstances. It seems unfair to denounce him for not anticipating and addressing concerns that have only recently been raised to a high level of consciousness. This is not to say, however, that we can appeal to Paul's apparent acceptance of discrimination in his day to justify discrimination in our own. It is the gospel that Paul preaches rather than his limited application and witness to it that is definitive for our time. And that gospel has far-reaching implications for the full and equal realization of all human life.

We have sketched only broad contours in the history of interpretation of Paul. Hundreds of variations could be written on the five positions outlined here. Someone is bound to ask, Is Paul worth all this attention? Millions of hours of devoted labor have gone into the copying, translation, study, and interpretation of his letters. Tons and tons of paper and thousands of barrels of ink have gone into books and articles about him and his writings. Vast material resources have gone into great church buildings that bear his name, and the influence he exerted on key individuals like Augustine, Luther, Wesley, and others have had enormous historical consequences. One can easily imagine that Paul would be embarrassed by all this attention and surprised if not horrified that his personal letters were canonized as scripture. And yet the labors on his letters and the place they assume in the New Testament seem wholly justified. For he raised hard questions that the church had to face. And he dealt with real issues most of which still lie near the heart of humankind. Does history have a purpose? Can a broken and alienated world be reconciled? What is the nature of the human? Can the whole human and nonhuman world be saved from its futility and grief? How can one live with partialities— partial sight, partial knowing, and partial being? And what does it mean to be alive "in Christ" and have Christ alive in oneself in an age of disbelief?

Notes

Introduction

1. Richard Rubenstein, *My Brother Paul* (New York: Harper & Row, 1972), pp. 6ff.

Chapter 1:
Paul and His World

1. Because of Paul's gravitation toward Damascus at critical times, some scholars believe that city was Paul's boyhood home. They note that nowhere in the undisputed letters does Paul refer to Tarsus, which seems strange if he was raised there. However, Luke's reference to Paul's origin in Tarsus (Acts 9:11; 21:39) seems credible because it could not conceivably serve Luke's theological interests.

2. This has been proven by J. A. L. Lee in his *LXX, A Lexical Study of the Septuagint Version of the Pentateuch* (Chico, Calif.: Scholars Press, 1983).

3. For this important story, see *The Letter of Aristeas,* found in *The Old Testament Pseudepigrapha,* ed. James H. Charlesworth (Garden City, N.Y.: Doubleday & Co., 1985), 2:7–34.

4. Charlesworth, *The Old Testament Pseudepigrapha,* 2:177–201.

5. Ibid., 2:831–842.

6. See C. H. Dodd, *The Bible and the Greeks* (London: Hodder & Stoughton, 1935), pp. 65–69.

7. Richard B. Hays, *Echoes of Scripture in the Letters of Paul* (New Haven, Conn.: Yale University Press, 1989), has drawn attention to the dynamic of this intertextual relationship.

8. In adopting and using this tradition, we must assume Paul shares the views expressed here even if he did not author the passage.

9. For a survey of the literature, see Hans Dieter Betz, *Galatians: A Commentary on Paul's Letter to the Churches in Galatia* (Philadelphia: Fortress Press, 1979), pp. 281–283.

10. For other lists in the Pauline letters see Rom. 1:29–31; 13:13; 1 Cor. 5:10–11; 6:9–10; 2 Cor. 12:20–21, etc.

11. First noted by Abraham J. Malherbe, " 'Gentle as a Nurse' The Cynic Background to I Thess. ii," *Novum Testamentum* 12 (1970): 203–217.

12. See especially Victor C. Pfitzner, *Paul and the Agon Motif: Traditional Athletic Imagery in the Pauline Literature* (New York: Humanities Press, 1967).

13. Not "true circumcision" as in the RSV.

14. Rudolf Bultmann, *Der Stil der paulinischen Predigt und die kynisch-stoische Diatribe* (Göttingen: Vandenhoeck & Ruprecht, 1910).

15. See Stanley K. Stowers, *The Diatribe and Paul's Letter to the Romans* (Chico, Calif.: Scholars Press, 1981), for an excellent discussion.

16. Betz, *Galatians.*

17. See ibid., pp. 16–23, for the full development of this outline.

18. See, for example, Hans Hübner's review of Betz's commentary on Galatians, "Der Galaterbrief und das Verhältnis von antiker Rhetorik und Epistolographie," *Theologische Literaturzeitung* 109 (1984): 241–250.

19. Wilhelm Wuellner, "Where Is Rhetorical Criticism Taking Us?" *Catholic Biblical Quarterly* 49 (1987): 448–463, offers a positive assessment of this approach and a helpful bibliography.

20. Here I am following Johannes Munck, *Paul and the Salvation of Mankind,* trans. Frank Clarke (Richmond: John Knox Press, 1959).

21. Helmut Koester, *Introduction to the New Testament, History, Culture, and Religion of the Hellenistic Age* (Philadelphia: Fortress Press, 1982), 1:170.

22. Martin P. Nilsson, *Greek Piety* (Oxford: Clarendon Press, 1948), p. 188.

23. Gilbert Murray, *Five Stages of Greek Religion* (Garden City, N.Y.: Doubleday & Co., 1955), p. 4.

24. It is inappropriate to call these expressions *"new* religious movements" as Koester suggests, because a religion like the Isis-Osiris cult comes from the very dawn of Egyptian history, predating Greek religions by a millennium or more. A vast literature on the mystery religions is available. One of the best of all secondary sources is Walter Burkert's *Ancient Mystery Cults* (Cambridge, Mass.: Harvard University Press, 1987).

25. The use of the term "mystery religion," though problematic, is used here for the sake of convenience. No definition of the mysteries is without objection. For example, if one defines the mysteries as religions of secret rites, one can point to Christianity and the cult of Dionysus with public rites and festivals. If one uses the term to refer to religions whose rites brought its devotees into a mystical union with the god, one may note the Christian union with Jesus but not God. If one thinks of the mysteries as those promising to their initiates esoteric wisdom that sets them apart from the masses, and offering a new life or conversion that transcends human limit, mortality, or culpability, then the definition is so broad that it fits almost all religious movements and is, therefore, useless. Here we accept the self-description of the movements themselves—that is, as those that are privy to the divine mysteries, and as such can offer deliverance from this mortal web of fate, matter, and mortality.

26. See Frederick C. Grant, ed., *Ancient Roman Religion* (New York: Bobbs-Merrill Co., 1957), p. xxiv. For materials ascribed to the mystery religions see Charles K. Barrett, ed., *The New Testament Background: Selected Documents* (New York: Macmillan Co., 1957), pp. 92–104.

27. Rudolf Bultmann, *Primitive Christianity in Its Contemporary Setting,* trans. R. H. Fuller (New York: World Publishing Co., 1947), p. 159.

28. Cicero, *De leg.* 2.38.

29. An old but still highly instructive work on Egyptian religion is Henri Frankfort's *Ancient Egyptian Religion* (New York: Columbia University Press, 1948). On Isis and Osiris see esp. pp. 104–123.

30. Ibid., p. 106.

31. See Koester, *Introduction to the New Testament,* p. 191.

32. See Apuleius, *Metamorphoses* 11.5.1.

33. Martin P. Nilsson, *The Dionysiac Mysteries of the Hellenistic Roman Age* (Lund: C. W. K. Gleerup, 1957), followed by Koester, traces Dionysus's origins back to Thrace, south of the River Danube, and Phrygia of northwest Asia Minor. Walter Friedrich Otto, *Dionysus, Myth and Cult* (Bloomington, Ind.: Indiana University Press, 1965), p. 58, disputes Nilsson's claim, arguing that Dionysus was always a native of Greece.

34. See Albert Henrichs, "Greek and Roman Glimpses of Dionysos," in Caroline Houser, *Dionysos and His Circle, Ancient Through Modern* (Cambridge, Mass.: Fogg Art Museum, Harvard University, 1979), p. 6.

35. Nilsson, *The Dionysiac Mysteries,* provides a useful summary of the Dionysiac mystery religion, pp. 143–147; however, he overemphasizes its elitist appeal primarily to rich, cultured conservatives. Caroline Houser's position is more convincing.

36. Caroline Houser, "Changing Views of Dionysos," in idem, ed., *Dionysos and His Circle, Ancient Through Modern,* p. 24.

37. *Inscriptiones Graecae* (Berlin, 1902), vol. 4, no. 951, 11.36–41, cited in Frederick C. Grant, ed., *Hellenistic Religions: The Age of Syncretism* (New York: Liberal Arts Press, 1953), p. 57, but also see pp. 49–59. See also Howard C. Kee, *Medicine, Miracle and Magic in New Testament Times* (Cambridge, Mass.: Harvard University Press, 1986), and E. J. and L. Edelstein, *Asclepius: A Collection and Interpretation of the Testimonies,* 2 vols. (Baltimore: Johns Hopkins Press, 1945).

38. See Edwyn Bevan, *Stoics and Sceptics* (Oxford: Clarendon Press, 1913), p. 41.

39. As cited in Edward Vernon Arnold, *Roman Stoicism* (Freeport, N.Y.: Books for Libraries, 1971), p. 86.

40. Bultmann, *Primitive Christianity,* p. 159.

41. See the discussion of "Methods of Argumentation," above.

42. Diogenes Laertius, "Diogenes," in idem, *Lives of Eminent Philosophers,* trans. R. D. Hicks (London: William Heinemann, 1925), 4.39.

43. Ibid., 6.41.

44. Seneca, *Ad Lucilium Epistulae Morales,* trans. Richard M. Gummere, Loeb Classical Library (Cambridge, Mass.: Harvard University Press, 1979), V, 21.

45. Hans Dieter Betz, *Der Apostel Paulus und die sokratische Tradition* (Tübingen: J. C. B. Mohr [Paul Siebeck], 1972), p. 98.

46. Pythagoras lived and taught in the sixth century B.C.E. Epicureanism and the Imperial cult, while they were important features of the landscape, are not discussed here because their influence on Paul's hearers was minimal.

47. This is not to dispute the views of Tarn and Dodds that astrology came from the East. Not its origin but its manifestation in Greece is what concerns us here.

48. Walter Burkert, *Lore and Science in Ancient Pythagoreanism,* trans. Edwin L. Minar, Jr. (Cambridge, Mass.: Harvard University Press, 1972), p. 482.

49. Although this phrase was meant to describe Gnosticism and its understanding of the cosmos, it could equally well be used to describe the developing mood of first-century Hellenism. Hans Jonas, *The Gnostic Religion: The Message of the Alien God and the Beginnings of Christianity,* 2nd ed. (Boston: Beacon Press, 1963), p. 328.

50. F. E. Peters, *The Harvest of Hellenism* (New York: Simon & Schuster, 1971), p. 431; H. J. Leon, *The Jews of Ancient Rome* (Philadelphia: Jewish Publication Society of America, 1961), pp. 243–257, 350–356; Victor Tcherikover, *Hellenistic Civilization and the Jews,* trans. S. Applebaum (New York: Atheneum Press, 1970), pp. 301–308.

51. Pliny, *Natural History,* trans. Harris Rackham, Loeb Classical Library (Cambridge, Mass.: Harvard University Press, 1938), 2.5.22.

52. Philostratus, *The Life of Apollonius of Tyana,* trans. F. C. Conybeare, Loeb Classical Library (Cambridge, Mass.: Harvard University Press, 1960). E. R. Dodds, *The Greeks and the Irrational* (Boston: Beacon Press, 1951), pp. 135–146, shows how interest grew in the philosophers as workers of miracles. David L. Tiede, *The Charismatic Figure as Miracle Worker* (Missoula, Mont.: Society of Biblical Literature, 1972), pp. 16ff., sees real tension between those traditions that view Pythagoras as a divine philosopher and those that remember him as a miracle worker. Tiede is right, of course, but it appears that the miracle worker view was predominant in the first century.

53. Philostratus, *Life of Apollonius* 8.7, vol. II, p. 315.

54. See Holger Thesleff, *An Introduction to the Pythagorean Writings of the Hellenistic Period* (Abo [Turku], Finland: Abo Akademi, 1961).

55. A translation of most of these documents is available in *The Nag Hammadi Library,* ed. James M. Robinson (San Francisco: Harper & Row, 1977). For an older account now in need of some correction, see the description by Hans Jonas, *The Gnostic Religion.*

56. See Elaine Pagels, *The Gnostic Paul: Gnostic Exegesis of the Pauline Letters* (Philadelphia: Fortress Press, 1975).

57. *Sympatheia* stands behind our word *sympathy,* meaning to suffer with

someone. Here the word means to feel with or acknowledge kinship or relationship to all things so that what affects one part affects all of creation.

58. John Knox, *Chapters in a Life of Paul* (Nashville: Abingdon Press,
1950), ch. 2.

59. In the Gospel of Matthew, for instance, the Pharisees appear as "vipers"
(3:7; 12:34; 23:33), "hypocrites" (23:27), "blind guides" (23:16), keepers of the
minutiae of the law who neglect "justice and mercy and faith" (23:23), murder-
ers of the prophets (23:30), and "whitewashed tombs" (23:27).

60. Jacob Neusner, *From Politics to Piety: The Emergence of Pharisaic
Judaism* (Englewood Cliffs, N.J.: Prentice-Hall, 1973), p. 89. Neusner's writings have totally altered our former caricatures of Pharisaism.

61. Josephus, *The Jewish War,* trans. H. St. J. Thackeray (Cambridge,
Mass.: Harvard University Press, 1976) 2.162–63, pp. 385, 387.

62. Josephus, *Antiquities,* trans. R. Marcus (Cambridge, Mass.: Harvard
University Press, 1957), 13.171–173, pp. 311, 313.

63. Ellis Rivkin, *A Hidden Revolution: The Pharisees' Search for the Kingdom Within* (Nashville: Abingdon Press, 1978), pp. 72–75, 242.

64. Joachim Jeremias, "Paulus als Hillelit," in *Neotestamentica et Semitica:
Studies in Honour of Principal Matthew Black,* ed. Edward Earle Ellis and
Max Wilcox (Edinburgh: T. & T. Clark, 1969), pp. 88–94. Cf. the classic work
of Joseph Bonsirven, *Exégèse rabbinique et exégèse paulienne* (Paris: Beauchesne, 1939).

65. For a list of passages, see my *Judgement in the Community: A Study of
the Relationship Between Eschatology and Ecclesiology in Paul* (Leiden: E. J.
Brill, 1972), pp. 153–154.

66. See Jeremias, "Paulus als Hillelit" (cited above), as well as Otto Michel,
Paulus und seine Bibel (Gütersloh: C. Bertelsmann, 1929).

67. In the view of Jeremias, "Paulus als Hillelit," p. 93, the distinction drawn
between general and specific commandments seen in Romans 13:9 reflects
Paul's use of the fifth rule of Hillel. It is more likely, however, that the
distinction between the "love commandment" and the Ten Commandments
comes from early church tradition.

68. Our word "eschatology" comes from two Greek words *(eschaton* and
logos), which when taken together mean literally "thought about the end." The
word as it is used by biblical critics has come to denote God's decisive or final
act in history. Apocalyptic literature is a highly imaginative literary account
of God's revelation. In fact, the noun "apocalypticism" comes from the Greek
word *apokalypsis,* which means "revelation." Usually apocalypticism is more
explosive than other eschatological pronouncements. Jesus' proclamation that
the kingdom of God is at hand is eschatological. The vision of the beasts, fire,
and astral pyrotechnics in the book of Revelation is apocalypticism. At the risk
of oversimplification, we could say that all apocalyptic literature is eschatological (dealing with the end), not all eschatological materials are apocalyptic. The
term, eschatology, therefore, is the more general term. For a good discussion
of apocalypticism, see the *Interpreter's Dictionary of the Bible* (Nashville:

Abingdon Press, 1962), 1:157–161. A vast literature on apocalyptic thinking is available. A helpful summary of the setting and message of many apocalyptic writings is found in John J. Collins, *The Apocalyptic Imagination, An Introduction to the Jewish Matrix of Christianity* (New York: Crossroad, 1984). For an outline of major issues involved in the interpretation of apocalypticism and a useful proposal to guide future interpretation, see Klaus Koch, *The Rediscovery of Apocalyptic* (Naperville, Ill.: Alec R. Allenson, 1970). A collection of useful essays on the nature, meaning, and function of apocalypticism is available in *Visionaries and Their Apocalypses,* ed. Paul D. Hanson (Philadelphia: Fortress Press, 1983).

69. Johannes Munck, *Paul and the Salvation of Mankind,* trans. Frank Clarke (Richmond: John Knox Press, 1959).

70. Hans Joachim Schoeps, *Paul: The Theology of the Apostle in the Light of Jewish Religious History,* trans. Harold Knight (Philadelphia: Westminster Press, 1961), p. 38.

71. See Victor Tcherikover, *Hellenistic Civilization and the Jews,* pp. 349ff. and 303ff.

72. Edwin R. Goodenough, *Jewish Symbols in the Greco-Roman Period* (New York: Pantheon Books, 1953), 1:61ff.

73. W. D. Davies, "Paul and the Dead Sea Scrolls: Flesh and Spirit," in *The Scrolls and the New Testament,* ed. Krister Stendahl (New York: Harper & Brothers, 1957), p. 157.

74. Martin Hengel, *Judentum und Hellenismus* (Tübingen: J. C. B. Mohr [Paul Siebeck], 1969), esp. pp. 458–463. English translation: *Judaism and Hellenism* (Philadelphia: Fortress Press, 1974).

75. On this point Willem C. van Unnik is swimming against the stream when he juxtaposes Tarsus, "a typically Hellenistic city . . . the intellectual centre of a flourishing Stoic School," and Jerusalem, in which "syncretism secured no footing . . . and Hellenistic culture could force a way in only with difficulty and only very superficially" (*Tarsus or Jerusalem: The City of Paul's Youth* [London: Epworth Press, 1962], pp. 3–4). Van Unnik then argues that although Paul was born in Tarsus he was reared in Jerusalem where he received rabbinic training (p. 52).

76. See Ralph Philip Martin, *Carmen Christi: Philippians ii.5–11 in Recent Interpretation and in the Setting of Early Christian Worship* (Cambridge: Cambridge University Press, 1967) for a dated but still excellent survey of the problems associated with this passage and the scholarly opinion.

77. Salo W. Baron, *A Social and Religious History of the Jews* (New York: Columbia University Press, 1952), 1:171.

78. Juvenal in his *Satires* 14, as cited by Baron, *History of the Jews,* 1:179.

79. Ibid., p. 173.

80. Ibid., p. 171.

81. Philo, *The Life of Moses* 2.27, trans. R. H. Colson, Loeb Classical Library (Cambridge, Mass.: Harvard University Press, 1959), vol. VI, p. 463.

82. Munck, *Paul and the Salvation of Mankind,* pp. 11–35.

83. If Paul has a favorite prophet, it would appear to be Isaiah, whom he cites or alludes to more than twice as often as to Jeremiah. See the discussion in my *Judgement in the Community* (Leiden: E. J. Brill, 1972), pp. 153ff.

84. See esp. Knox, *Chapters in a Life of Paul,* and more recently John C. Hurd, Jr., *The Origin of 1 Corinthians* (New York: Seabury Press, 1965).

Chapter 2:
The Anatomy of the Letters

1. For an up-to-date summary of the discussion so far, see William Doty, *Letters in Primitive Christianity* (Philadelphia: Fortress Press, 1973). An excellent survey of recent scholarship and the emerging consensus was done by John L. White, *Light from Ancient Letters* (Philadelphia: Fortress Press, 1986).

2. B. G. U. 27 (H. E. 1 13) as cited by Charles K. Barrett, *New Testament Background: Selected Documents* (New York: Macmillan Co., 1957), p. 29.

3. Since there had been no attempt at this time to define life in Christ in terms of a system of belief, I realize the inappropriateness of the term "orthodoxy." I use it, nevertheless, to show that some distinctions were being made between "true" and "false" apostles, prophets, etc. Paul himself rejected certain rival teachings as false.

4. Paul Schubert, *The Form and Function of the Pauline Thanksgivings* (Berlin: Alfred Töpelmann, 1939).

5. See Erich Fascher, "Briefliteratur, urchristliche, formgeschichtlich," in *Die Religion in Geschichte und Gegenwart* (Tübingen: J. C. B. Mohr [Paul Siebeck], 3rd ed. 1957), 1:1412–1416.

6. The situation in 2 Corinthians is complicated by the likelihood that it is a composite of two or more letters. For a good discussion of the various possibilities, see the English summary of Günther Bornkamm's "Die Vorgeschichte des sogenannten Zweiten Korintherbriefs," in *New Testament Studies* 8 (1962): 258–264.

7. See Fascher, "Briefliteratur," loc. cit., 1:1413.

8. James M. Robinson, "The Historicality of Biblical Language," in *The Old Testament and Christian Faith,* ed. Bernhard W. Anderson (New York: Harper & Row, 1963), pp. 132–149.

9. Robert W. Funk, *Language, Hermeneutic, and Word of God* (New York: Harper & Row, 1966), p. 270. He thinks Galatians and Romans are exceptions to this rule for good and sufficient reasons.

10. Ibid., p. 268. Funk also believes that the location of the announcement of his travel plans at the end of the letter is explicable in terms of Paul's imminent visit to Rome and the purpose the letter serves in preparing for that visit.

11. Ibid., p. 249.

12. Martin Dibelius, *Der Brief des Jakobus,* 11th ed. (Göttingen: Vandenhoeck & Ruprecht, 1964), pp. 15ff.

13. For Hellenistic influence see Francis W. Beare, "The Epistle to the

Colossians, Introduction," in *The Interpreter's Bible,* ed. George A. Buttrick et al. (Nashville: Abingdon Press, 1955), 11:133ff. For Jewish and Hellenistic background, see Siegfried Wibbing, *Die Tugend- und Lasterkataloge in Neuen Testament* (Berlin: Alfred Töpelmann, 1959).

14. David G. Bradley, "The Topos as a Form in the Pauline Paraenesis," *Journal of Biblical Literature* 72 (1953): 238–246.

15. Gordon Wiles, *Paul's Intercessory Prayers* (Cambridge: Cambridge University Press, 1973); William Doty, *Letters in Primitive Christianity;* and my "1 Thessalonians 5:12–28: A Case Study," *Proceedings of the Society of Biblical Literature,* 108 (1972): 11, 367–383. See Harry Y. Gamble, *The Textual History of the Letter to the Romans* (Grand Rapids: Wm. B. Eerdmans Publishing Co., 1977).

16. *The Oxyrhynchus Papyri,* ed. Bernard Grenfell and Arthur Hunt (London: Oxford University Press, 1910), 3:261–262.

17. Heikki Koskenniemi, *Studien zur Idee und Phraseologie des griechischen Briefes bis 400 nach Christus* (Helsinki: Akateeminen Kirjakauppa, 1956), pp. 169–180.

18. See my *Judgement in the Community* (Leiden: E. J. Brill, 1972), pp. 145, 161.

19. Even in the letter to Philemon Paul addresses "the church in your house" (v. 2).

20. Victor Paul Furnish, *Theology and Ethics in Paul* (Nashville: Abingdon Press, 1968), p. 55.

21. See my *Judgement in the Community,* pp. 145ff., 161.

22. Paul sometimes dictates his letters to a secretary (amanuensis), appending a conclusion in his own hand. For instance, in Galatians 6:11ff., after he summarizes the central argument of the letter, he adds the conclusion with his "own hand." 1 Corinthians 16:21–24 likewise displays an autograph. Although the secretary identifies himself in Romans 16:22, doubt persists whether chapter 16 was part of the original letter (see ch. 4 below). On the strength of these two (or three) references it seems arbitrary to conclude that Paul dictated all his letters.

Chapter 3:
Traditions Behind the Letters

1. C. H. Dodd, *The Apostolic Preaching and Its Developments* (London: Hodder & Stoughton, 1936), pp. 21–23.

2. My translation follows Ernst Lohmeyer's arrangement in his *Der Brief an die Philipper* (Göttingen: Vandenhoeck & Ruprecht, 19th ed. 1954), pp. 96ff.

3. "Even death on a cross" was probably inserted here by Paul.

4. The Greek may suggest an unreal past condition, "even if I had known him (which of course I didn't). . . ." Since we cannot be sure that such was Paul's intention, the following discussion is necessary.

5. Victor Paul Furnish, *Theology and Ethics in Paul* (Nashville: Abingdon Press, 1968), p. 55.

6. Joseph F. Fitzmyer, *Pauline Theology: A Brief Sketch* (Englewood Cliffs, N.J.: Prentice-Hall, 1967), p. 13.

7. Lloyd Gaston, *No Stone on Another* (Leiden: E. J. Brill, 1970), pp. 407–408, makes a good case for the authenticity of this saying.

8. Martin Dibelius, *A Fresh Approach to the New Testament and Early Christian Literature* (New York: Charles Scribner's Sons, 1936), p. 143.

9. Dibelius correctly notes this in *A Fresh Approach,* pp. 143ff. W. D. Davies, *Paul and Rabbinic Judaism* (London: SPCK, 1948), p. 136, and Archibald M. Hunter, *Paul and His Predecessors* (London: SCM Press, 1961), pp. 52ff., go along with this view.

10. Robert W. Funk, *Language, Hermeneutic, and Word of God* (New York: Harper & Row, 1966), p. 270, and Furnish, *Theology and Ethics in Paul,* pp. 69ff., have forced a qualification of this earlier view.

11. Funk, *Language, Hermeneutic, and Word of God,* pp. 33–34.

12. Furnish, *Theology and Ethics in Paul,* pp. 84–85.

13. David G. Bradley, "The Topos as a Form in the Pauline Paraenesis," *Journal of Biblical Literature* 72 (1953): 246.

14. Of course those who argue for the authenticity of Colossians and Ephesians would add another category—rules for domestic life *(Haustafeln)*: for example, see Colossians 3:18–22: "Wives be subject to your husbands, as is fitting in the Lord. Husbands, love your wives, and do not be harsh with them. Children, obey your parents in everything, for this pleases the Lord. Fathers, do not provoke your children, lest they become discouraged. Slaves, obey in everything those who are your earthly masters" (see also Eph. 5:21–6:9). Such instruction is unparalleled in the undisputed Pauline letters.

Chapter 4:
The Letters as Conversations

1. Joseph F. Fitzmyer's *Pauline Theology: A Brief Sketch*, 2nd ed. (Englewood Cliffs, N.J.: Prentice-Hall, 1989), is excellent. Rudolf Bultmann's *Theology of the New Testament,* trans. Kendrick Grobel (New York: Charles Scribner's Sons, 1951), vol. I, is now almost a classic. Victor Paul Furnish, *Theology and Ethics in Paul* (Nashville: Abingdon Press, 1968), gives a good treatment of the major currents of Pauline interpretation.

2. Two discussions of Pauline chronology inform recent discussion of the dating of the letters. See Robert Jewett, *A Chronology of Paul's Life* (Philadelphia: Fortress Press, 1979), and Gerd Lüdemann, *Paulus, Der Heidenapostel,* vol. 1: *Studien zur Chronologie* (Göttingen: Vandenhoeck & Ruprecht, 1980). For the relevance of this discussion for our understanding of Paul's theology, see John C. Hurd, Jr., "Pauline Chronology and Pauline Theology," in William R. Farmer, ed., *Christian History and Interpretation* (Cambridge: Cambridge University Press, 1967), pp. 225–248.

3. Richard B. Hays, *The Faith of Jesus Christ* (Chico, Calif.: Scholars Press, 1983), has given an excellent discussion of the narrative structure of Paul's gospel behind its application in Galatians.

4. The Greek word *ataktoi* refers not just to the idle, as is often assumed, but to those who create disorder. See 1 Corinthians 14:40.

5. If the Thessalonians sent a letter to Paul with Timothy, it probably contained requests for guidance on three items: (1) Paul had taught the members of the church to love one another. But it became a hot question whether one could love those who, expecting the end, had stopped work. Does love require that some be free at the expense of others? (2) Some members of the congregation had died. They were sincere when they accepted the gospel; they seemed to be as strong in their faith as anyone else. Does their death mean they were judged unworthy to enter the kingdom of God? If they were judged unworthy, how will anyone be saved? (3) Paul had taught that the end was near, and the church had tried to prepare for it, but the end had not come. When would the end come?

Elsewhere (1 Corinthians) Paul uses the phrase "now, concerning" to identify topics one by one that the churches had asked guidance on. A similar phrase appears in 1 Thessalonians 4:9 and 4:13, and a variation of the phrase appears in 5:1, leading some scholars to conclude that indeed the Thessalonians did write Paul a letter.

6. A useful summary of recent secondary literature and discussion of issues may be found in Gordon D. Fee, *The First Epistle to the Corinthians* (Grand Rapids: Wm. B. Eerdmans Publishing Co., 1987).

7. Some see 2 Corinthians 6:14–7:1 as a fragment of the missing letter since it clearly is an insertion and since it deals with immorality—which Paul himself writes was the theme of his first letter (1 Cor. 5:9). Joseph A. Fitzmyer, however, has argued convincingly that the language is more characteristic of Qumran than of Paul: see his "Qumran and the Interpolated Paragraph in 2 Corinthians 6:14–7:1," *Catholic Biblical Quarterly* 23 (1961): 271ff.

8. In this discussion of 1 Corinthians, I am for the most part following John C. Hurd, Jr., *The Origin of 1 Corinthians* (New York: Seabury Press, 1965).

9. Note especially Luke 20:34–36, which seems to suggest the same view: "And Jesus said to them, 'Those who belong to this age marry and are given in marriage; but those who are considered worthy of a place in that age and in the resurrection from the dead neither marry nor are given in marriage. Indeed they cannot die anymore, because they are like angels and are children of God, being children of the resurrection' " (author's trans.).

10. Dieter Georgi's *Die Gegner des Paulus im 2. Korintherbrief: Studien zur religiösen Propaganda in der Spätantike* (Neukirchen-Vluyn: Neukirchener Verlag, 1964), English translation, *The Opponents of Paul in Second Corinthians* (Philadelphia: Fortress Press, 1985), has profoundly affected our understanding of the nature of this opposition.

11. Two recent commentaries are exceedingly useful in different ways: Victor Paul Furnish, *II Corinthians,* Anchor Bible (Garden City, N.Y.: Double-

day & Co., 1984), and Ralph P. Martin, *2 Corinthians* (Waco, Tex.: Word Books, 1986).

12. Because of the abrupt appearance of a new topic in the text, and because the command that women keep silent in church contradicts Paul's understanding of their role in 1 Corinthians 11:5, it is widely assumed that 1 Corinthians 14:33b–36 was inserted by a later hand to make the Corinthian letter conform to the viewpoint of the Pastoral epistles, especially 1 Timothy 2:11, "Let a woman learn in silence. . . ."

13. If 2 Corinthians 10–13 originally belonged with chapters 1–9, then it was probably dictated a few days later. Notice the sharp change in tone between the end of chapter 9 and chapters 10–13. Bornkamm sees further divisions in chapters 1–9. For our purposes, however, whether chapters 1–9 (minus 6:14–7:1) were written at the same time or different times is unimportant. The period of time over which 1–9 were written was so short that the practical result is a unified composition.

14. An exceedingly useful discussion of the history of scholarship of Galatians and the major issues of interpretation may be found in Hans Dieter Betz, *Galatians, A Commentary on Paul's Letter to the Churches in Galatia,* Hermeneia (Philadelphia: Fortress Press, 1979).

15. Scholars disagree on the location of these churches. According to the Southern Galatian theory, they were in the region through which Paul traveled on his first missionary journey (Acts 13 and 14). This theory has the advantage of harmonizing Paul's letters with the Acts account. Those holding the Northern Galatian theory point to other discrepancies between Acts and Paul's letters and argue further that Paul uses the ethnic name "Galatians" (3:1) to refer to his readers, which would better befit the inhabitants of the north where the Galatians had settled than residents in the southern part of the Roman province of Galatia. Those opting for the Southern theory tend to date Galatians among the earliest of Paul's epistles since it is assumed that he founded the church on the first journey. Those supporting the Northern theory date Galatians later since it is assumed that it was on a later journey than the one described in Acts 13 and 14 that Paul penetrated to the heart of the old Celtic kingdom of Galatia (near modern Ankara, Turkey). The dating would also be of some significance if one were interested in trying to trace development in Paul's thought.

16. Johannes Munck, *Paul and the Salvation of Mankind,* trans. Frank Clarke (Richmond: John Knox Press, 1959), pp. 87–134.

17. See Lloyd Gaston, "Paul and the Law in Galatians 2 and 3," in idem, *Paul and the Torah* (Vancouver: University of British Columbia Press, 1987), pp. 64–79.

18. Ignatius, *Epistle to the Philadelphians,* trans. Kirsopp Lake, Loeb Classical Library (Cambridge, Mass.: Harvard University Press, 1949), 1.245.

19. Gaston, "Paul and the Law in Galatians 2 and 3," pp. 73–76.

20. I am indebted to Professor Nils Dahl for this insight, which he put forth in a paper for the Paul seminar of the Society of Biblical Literature at the 1973

annual meeting. The paper was entitled "Paul's Letter to the Galatians: Epistolary Genre, Content, and Structure."

21. For the best defense of the hypothesis that Romans 16 was a part of Paul's original letter to the Roman church, see Harry Y. Gamble, *The Textual History of the Letter to the Romans.*

22. W. H. Auden, *A Selection by the Author* (London: Faber & Faber, 1958), p. 116.

23. Victor Paul Furnish, *Theology and Ethics in Paul,* has shown that the ethical instruction in Paul's letters is hardly restricted to the closing sections.

24. Arguments for Roman authorship: Paul mentions the "praetorian guard," and "those of Caesar's household" and expects that the verdict will come soon. He realizes he may be executed. From the second to the eighteenth century, tradition held that Paul wrote Philippians from Rome.

Against Roman authorship: Members of the "praetorian guard" were present in most large population centers in the Empire. Likewise, "servants of the Emperor" (public as well as private) were present in other Mediterranean cities. In the letter Paul expresses the hope to visit Philippi soon, which if written from Rome would take him back east to Philippi. But we know from Paul's letter to the Romans that he fervently hoped to go from Rome to Spain (west). Finally, five communications between Paul and the Philippian church are assumed in the letter (the Philippians hear that Paul is in prison; they send Epaphroditus to minister to him; they hear later that Epaphroditus is ill; they communicate their concern to Paul, and he, in turn, communicates via letter with them). It would have taken approximately eight weeks to travel the distance between Rome and Philippi (some 730 miles by land). Would Paul have been able to speak of "coming soon" if his prospective visit to Philippi were at the very least months away?

Although Ephesus is the leading rival to Rome as the place of Paul's imprisonment, a major objection to it is that neither Paul nor Acts anywhere explicitly speaks of an imprisonment in Ephesus. However, Paul himself does say he was imprisoned many times (2 Cor. 11:23) and suffered a "great affliction" in Asia. He recalls that he was so "unbearably crushed" that he despaired of surviving (2 Cor. 1:8). Moreover, Clement of Rome wrote a generation later that Paul "wore chains seven times" and the later *Acts of Paul* speaks of an Ephesian imprisonment (see *New Testament Apocrypha* [Philadelphia: Westminster Press, 1964], II, 338). Although these late traditions cannot be invoked as primary evidence, they do offer secondary support that an Ephesian imprisonment was probable. The decision on the provenance of the letter affects the dating of the letter (55–56 in Ephesus, or 58–60 in Rome) and is relevant for the discussion of development in Pauline theology. See my discussion of "Philippians, letter of," in the *Dictionary of Biblical Interpretation* (Nashville: Abingdon Press, forthcoming).

25. Philippians is so loosely structured that many have suggested that it is a patchwork of at least three fragments. Johannes Weiss observed that instead of a conclusion one would expect after 3:1 (*"Finally,* my brothers and sisters,

rejoice in the Lord."), one finds an acrimonious warning "Look out for the dogs . . ." in 3:2. This jarring non sequitur, Weiss argued, cannot be explained on any other grounds than that it is from another letter. The most common reconstructions are those of: Schmithals (A: 4:10–23 [a letter of thanksgiving]; B: 1:1–3:1; 4:4–7 [a prison letter]; C: 3:2–4:3; 4:8–9 [a warning letter]); Bornkamm (A: 1:1–3:1; 4:4–7; 4:21–23; B: 3:2–4:3; C: 4:10–20); Rahtjen (A: 4:10–20; B: 1:1–2:30; 4:21–23; C: 3:1–4:9); and Marxsen (A: 4:10–20; B: 1:1–3:1; 4:4–7; 4:21–23; C: 3:2–4:3; 4:8–9). Helmut Koester, "The Purpose of the Polemic of a Pauline Fragment (Philippians iii)," *New Testament Studies* 8 (1962): 317 n. 1, has a good survey of the literature on the subject. His article offers a slightly different construction. However, even if we do have fragments from several letters, and they are arranged in a different order, the essential elements in the conversation remain.

26. See Walter Schmithals, "Die Irrlehrer des Philipperbriefs," *Zeitschrift für Theologie und Kirche* 54 (1957): 279ff.

27. Norman R. Petersen, *Rediscovering Paul, Philemon and the Sociology of Paul's Narrative World* (Philadelphia: Fortress Press, 1985), argues that Paul's request that Philemon treat Onesimus like a brother implies that Onesimus is to be set free.

Chapter 5:
Paul and His Myths

1. This is Søren Kierkegaard's phrase, from *Philosophical Fragments,* trans. David F. Swenson (Princeton: Princeton University Press, 1962), pp. 68ff.

2. Henri Frankfort, *Before Philosophy* (Baltimore: Penguin Books, 1963), p. 16.

3. Gerardus van der Leeuw, *Religion in Essence and Manifestation,* trans. J. E. Turner (New York: Macmillan Co., 1938), p. 413.

4. *The Haggadah of Passover,* trans. Cecil Roth (London: Soncino Press, 1934), pp. 11–12.

5. Jacob Neusner, *The Way of Torah: An Introduction to Judaism* (Belmont, Calif.: Dickenson Publishing Co., 1970), p. 17. These ideas Neusner develops at much greater length; see especially his first chapter.

6. Mircea Eliade, *The Myth of the Eternal Return,* trans. Willard R. Trask (New York: Pantheon Books, 1954), p. 21.

7. Ernst Käsemann, "The Pauline Doctrine of the Lord's Supper" in idem, *Essays on New Testament Themes* (London: SCM Press, 1964), p. 124.

8. Richard Rubenstein, *My Brother Paul* (New York: Harper & Row, 1972), p. 173.

9. Robin Scroggs, *The Last Adam* (Philadelphia: Fortress Press, 1966), p. 84.

10. H. Richard Niebuhr, *The Meaning of Revelation* (New York: Macmillan Co., 1941), pp. 71–72.

Chapter 6:
The First Interpreters of Paul

1. See R. H. Charles, *The Apocrypha and Pseudepigrapha of the Old Testament* (Oxford: Clarendon Press, 1963–64), vol. 2.

2. See Werner Georg Kümmel, *Introduction to the New Testament* (Nashville: Abingdon Press, 1966), p. 241.

3. Eduard Lohse, *Colossians and Philemon: A Commentary on the Epistles to the Colossians and to Philemon,* trans. William R. Poehlmann and Robert J. Karris (Philadelphia: Fortress Press, 1971), pp. 81ff., has pointed out how the author of Colossians integrates major motifs from the genuine letters. Especially noteworthy are the similarities of epistolary style, their view of Paul as the apostle to the Gentiles, the use of traditional ethical materials, the understanding of wisdom, and the significance of the suffering of the apostle.

4. See note 3.

5. Günther Bornkamm, "The Heresy of Colossians," in *Conflict at Colossae: A Problem in the Interpretation of Early Christianity Illustrated by Selected Modern Studies,* ed. and trans. Fred O. Francis and Wayne A. Meeks (Missoula, Mont.: Scholars Press, 1973), p. 130.

6. Fred O. Francis, "Humility and Angelic Worship in Col. 2:18," in *Conflict at Colossae,* pp. 163–195; and Eduard Schweizer, *Der Brief an die Kolosser* (Zurich: Benziger Verlag, 1976), p. 104.

7. See Wayne A. Meeks and Fred O. Francis, "Epilogue," in *Conflict at Colossae,* pp. 209–218.

8. The notable exception is Fred O. Francis. See note 6.

9. Ernst Käsemann, in *Theologische Literaturzeitung* 86 (1961): 3.

10. J. Paul Sampley, "The Letter to the Ephesians," in Sampley et al., *Ephesians, Colossians, 2 Thessalonians, the Pastoral Epistles* (Philadelphia: Fortress Press, 1978), p. 10.

11. Edgar Johnson Goodspeed, *The Key to Ephesians* (Chicago: University of Chicago Press, 1956).

12. N. A. Dahl, "Address and Prooemium des Epheserbriefes," *Theologische Zeitschrift* 7 (1951): 241–264, esp. pp. 261ff.

13. H. Chadwick, "Die Absicht des Epheserbrief," *Zeitschrift für die neutestamentliche Wissenschaft* 51 (1960): 145–153.

14. For this insight I am indebted to Karl Martin Fischer, *Tendenz und Absicht des Epheserbriefs* (Göttingen: Vandenhoeck & Ruprecht, 1973).

15. Ibid., p. 107.

16. Gerhard Krodel, "2 Thessalonians," in Sampley et al., *Ephesians, Colossians, 2 Thessalonians, the Pastoral Epistles,* p. 80.

17. See Birger Pearson, *Harvard Theological Review* 64 (1971): 79–94, and Hendrikus Boers, *New Testament Studies* 22 (1976): 151–152.

18. The word "pseudepigraphy" means falsely assigning a writing to an author.

19. Krodel, "2 Thessalonians," in Sampley et al., *Ephesians, Colossians, 2 Thessalonians, the Pastoral Epistles,* p. 75.

20. More than 30 percent of 2 Thessalonians comes from 1 Thessalonians.

21. Although Philippians mentions bishops and deacons (1:1), it is generally agreed that these terms refer to charismatic leaders and not an ordained clergy as in the Pastorals.

22. Martin Dibelius and Hans Conzelmann, *The Pastoral Epistles,* trans. Philip Buttolph and Adela Yarbro (Philadelphia: Fortress Press, 1972), pp. 22–25; 39–41.

23. It is interesting that those who oppose the ordination of women or who seek to assign women a subordinate role in the society most often appeal to the Pastorals rather than the undisputed Pauline letters.

24. Kümmel, *Introduction to the New Testament,* p. 269.

25. The expression "eschatological reservation" refers to the partial experience of salvation in the present with the full realization reserved for the future, in the eschaton.

26. It is clear from Luke's extended treatment of Paul's mission in Acts, the collection of Paul's letters noted in 2 Peter 3:16, and the imitation of his epistolary style in Colossians and Ephesians, that Paul, who was unwelcome in many quarters during his life, was widely hailed in Asia Minor and Greece after his death.

Chapter 7:
Currents and Crosscurrents

1. Edgar Hennecke, *New Testament Apocrypha,* ed. Wilhelm Schneemelcher (Philadelphia: Westminster Press, 1964), 2:122.

2. This unfortunate juxtaposition of Paul and Jesus is discussed below.

3. Hennecke, *New Testament Apocrypha,* 2:133ff., 322ff., 755ff.

4. Since there was no sharp line between orthodoxy and heresy at this time, I realize a certain inappropriateness in using this term. I use it, nevertheless, for the sake of convenience.

5. *The Nag Hammadi Library,* ed. James M. Robinson (New York: Harper & Row, 1977), p. 134.

6. From a "Life of Rabbula" composed by a colleague of the bishop and cited in Walter Bauer, *Orthodoxy and Heresy in Earliest Christianity,* ed. Robert A. Kraft and Gerhard Krodel, 2nd ed. (Philadelphia: Fortress Press, 1971), pp. 26–27.

7. Church leaders of both East and West whose writings were the chief sources of the emerging doctrine and observances of the church.

8. Origen, *Contra Celsum,* trans. Henry Chadwick (Cambridge: Cambridge University Press, 1965), 3.42; 4.66.

9. See Maurice F. Wiles, *The Divine Apostle* (Cambridge: Cambridge University Press, 1967), p. 39.

10. See all six in Wiles, *The Divine Apostle,* p. 50.

11. Alexander Souter, *Pelagius's Expositions of Thirteen Epistles of St. Paul* (Cambridge: Cambridge University Press, 1926), vol. II, gives 120 pages of Latin text for the Roman commentary and 177 pages of commentary on the Corinthian letters.

12. J. N. D. Kelly, *Early Christian Doctrines* (London: Adam & Charles Black, 1958), p. 357.

13. Souter, *Pelagius's Expositions,* 2:45.

14. As cited in Jaroslav Pelikan, *The Christian Tradition, A History of the Development of Doctrine* (Chicago: University of Chicago Press, 1971), 1:315.

15. Augustine, *Confessions* 10.29.

16. Heiko A. Obermann, *Forerunners of the Reformation* (New York: Holt, Rinehart & Winston, 1966), p. 126.

17. Ibid., p. 127.

18. William Wrede, "Paulus," in *Das Paulusbild in der neueren deutschen Forschung,* ed. Karl Heinrich Rengstorf (Darmstadt: Wissenschaftliche Buchgesellschaft, 1964), p. 94.

19. For a good critical assessment of Schweitzer's work on Jesus, see James M. Robinson's introduction to the 1968 edition of Albert Schweitzer, *The Quest of the Historical Jesus* (New York: Macmillan Co., 1968), pp. xi–xxxiii. W. D. Davies, *Paul and Rabbinic Judaism* (New York: Harper & Row, 1967), pp. vii–xv, has an incisive statement on Schweitzer's estimation of Paul.

20. Augustine, *Confessions* 8.12.29.

21. André Dupont-Sommer, *The Essene Writings from Qumran,* trans. Geza Vermes (Cleveland: World Publishing Co., 1962), p. 102.

22. See Rudolf Bultmann, *Theology of the New Testament,* trans. Kendrick Grobel (New York: Charles Scribner's Sons, 1951), 1:190–352.

23. Ibid., 1:285.

24. See the review of his book by William D. Davies in *New Testament Studies* 2 (1955): 60–72.

25. By restricting my comments to Munck's work, I do not mean to slight the work of such eminent scholars as Ernst Käsemann, Krister Stendahl, C. Müller, P. Stuhlmacher, W. D. Davies, and others who differ from Bultmann. Munck was chosen here mainly to pose a sharp alternative to Bultmann's position.

26. George Bernard Shaw, "The Monstrous Imposition Upon Jesus," quoted in *The Writings of St. Paul,* ed. Wayne A. Meeks (New York: W. W. Norton & Co., 1972), p. 299.

27. Ibid.

28. Robin Scroggs, "Paul: Chauvinist or Liberationist?" *The Christian Century* 89 (1972): 307–309; "Paul and the Eschatological Woman," *Journal of the American Academy of Religion* 40 (1972): 283–303; and most recently "Paul and the Eschatological Woman Revisited," *Journal of the American Academy of Religion* 42 (1974): 532–537. Lately various authors have sought to show that 1 Corinthians 11:2–16 is a non-Pauline insertion. See W. O.

Walker, "The Non-Pauline Character of 1 Corinthians 11:2–16?" *Journal of Biblical Literature* 95 (1976): 615–621; Lamar Cope, "1 Cor. 11:2–16: One Step Further," *JBL* 97 (1978): 435–436; and now, G. W. Trompf, "On Attitudes Toward Women in Paul and Paulinist Literature: 1 Cor 11:3–6 and Its Context," *Catholic Biblical Quarterly* 42 (1980): 196–215. However, the removal of this passage would not alter the basic point of Scroggs, given the exhortation elsewhere on the equality of the sexes. J. Murphy-O'Connor has cogently argued that 1 Corinthians 11:2–16 makes sense as genuine Pauline material. See his "Sex and Logic in 1 Cor. 11:2–16," *Catholic Biblical Quarterly* 42 (1980): 482–500.

29. See especially Charles K. Barrett, *The First Epistle to the Corinthians* (New York: Harper & Row, 1968), pp. 330–332.

30. See the relevant discussion above in chapter 4, "The Letters as Conversations."

31. Scroggs, "Paul and the Eschatological Woman Revisited," p. 533.

32. Ibid. See Philippians 4:2–3 (Euodia and Syntyche, who have "labored side by side with me in the gospel") and Romans 16, if genuine. See 1 Corinthians 16:19, which is certainly Paul's.

33. Elaine Pagels, "Paul and Women: A Response to Recent Discussion," *Journal of the American Academy of Religion* 42 (1974): 538–549.

34. S. Scott Bartchy, *First-Century Slavery and 1 Corinthians 7:21* (Missoula, Mont.: Society of Biblical Literature, 1973), pp. 161–172, makes a strong case for this view.

35. Pagels, "Paul and Women," p. 545.

36. Ibid., p. 544.

37. Ibid., p. 544.

38. David Daube, "Pauline Contributions to a Pluralistic Culture: Re-creation and Beyond" in *Jesus and Man's Hope,* ed. Donald G. Miller and Dikran Y. Hadidian (Pittsburgh: Pittsburgh Theological Seminary, 1971), pp. 223–245.

Selected Bibliographies

CHAPTER 1:
PAUL AND HIS WORLD

1. Hellenistic World (Introductory)

Bultmann, Rudolf. *Primitive Christianity in Its Contemporary Setting.* Trans. R. H. Fuller. New York: World Publishing Co., Living Age Books, 1957.

Dodds, E. R. *The Greeks and the Irrational.* Berkeley: University of California Press, 1951 and 1966.

Hadas, Moses. *Hellenistic Culture.* New York: W. W. Norton & Co., 1959.

Hengel, Martin. *Judaism and Hellenism.* Trans. John Bowden. 2 vols. Philadelphia: Fortress Press, 1974.

Nock, Arthur Darby. *Early Gentile Christianity and Its Hellenistic Background.* New York: Harper & Row, 1964.

Peters, F. E. *The Harvest of Hellenism.* New York: Simon & Schuster, 1971.

Schürer, Emil. *The History of the Jewish People in the Age of Jesus Christ.* Rev. and ed. Geza Vermes, Fergus Millar, and Martin Goodman. 4 vols. Edinburgh: T. & T. Clark, 1973–87.

Tarn, W. W. *Hellenistic Civilization.* 3rd ed. with G. T. Griffith. New York: World Publishing Co., 1952.

Tcherikover, Victor. *Hellenistic Civilization and the Jews.* Trans. S. Applebaum. New York: Atheneum Publishers, 1970.

2. The Greek Translation of the Bible (The Septuagint)

Bickerman, E. *Studies in Jewish and Christian History.* 2 vols. Leiden: E. J. Brill, 1976–80.

Dodd, C. H. *The Bible and the Greeks.* London: Hodder & Stoughton, 1935.

Harl, Marguerite. *La Bible grecque des Septante, du Judaïsme hellénistique au Christianisme ancien.* Paris: Éditions du Cerf, 1988.

Hays, Richard B. *Echoes of Scripture in the Letters of Paul.* New Haven, Conn.: Yale University Press, 1989.

Jellicoe, S. *The Septuagint and Modern Study.* Oxford: Clarendon Press, 1968.

———. *Studies in the Septuagint: Origins, Recensions, and Interpretation.*

New York: KTAV Publishing House, 1974. See the *Bulletin of the International Organization for Septuagint and Cognate Studies.*

3. Argumentation

a. Diatribe

Stowers, Stanley K. *The Diatribe and Paul's Letter to the Romans.* Chico, Calif.: Scholars Press, 1981.

b. Rhetoric

Betz, Hans Dieter. *Galatians.* Philadelphia: Fortress Press, 1979.
Marrou, H. I. *A History of Education in Antiquity.* London: Sheed & Ward, 1956.
————. "Education and Rhetoric." In *The Legacy of Greece: A New Appraisal,* ed. M. I. Finley, pp. 185–201. Oxford: Clarendon Press, 1981.
Wuellner, Wilhelm. "Where Is Rhetorical Criticism Taking Us?" *Catholic Biblical Quarterly* 49 (1987): 448–463. Excellent recent bibliography.

c. Allegory

Barr, James. "Typology and Allegory." In idem, *Old and New in Interpretation, A Study of the Two Testaments,* pp. 103–148. London: SCM Press, 1966.
Sowers, Sidney G. *The Hermeneutics of Philo and Hebrews: A Comparison of the Interpretation of the Old Testament in Philo Judaeus and the Epistle to the Hebrews.* Richmond: John Knox Press, 1965.

4. Hellenistic Religion and Philosophy

a. General

Bevan, E. "Hellenistic Popular Philosophy." In *The Hellenistic Age,* ed. J. B. Bury. Cambridge: Cambridge University Press, 1923.
Burkert, Walter. *Greek Religion.* Trans. John Raffan. Cambridge, Mass.: Harvard University Press, 1977.
Dietrich, B. C. *The Origins of Greek Religion.* Berlin and New York: Walter de Gruyter, 1974.
Festugiere, A. J. *Personal Religion Among the Greeks.* Berkeley and Los Angeles: University of California Press, 1954.
————. *A History of Greek Religion.* 2nd ed. Trans. F. J. Fielden. New York: W. W. Norton & Co., 1964.
Grant, Fred C., ed. *Hellenistic Religions: The Age of Syncretism.* New York: Liberal Arts, 1953.

Guthrie, W. K. C. *The Greeks and Their Gods.* Boston: Beacon Press, 1951.

Nilsson, Martin. *Greek Piety.* Oxford: Clarendon Press, 1948.

———. *Greek Popular Religion.* New York: Columbia University Press, 1940.

Teixidor, Javier. *The Pagan God: Popular Religion in the Greco-Roman Near East.* Princeton: Princeton University Press, 1977.

b. Mystery Religions

Bianchi, Ugo. *The Greek Mysteries.* Leiden: E. J. Brill, 1976.

Godwin, Joscelyn. *Mystery Religions in the Ancient World.* New York: Harper & Row, 1981.

Guthrie, W. K. C. *The Greeks and Their Gods.* Boston: Beacon Press, 1961.

Metzger, Bruce M. "A Classified Bibliography of the Graeco-Roman Mystery Religions 1924–1973 with a Supplement 1974–1979." In *Aufstieg und Niedergang der römischen Welt,* eds. Hildegard Temporini and Wolfgang Haase, II, 17.3, pp. 1259–1423. Berlin: Walter de Gruyter, 1984.

Nock, A. D. *Conversion.* London: Oxford University Press, 1933.

———. "Mysteries." In *Encyclopedia of the Social Sciences,* ed. E. R. A. Seligman, 2:172–175. New York: Macmillan Co., 1930–35.

Reitzenstein, R. *Hellenistic Mystery Religions: Their Basic Ideas and Significance.* Trans. J. E. Steely. Pittsburgh: Pickwick Press, 1978.

(1) *The Eleusinian Mystery*

Kerenyi, C. *Eleusis: Archetypal Image of Mother and Daughter.* Trans. Ralph Manheim. New York: Pantheon Books, 1967.

Mylonas, George E. *Eleusis and the Eleusinian Mysteries.* Princeton: Princeton University Press, 1961.

(2) *Isis and Osiris Mystery (and Serapis Cult)*

Brady, Thomas Allen. *The Reception of the Egyptian Cults by the Greeks (330–30 B.C.).* Columbia, Mo.: University of Missouri, 1935.

Frankfort, Henri. *Ancient Egyptian Religion.* New York: Columbia University Press, 1948.

Heyob, Sharon Kelley. *The Cult of Isis Among Women in the Graeco-Roman World.* Leiden: E. J. Brill, 1975.

Plutarch. *De Iside et Osiride.* In *Moralia,* vol. V, trans. Frank C. Babbitt. Loeb Classical Library. Cambridge, Mass.: Harvard University Press, 1936.

Solmsen, Friedrich. *Isis Among the Greeks and Romans.* Cambridge, Mass.: Harvard University Press, 1979.

Stambaugh, John E. *Serapis Under the Early Ptolemies.* Leiden: E. J. Brill, 1972.

Witt, R. E. *Isis in the Graeco-Roman World.* Ithaca, N.Y.: Cornell University Press, 1971.

(3) *The Dionysiac Mystery*

Euripides. *The Bacchae.* Trans. William Arrowsmith. In *The Complete Greek Tragedies,* vol. IV, ed. David Grene and Richard Lattimore. Chicago: University of Chicago Press, 1960.

Houser, Caroline. *Dionysos and His Circle, Ancient Through Modern.* Cambridge, Mass.: Fogg Art Museum, Harvard University, 1979.

Kerenyi, C. *Dionysos: Archetypal Image of the Indestructible Life.* Trans. Ralph Manheim. Princeton: Princeton University Press, 1976.

Nilsson, Martin. *The Dionysiac Mysteries of the Hellenistic and Roman Age.* Lund: C. W. K. Gleerup, 1957.

Walter, Friedrich Otto. *Dionysus, Myth and Cult.* Bloomington, Ind.: Indiana University Press, 1965.

c. The Healing Cult of Asclepius

Ackerknecht, Erwin H. *The World of Asclepios.* Bern: H. Huber, 1963.

Edelstein, E. J. and L. *Asclepius; A Collection and Interpretation of the Testimonies.* 2 vols. Baltimore: Johns Hopkins Press, 1945.

Kee, Howard C. *Medicine, Miracle and Magic in New Testament Times.* Cambridge: Cambridge University Press, 1986.

Kerenyi, C. *Asklepios: Archetypal Image of the Physician's Existence.* Trans. Ralph Manheim. Princeton: Princeton University Press, 1959.

Walton, Alice. *The Cult of Asklepios.* Boston: Ginn & Co., 1894. Reprinted as *Asklepios: The Cult of the Greek God of Medicine.* New York: Johnson Reprint Corp., 1979.

d. Stoicism

Colish, Marcia L. *The Stoic Tradition from Antiquity to the Middle Ages.* Leiden: E. J. Brill, 1985.

Long, A. A. *Hellenistic Philosophy: Stoics, Epicureans, Sceptics.* New York: Humanities Press, 1958.

Rist, John M. *Stoic Philosophy.* London: Cambridge University Press, 1969.

Wenley, R. M. *Stoicism and Its Influence.* New York: Cooper Square Publishers, 1963.

e. Cynicism

Attridge, Harold W. *First-Century Cynicism in the Epistles of Heraclitus.* Missoula, Mont.: Scholars Press, 1976.

———. "The Philosophical Critique of Religion Under the Early Empire." in *Aufstieg und Niedergang der römischen Welt,* ed. Hildegard Temporini and Wolfgang Haase. Berlin: Walter de Gruyter, 1984.

Dudley, D. R. *A History of Cynicism from Diogenes to the Sixth Century A.D.* London: Methuen & Co., 1937.

Malherbe, A. J. *The Cynic Epistles: A Study Edition.* Missoula, Mont.: Scholars Press, 1977.

Sloterdijk, Peter. *Critique of Cynical Reason.* Trans. Michael Eldred. Minneapolis: University of Minnesota Press, 1987. Esp. pp. 101–106 and 155–168.

f. Neo-Pythagoreanism

Burkert, Walter. *Lore and Science in Ancient Pythagoreanism.* Trans. Edwin L. Minar, Jr. Cambridge, Mass.: Harvard University Press, 1972.
Philostratus. *The Life of Apollonius of Tyana.* Trans. F. C. Conybeare. Loeb Classical Library. Cambridge, Mass.: Harvard University Press, 1960.
Thesleff, Holger. *An Introduction to the Pythagorean Writings of the Hellenistic Period.* Abo [Turku], Finland: Abo Akademi, 1961.

g. Gnosticism

Haardt, R. *Gnosis, Character and Testimony.* Leiden: E. J. Brill, 1971.
Jonas, Hans. *The Gnostic Religion: The Message of the Alien God and the Beginnings of Christianity.* 2nd ed. Boston: Beacon Press, 1963.
Pagels, Elaine H. *The Gnostic Paul: Gnostic Exegesis of the Pauline Letters.* Philadelphia: Fortress Press, 1975.
Robinson, James M., ed. *The Nag Hammadi Library in English.* New York: Harper & Row, 1977. Rev. ed., Leiden: E. J. Brill, 1988.
Rudolph, Kurt. *Gnosis: The Nature and History of Gnosticism.* Trans. Robert McL. Wilson. San Francisco: Harper & Row, 1983.

5. Paul's Jewish Environment

Baron, Salo W. *A Social and Religious History of the Jews.* 2 vols. 2nd ed. New York: Columbia University Press, 1952–80.
Borgen, Peder. "Philo of Alexandria: A Critical and Synthetical Survey of Research Since World War II." In *Aufstieg und Niedergang der römischen Welt,* ed. Hildegard Temporini and Wolfgang Haase, II, 21.2, pp. 98–154. Berlin: Walter de Gruyter, 1984.
Green, William Scott. *Approaches to Ancient Judaism.* Vol. II. Chico, Calif.: Scholars Press, 1980.
———. *Approaches to Ancient Judaism.* Vol. III. Chico, Calif.: Scholars Press, 1981.
———. *Approaches to Ancient Judaism.* Vol. IV. Chico, Calif.: Scholars Press, 1983.
———. *Approaches to Ancient Judaism.* Vol. V. *Studies in Judaism and Its Greco-Roman Context.* Decatur, Ga.: Scholars Press, 1985.
Hengel, Martin. *Judaism and Hellenism.* 2 vols. Trans. John Bowden. Philadelphia: Fortress Press, 1974.
Neusner, Jacob. *Formative Judaism: Religious, Historical and Literary Studies, Torah, Pharisees, and Rabbis.* Chico, Calif.: Scholars Press, 1983.
Safrai, Shemuel, and M. Stern, eds. *The Jewish People in the First Century.*

Historical Geography, Political History, Social, Cultural and Religious Life and Institutions. Vol. 1. Philadelphia: Fortress Press, 1974.

Schürer, Emil. *The History of the Jewish People in the Age of Jesus Christ.* Rev. and ed. G. Vermes, Fergus Millar, and Martin Goodman. 4 vols. Edinburgh: T. & T. Clark, 1973–1987.

Smallwood, E. Mary. *The Jews Under Roman Rule: From Pompey to Diocletian.* Leiden: E. J. Brill, 1976.

Tcherikover, Victor. *Hellenistic Civilization and the Jews.* Trans. S. Applebaum. New York: Atheneum Press, 1970.

Williamson, Ronald. *Jews in the Hellenistic World: Philo.* Cambridge: Cambridge University Press, 1989.

a. Pharisaism

Baeck, Leo. *The Pharisees, and Other Essays.* New York: Schocken Books, 1966.

Finkelstein, Louis. *The Pharisees: the Sociological Background of Their Faith.* 2 vols. 3rd ed. Philadelphia: Jewish Publication Society of America, 1962.

Neusner, Jacob. *The Rabbinic Traditions About the Pharisees Before 70.* 3 vols. Leiden: E. J. Brill, 1971.

———. *From Politics to Piety: The Emergence of Pharisaic Judaism.* Englewood Cliffs, N.J.: Prentice-Hall, 1973.

Rivkin, Ellis. *A Hidden Revolution: The Pharisees' Search for the Kingdom Within.* Nashville: Abingdon Press, 1978.

b. Scripture Interpretation

Bonsirven, Joseph. *Exégèse rabbinique et exégèse paulienne.* Paris: Beauchesne, 1939.

Carson, D. A., and H. G. M. Williamson, eds. *It Is Written: Scripture Citing Scripture.* Cambridge: Cambridge University Press, 1988.

Jeremias, Joachim. "Paulus als Hillelit." In *Neotestamentica et Semitica: Studies in Honour of Principal Matthew Black,* ed. Edward Earle Ellis and Max Wilcox. Edinburgh: T. & T. Clark, 1969.

Michel, Otto. *Paulus und seine Bibel.* Gütersloh: C. Bertelsmann, 1929.

c. Apocalypticism

(1) *Nature and Function*

Collins, John J. *The Apocalyptic Imagination: An Introduction to the Jewish Matrix of Christianity.* New York: Crossroad, 1984.

Hanson, Paul D., ed. *Visionaries and Their Apocalypses.* Philadelphia: Fortress Press, 1983.

Hellholm, David, ed. *Apocalypticism in the Mediterranean World and the Near East.* Tübingen: J. C. B. Mohr (Paul Siebeck), 1983.

Koch, Klaus. *The Rediscovery of Apocalyptic.* Naperville, Ill.: Alec R. Allenson, Inc., 1970.

Rist, M. "Apocalypticism." In *Interpreter's Dictionary of the Bible*, 1:157–161. Nashville: Abingdon Press, 1962.

Rowland, Christopher. *The Open Heaven: A Study of Apocalyptic in Judaism and Early Christianity*. New York: Crossroad, 1982.

Schmithals, Walter. *The Apocalyptic Movement: Introduction and Interpretation*. Trans. John E. Steely. Nashville: Abingdon Press, 1975.

(2) Qumran Community

Fitzmyer, J. A. *The Dead Sea Scrolls: Major Publications and Tools for Study*. Missoula, Mont.: Scholars Press, 1975.

————. "The Dead Sea Scrolls and the New Testament After Thirty Years." *Theology Digest* 29 (1981): 351–367.

Koester, Craig. "A Qumran Bibliography: 1974–1984." *Biblical Theological Bulletin* 15 (1985): 110–120.

Vermes, Geza. *The Dead Sea Scrolls in English*. 3rd ed. New York: Penguin Books, 1987.

CHAPTER 2:
THE ANATOMY OF THE LETTERS

Aune, David. *The New Testament in Its Literary Environment*. Philadelphia: Westminster Press, 1987.

Dahl, Nils A. "Letter." In *The Interpreter's Dictionary of the Bible, Supplementary Volume*, pp. 538–541. Nashville: Abingdon Press, 1976.

Doty, William G. *Letters in Primitive Christianity*. Philadelphia: Fortress Press, 1973.

Funk, Robert W. "The Letter: Form and Style." In idem, *Language, Hermeneutic, and the Word of God*, pp. 250–274. New York: Harper & Row, 1966.

————. "The Apostolic Parousia." In *Christian History and Interpretation: Studies Presented to John Knox*, ed. W. R. Farmer et al., pp. 249–268. Cambridge: Cambridge University Press, 1967.

Malherbe, Abraham J. "Ancient Epistolary Theorists." *Ohio Journal of Religious Studies* 5 (1977): 3–77.

Schubert, Paul. *The Form and Function of the Pauline Thanksgivings*. Berlin: Alfred Töpelmann, 1939.

Stowers, Stanley K. *Letter Writing in Greco-Roman Antiquity*. Philadelphia: Westminster Press, 1986.

White, John L. *Light from Ancient Letters*. Philadelphia: Fortress Press, 1986.

————. *The Form and Function of the Body of the Greek Letter: A Study of the Letter-body in the Non-literary Papyri and in Paul the Apostle*. Missoula, Mont.: Scholars Press, 1972.

————. "New Testament Epistolary Literature in the Framework of Ancient Epistolography." In *Aufstieg und Niedergang der römischen Welt*, ed.

Hildegard Temporini and Wolfgang Haase, II, 25.2, pp. 1730–1756. Berlin: Walter de Gruyter, 1984.

CHAPTER 3:
TRADITIONS BEHIND THE LETTERS

Allison, D. C., Jr. "The Pauline Epistles and the Synoptic Gospels: The Pattern of the Parallels." *New Testament Studies* 28 (1982): 1–32.

Betz, Hans Dieter. "A Catalogue of Vices and Virtues." In idem, *Galatians: A Commentary on Paul's Letter to the Churches in Galatia,* 281–283. Philadelphia: Fortress Press, 1979.

Bornkamm, Günther. "Lord's Supper and Church in Paul." In idem, *Early Christian Experience,* ch. 9. New York: Harper & Row, 1969.

Bradley, David G. "The Topos as Form in the Pauline Paraenesis." *Journal of Biblical Literature* 72 (1953): 283–296.

Carson, D. A., and H. G. M. Williamson, eds. *It Is Written: Scripture Citing Scripture.* Cambridge: Cambridge University Press, 1988.

Davies, W. D. "Ethics in the New Testament." In *The Interpreter's Dictionary of the Bible,* II, 167–176. Nashville: Abingdon Press, 1962.

Dibelius, Martin. *A Fresh Approach to the New Testament and Early Christian Literature.* New York: Charles Scribner's Sons, 1936.

Dodd, C. H. *The Apostolic Preaching and Its Developments.* London: Hodder & Stoughton, 1963.

Furnish, Victor P. *Theology and Ethics in Paul.* Nashville: Abingdon Press, 1968.

Hodgson, R. "Paul the Apostle and First Century Tribulation Lists." *Zeitschrift für die neutestamentliche Wissenschaft* 74 (1983): 59–80.

Hooker, Morna D. "Phil 2, 6–11." In *Jesus und Paulus: Festschrift für W. G. Kümmel,* pp. 151–164. Göttingen: Vandenhoeck & Ruprecht, 1975.

Horsley, R. A. "The Background of the Confessional Formula in 1 Kor 8, 6." *Zeitschrift für die neutestamentliche Wissenschaft* 69 (1978): 130–135.

Hunter, Archibald M. *Paul and His Predecessors.* London: SCM Press, 1961.

Jeremias, Joachim. *The Eucharistic Words of Jesus.* New York: Charles Scribner's Sons, 1966.

Lindars, Barnabas. *New Testament Apologetic.* Philadelphia: Westminster Press, 1961.

Martin, Ralph P. *Carmen Christi: Philippians ii. 5–11 in Recent Interpretation and in the Setting of Early Christian Worship.* Cambridge: Cambridge University Press, 1967.

Richardson, R. D. "Supplementary Essay: A Further Inquiry Into Eucharistic Origins with Special Reference to New Testament Problems." In *Mass and Lord's Supper; A Study of the History of Liturgy,* ed. H. Lietzmann, pp. 217–253. Leiden: E. J. Brill, 1979.

Sanders, Jack T. *The New Testament Christological Hymns; Their Historical Religious Background.* Cambridge: Cambridge University Press, 1971.

Schnackenburg, R. *Baptism in the Thought of St. Paul, A Study in Pauline Theology.* Trans. G. R. Beasley-Murray. New York: Herder & Herder, 1964.

Schweizer, Eduard. *The Lord's Supper According to the New Testament.* Trans. James M. Davis. Philadelphia: Fortress Press, 1967.

CHAPTER 4:
THE LETTERS AS CONVERSATIONS

1 Thessalonians

Beker, J. Christiaan. *Paul the Apostle: The Triumph of God in Life and Thought.* Philadelphia: Fortress Press, 1980.

Boers, Hendrikus. "The Form-Critical Study of Paul's Letters: I Thessalonians as a Test Case." *New Testament Studies* 22 (1975): 140–158.

Conzelmann, Hans. *1 Corinthians; A Commentary on the First Epistle to the Corinthians.* Trans. James W. Leitch. Philadelphia: Fortress Press, 1975.

Dahl, Nils A. "Paul and the Church at Corinth According to I Corinthians 1:10–4:21." In *Christian History and Interpretation: Studies Presented to John Knox,* ed. W. R. Farmer et al., pp. 313–335. Cambridge: Cambridge University Press, 1967.

Jewett, Robert. *The Thessalonian Correspondence: Pauline Rhetoric and Millenarian Piety.* Philadelphia: Fortress Press, 1986.

Malherbe, Abraham J. *Paul and the Thessalonians, The Philosophic Tradition and Pastoral Care.* Philadelphia: Fortress Press, 1987.

Marshall, I. Howard. *1 and 2 Thessalonians.* Grand Rapids: Wm. B. Eerdmans Publishing Co., 1983.

Munck, Johannes. "I Thess. 1:9–10 and the Missionary Preaching of Paul." *New Testament Studies* 9 (1962–63): 95–110.

Pearson, B. A. "I Thess. 2:13–16: A Deutero-Pauline Interpolation." *Harvard Theological Review* 14 (1971): 79–94.

Schmidt, D. "I Thess. 2:13–16: Linguistic Evidence for an Interpolation." *Journal of Biblical Literature* 102 (1983): 269–279.

1 Corinthians

Barrett, C. K. *A Commentary on the First Epistle to the Corinthians.* New York: Harper & Row, 1968.

Bartchy, S. Scott. *First-Century Slavery and 1 Corinthians 7:21.* Missoula, Mont.: Scholars Press, 1973.

Daube, David. "Pauline Contributions to a Pluralistic Culture: Re-creation and Beyond." In *Jesus and Man's Hope,* ed. Donald G. Miller and D. Y. Hadidian, pp. 223–245. Pittsburgh: Pittsburgh Theological Seminary, 1971.

Fee, Gordon D. *The First Epistle to the Corinthians.* Grand Rapids: Wm. B. Eerdmans Publishing Co., 1987. Good bibliography.

Horsley, R. A. " 'How Can Some of You Say There Is No Resurrection of the Dead?' Spiritual Elitism in Corinth." *Novum Testamentum* 20 (1978): 203–240.

———. "Gnosis in Corinth: I Cor. 8:1–6." *New Testament Studies* 27 (1980): 32–51.

Hurd, John C., Jr. *The Origin of 1 Corinthians.* New York: Seabury Press, 1965. Reprinted 1983.

Neyrey, J. H. "Body Language in 1 Corinthians: The Use of Anthropological Models for Understanding Paul and His Opponents." *Semeia* 35 (1986): 129–170.

Pagels, Elaine H. "Paul and Women: A Response to Recent Discussion." *Journal of the American Academy of Religion* 42 (1974): 538–549.

Patte, D. *Paul's Faith and the Power of the Gospel: A Structural Introduction to the Pauline Letters.* Philadelphia: Fortress Press, 1983.

Scroggs, Robin. "Paul and the Eschatological Woman." *Journal of the American Academy of Religion* 40 (1972): 283–303.

———. "Paul and the Eschatological Woman Revisited." *Journal of the American Academy of Religion* 42 (1974): 532–537.

Sellin, Gerhard. "Hauptprobleme des Ersten Korintherbriefes." In *Aufstieg und Niedergang der römischen Welt,* ed. Hildegard Temporini and Wolfgang Haase, II, 25.4, pp. 2940–3044. Berlin: Walter de Gruyter, 1987. Excellent bibliography.

Theissen, Gerd. *The Social Setting of Pauline Christianity: Essays on Corinth.* Ed. and trans. J. H. Schütz. Philadelphia: Fortress Press, 1982.

2 Corinthians

Furnish, Victor Paul. *II Corinthians.* Garden City, N. Y.: Doubleday, 1984.

Georgi, Dieter. *The Opponents of Paul in Second Corinthians.* Philadelphia: Fortress Press, 1986.

Martin, Ralph P. *2 Corinthians.* Waco, Tex.: Word, 1986.

Schmithals, Walter. *Gnosticism in Corinth: An Investigation of the Letters to the Corinthians.* Trans. John E. Steely. Nashville: Abingdon Press, 1971.

Galatians

Betz, Hans Dieter. *Galatians.* Philadelphia: Fortress Press, 1979.

———. "The Literary Composition and Function of Paul's Letter to the Galatians." *New Testament Studies* 21 (1974–75): 353–373.

Fiorenza, Elisabeth Schüssler. "Neither Male Nor Female: Galatians 3:28— Alternative Vision and Pauline Modification." In idem, *In Memory of Her, A Feminist Theological Reconstruction of Christian Origins,* 205–241. New York: Crossroad, 1983.

Hays, Richard B. *The Faith of Jesus Christ.* Chico, Calif.: Scholars Press, 1983.

Howard, George. *Paul: Crisis in Galatia.* Cambridge: Cambridge University Press, 1979.

Jewett, Robert. "The Agitators and the Galatian Community." *New Testament Studies* 17 (1970): 198–212.

Lull, D. J. *The Spirit in Galatia.* Chico, Calif.: Scholars Press, 1980.

Munck, J. *Paul and the Salvation of Mankind.* Trans. F. Clarke. Richmond: John Knox Press, 1959.

Romans

Badenas, Robert. *Christ the End of the Law: Romans 10.4 in Pauline Perspective.* Sheffield: JSOT Press, 1985.

Barrett, C. K. *The Epistle to the Romans.* New York: Harper & Brothers, 1957.

———. "Romans 9:30–10:21: Call and Responsibility in Israel." In idem, *Essays on Paul,* 132–153. Philadelphia: Westminster Press, 1982.

Bassler, Jouette. *Divine Impartiality: Paul and a Theological Axiom.* Chico, Calif.: Scholars Press, 1982.

Beker, J. Christiaan. *Paul the Apostle: The Triumph of God in Life and Thought.* Philadelphia: Fortress Press, 1980.

Campbell, W. S. "Romans 3 as a Key to the Structure and Thought of the Letter." *Novum Testamentum* 23 (1981): 22–40.

Cranfield, C. E. B. *The Epistle to the Romans.* 2 vols. Edinburgh: T. & T. Clark, 1985.

Dahl, Nils A. "The Missionary Theology in the Epistle to the Romans." In idem, *Studies in Paul,* 70–94. Minneapolis: Augsburg Publishing House, 1977.

———. "The Future of Israel." In idem, *Studies in Paul,* 137–158. Minneapolis: Augsburg Publishing House, 1977.

Davies, W. D. "Paul and the Law: Pitfalls in Interpretation." In idem, *Jewish and Pauline Studies,* 91–122. Philadelphia: Fortress Press, 1984.

Donfried, Karl P., ed. *The Romans Debate.* Minneapolis: Augsburg Publishing House, 1977.

Dunn, James D. G. *Romans.* Waco, Tex.: Word Books, 1988. 2 vols. of useful bibliography.

Gaston, Lloyd. "Israel's Enemies in Pauline Theology." *New Testament Studies* 28 (1982): 400–423.

Jewett, Robert. "Major Impacts in the Theological Interpretation of Romans Since Barth." *Interpretation* 34 (1980): 17–31.

Karris, Robert J. "Rom. 14:1–15:13 and the Occasion of Romans." *Catholic Biblical Quarterly* 35 (1973): 155–178.

Käsemann, Ernst. *Commentary on Romans.* Trans. Geoffrey W. Bromiley. Grand Rapids: Wm. B. Eerdmans Publishing Co., 1980.

———. "The Righteousness of God in Paul." In idem, *New Testament Questions of Today,* pp. 168–182. Philadelphia: Fortress Press, 1969.

————. "Principles of the Interpretation of Romans 13." In idem, *New Testament Questions of Today,* pp. 196–216. Philadelphia: Fortress Press, 1969.

Minear, Paul S. *The Obedience of Faith; The Purposes of Paul in the Epistle to the Romans.* Naperville, Ill.: Alec R. Allenson, 1971.

Munck, Johannes. *Christ and Israel: An Interpretation of Romans 9–11.* Philadelphia: Fortress Press, 1967.

Roetzel, Calvin J. "Romans, the Letter of Paul to the." In *Harper's Bible Dictionary,* ed. Paul J. Achtemeier et al., pp. 876–880. New York: Harper & Row, 1985.

Scroggs, Robin. *The Last Adam.* Philadelphia: Fortress Press, 1966.

Stendahl, Krister. "The Apostle Paul and the Introspective Conscience of the West." *Harvard Theological Review* 56 (1963): 199–215. Reprinted in Krister Stendahl, *Paul among Jews and Gentiles,* pp. 78–96. Philadelphia: Fortress Press, 1976.

————. "Hate, Non-Retaliation, and Love." *Harvard Theological Review* 55 (1962): 343–355.

Stowers, S. K. *The Diatribe and Paul's Letter to the Romans.* Chico, Calif.: Scholars Press, 1981.

Tannehill, Robert C. *Dying and Rising with Christ.* Berlin: Alfred Töpelmann, 1967.

Philippians

Bornkamm, Günther. "On Understanding the Christ-Hymn (Phil. 2:6–11)." In idem, *Early Christian Experience,* pp. 112–122. New York: Harper & Row, 1969.

Furnish, Victor P. "The Place and Purpose of Philippians III." *New Testament Studies* 10 (1963–64): 80–88.

Hooker, Morna D. "Philippians 2:6–11." In *Jesus und Paulus,* eds. E. E. Ellis and E. Grässer, pp. 151–164. Göttingen: Vandenhoeck & Ruprecht, 1975.

Howard, George. "Phil. 2:6–11 and the Human Christ." *Catholic Biblical Quarterly* 40 (1978): 368–387.

Jewett, Robert. "Conflicting Movements in the Early Church as Reflected in Philippians." *Novum Testamentum* 30 (1970): 361–390.

Koester, Helmut. "The Purpose of the Polemic of a Pauline Fragment (Phil. III)." *New Testament Studies* 8 (1961–62): 317–332.

Martin, Ralph P. *Carmen Christi: Philippians 2:5–11 in Recent Interpretation and in the Setting of Early Christian Worship.* Cambridge: Cambridge University Press, 1967.

Roetzel, Calvin J. "Philippians, book of." In *Dictionary of Biblical Interpretation.* Nashville: Abingdon Press, forthcoming.

Schmithals, Walter. "The False Teachers of the Epistle to the Philippians." In idem, *Paul and the Gnostics,* pp. 65–122. Trans. J. Steely. Nashville: Abingdon Press, 1972.

Philemon

O'Brien, Peter T. *Colossians, Philemon.* Waco, Tex.: Word, 1982.

Petersen, Norman R. *Rediscovering Paul: Philemon and the Sociology of Paul's Narrative World.* Philadelphia: Fortress Press, 1985.

White, J. L. "The Structural Analysis of Philemon: A Point of Departure in the Formal Analysis of the Pauline Letters." *Society of Biblical Literature Seminar Papers* (1971), 1:1–45.

Winter, S. C. "Paul's Letter to Philemon." *New Testament Studies* 33 (1987): 1–35.

CHAPTER 5:
PAUL AND HIS MYTHS

Bultmann, Rudolf. *Jesus Christ and Mythology.* New York: Charles Scribner's Sons, 1958.

Bultmann, Rudolf, et al. *Kerygma and Myth: A Theological Debate.* Ed. Hans Werner Bartsch. New York: Harper & Row, 1961.

Cassirer, Ernst. *Language and Myth.* Trans. Susanne K. Langer. New York: Harper & Brothers, 1946.

———. *The Philosophy of Symbolic Forms.* Vol. 2, *Mythical Thought.* New Haven, Conn.: Yale University Press, 1955.

Dodds, E. R. *The Greeks and the Irrational.* Berkeley and Los Angeles: University of California Press, 1951.

Doty, William G., and Wendell C. Beane. *Myths, Rites, Symbols—A Mircea Eliade Reader.* 2 vols. New York: Harper & Row, 1976.

———. *Mythography: The Study of Myths and Rituals.* Tuscaloosa, Ala.: University of Alabama, 1986.

Douglas, Mary. "Deciphering a Meal." In *Myth, Symbol, and Culture.* Ed. Clifford Geertz. New York: W. W. Norton & Co., 1971.

Eliade, Mircea. *The Myth of the Eternal Return.* Trans. Willard R. Trask. Princeton: Princeton University Press, 1971.

———. *The Sacred and the Profane.* Trans. Willard R. Trask. New York: Harcourt, Brace & Co., 1959.

———. *Rites and Symbols of Initiation.* New York: Harper & Row, 1965.

Forsyth, Neil. *The Old Enemy: Satan and the Combat Myth.* Princeton: Princeton University Press, 1987.

Frye, Northrop. *The Great Code: The Bible and Literature.* San Diego: Harcourt Brace Jovanovich, 1983.

———. *The Critical Path: An Essay on the Social Context of Literary Criticism.* Bloomington, Ind.: Indiana University Press, 1973.

———. "Archetypal Criticism: Theory of Myths." In idem, *Anatomy of Criticism,* pp. 131–242. Princeton: Princeton University Press, 1971.

Frye, Northrop; L. C. Knights; et al. *Myth and Symbol: Critical Approaches and Application.* Lincoln, Nebr.: University of Nebraska Press, 1963.

Geertz, Clifford. *The Interpretation of Cultures.* New York: Basic Books, 1973.

Harrison, Jane E. *Mythology.* 1924. Reprint. New York: Harcourt, Brace & World, 1963.

Kluckhohn, Clyde. "Myth and Ritual: A General Theory." *Harvard Theological Review* 35 (1942): 45ff.

Leach, Edmund. *Claude Lévi-Strauss.* New York: Viking Press, 1970.

————. *Genesis as Myth, and Other Essays.* New York: Grossman Publishers, 1970.

————, ed. *The Structural Study of Myth and Totemism.* London: Tavistock Publications, 1967.

————. "Two Essays Concerning the Symbolic Representation of Time." In *Reader in Comparative Religion, An Anthropological Approach,* ed. William A. Lessa and Evon Z. Vogt, 2nd ed., pp. 124–136. New York: Harper & Row, 1965.

————. "Lévi-Strauss in the Garden of Eden: An Examination of Some Recent Developments in the Analysis of Myth." In *Reader in Comparative Religion, An Anthropological Approach,* ed. William A. Lessa and Evon Z. Vogt, 2nd ed., pp. 574–581. New York: Harper & Row, 1965.

Luke, Helen M. *The Inner Story: Myth and Symbol in the Bible and Literature.* New York: Crossroad, 1982.

Rank, Otto. *The Myth of the Birth of the Hero.* 1914. Reprint. New York: Random House, 1964.

Ricoeur, Paul. "The 'Adamic' Myth and the 'Eschatological' Vision of History." In idem, *The Symbolism of Evil,* pp. 232–278. Boston: Beacon Press, 1967.

Turner, Victor W. *The Ritual Process: Structure and Anti-Structure.* Hawthorne, N.Y.: Aldine Publishing Co., 1982.

Wilder, Amos N. *Jesus' Parables and the War of Myths: Essays on Imagination in Scripture.* Philadelphia: Fortress Press, 1982.

CHAPTER 6:
THE FIRST INTERPRETERS OF PAUL

Colossians

Balch, David. *Let Wives Be Submissive: The Domestic Code in I Peter.* Chico, Calif.: Scholars Press, 1981.

Crouch, J. E. *The Origin and Intention of the Colossian Haustafeln.* Göttingen: Vandenhoeck & Ruprecht, 1972.

Dahl, Nils A. "Christ, Creation, and the Church." In idem, *Jesus in the Memory of the Early Church,* pp. 120–140. Minneapolis: Augsburg Publishing House, 1976.

Francis, Fred O., and Wayne A. Meeks, eds. and trans. *Conflict at Colossae.* Missoula, Mont.: Society of Biblical Literature, 1973.

Käsemann, Ernst. "A Primitive Christian Baptismal Liturgy." In idem, *Essays on New Testament Themes.* Philadelphia: Fortress Press, 1982.

Lohse, Eduard. *Colossians and Philemon: A Commentary on the Epistles to the Colossians and to Philemon.* Trans. William R. Poehlmann and Robert J. Karris. Philadelphia: Fortress Press, 1971.

Martin, Ralph P. *Colossians: The Church's Lord and the Christian's Liberty.* Grand Rapids: Zondervan Publishing House, 1973.

O'Brien, P. T. *Colossians, Philemon.* Waco, Tex.: Word, 1982.

Ephesians

Caird, G. B. *Principalities and Powers: A Study in Pauline Theology.* Oxford: Clarendon Press, 1956.

Dahl, Nils A. "Cosmic Dimensions and Religious Knowledge." In *Jesus und Paulus,* ed. E. E. Ellis and E. Grässer, 57–75. Göttingen: Vandenhoeck & Ruprecht, 1975.

———. "Address und Prooemium des Epheserbriefes." *Theologische Zeitschrift* 7 (1951): 241–264.

Fischer, Karl Martin. *Tendenz und Absicht des Epheserbriefes.* Göttingen: Vandenhoeck & Ruprecht, 1973.

Kirby, J. C. *Ephesians, Baptism, and Pentecost: An Inquiry Into the Structure and Purpose of the Epistle to the Ephesians.* Montreal: McGill University Press, 1968.

Roetzel, Calvin J. "Jewish Christian–Gentile Christian Relations, A Discussion of Ephesians 2:15a." *Zeitschrift für die neutestamentliche Wissenschaft* 74 (1983): 81–89.

Sampley, J. Paul. *Ephesians, Colossians, 2 Thessalonians, the Pastoral Epistles.* Philadelphia: Fortress Press, 1978.

———. *"And the Two Shall Become One Flesh": A Study of Traditions in Ephesians 5:21–23.* Cambridge: Cambridge University Press, 1971.

Schlier, Heinrich. *Principalities and Powers in the New Testament.* New York: Herder & Herder, 1961.

Wink, Walter. *Naming the Powers: The Language of Power in the New Testament.* Philadelphia: Fortress Press, 1984.

2 Thessalonians

Best, Ernest. *A Commentary on the First and Second Epistles of the Thessalonians.* New York: Harper & Row, 1972.

Holland, Glenn S. "The Tradition That You Received from Us: 2 Thessalonians in the Pauline Tradition." Ph.D. diss., University of Chicago, 1986.

Krentz, Edgar. "Through a Prism: The Theology of 2 Thessalonians as a Deutero-Pauline Letter." In *1986 Society of Biblical Literature Seminar Papers,* ed. David J. Lull, pp. 1–7. Atlanta: Scholars Press, 1986.

Schmithals, Walter. "The Historical Situation of the Thessalonian Epistles."
In idem, *Paul and the Gnostics.* Trans. John E. Steely. Nashville: Abingdon
Press, 1972.
Trilling, Wolfgang. *Der Zweite Brief an die Thessalonicher.* Neukirchen-
Vluyn: Neukirchener Verlag, 1980.

1 and 2 Timothy and Titus (The Pastorals)

Barrett, C. K. "Pauline Controversies in the Post-Pauline Period." *New Testa-
ment Studies* 20 (1973–74): 229–245.
Dibelius, Martin, and Hans Conzelmann. *The Pastoral Epistles.* Trans. Philip
Buttolph and Adela Yarbro. Philadelphia: Fortress Press, 1972.
Käsemann, Ernst. "Paul and Early Catholicism." In idem, *New Testament
Questions of Today,* pp. 236–251. Philadelphia: Fortress Press, 1969.
Quinn, Jerome. *I Timothy.* Anchor Bible. New York: Doubleday, forthcom-
ing.

CHAPTER 7:
CURRENTS AND CROSSCURRENTS

Bartchy, S. Scott. *First-Century Slavery and I Corinthians 7:21.* Missoula,
Mont.: Scholars Press, 1973.
Bauer, Walter. *Orthodoxy and Heresy in Earliest Christianity.* Ed. Robert A.
Kraft and Gerhard Krodel. Philadelphia: Fortress Press, 1971.
Brown, Peter. *The Making of Late Antiquity.* Cambridge, Mass.: Harvard
University Press, 1978.
Bultmann, Rudolf. *Theology of the New Testament.* Trans. Kendrick Grobel.
New York: Charles Scribner's Sons, 1951.
Davies, William D. *Paul and Rabbinic Judaism.* New York: Harper & Row,
1967.
Dodds, E. R. *Pagan and Christian in an Age of Anxiety.* Cambridge: Cam-
bridge University Press, 1968.
Fiorenza, Elisabeth Schüssler. *In Memory of Her: A Feminist Theological
Reconstruction of Christian Origins,* esp. pp. 205–241. New York: Cross-
road, 1988.
Gibbon, Edward. *The History of the Decline and Fall of the Roman Empire.*
Ed. J. B. Bury. 7 vols. London: Methuen, 1896–1900.
Grant, Robert M. *After the New Testament: Studies in Early Christian Litera-
ture and Theology.* Philadelphia: Fortress Press, 1967.
Harnack, Adolf. *The Mission and Expansion of Christianity in the First Three
Centuries.* Trans. James Moffatt. Intro. Jaroslav Pelikan. New York: Harper
& Row, 1962.
Hennecke, Edgar. *New Testament Apocrypha.* Ed. Wilhelm Schneemelcher. 2
vols. Philadelphia: Westminster Press, 1963–64.

Kelly, J. N. D. *Early Christian Doctrines.* London: Adam & Charles Black, 1958.

Meeks, Wayne A., ed. *The Writings of St. Paul.* New York: W. W. Norton & Co., 1972.

Munck, Johannes. *Paul and the Salvation of Mankind.* Trans. Frank Clarke. Richmond: John Knox Press, 1959.

Obermann, Heiko A. *Forerunners of the Reformation.* New York: Holt, Rinehart & Winston, 1966.

Pagels, Elaine. "Paul and Women: A Response to Recent Discussion." *Journal of the American Academy of Religion* 42 (1974): 538–549.

Pelikan, Jaroslav. *The Christian Tradition: A History of the Development of Doctrine.* 5 vols. Chicago: University of Chicago Press, 1971–.

———. *Jesus Through the Centuries: His Place in the History of Culture.* New Haven, Conn.: Yale University Press, 1985.

Scroggs, Robin. "Paul and the Eschatological Woman." *Journal of the American Academy of Religion* 40 (1972): 283–303.

Souter, Alexander. *Pelagius's Expositions of Thirteen Epistles of St. Paul.* Cambridge: Cambridge University Press, 1926.

Wiles, Maurice F. *The Divine Apostle.* Cambridge: Cambridge University Press, 1967.

Wilson, Robert McL., trans. *The Gospel of Philip.* New York: Harper & Row, 1962.

Index